T0248428

RADICALS AND ROGUES

RADICALS AND ROGUES

THE WOMEN WHO MADE NEW YORK MODERN

Lottie Whalen

REAKTION BOOKS

In memory of EH, for encouraging me to tell stories, and JK,
for showing me how to be an indomitable woman

Published by
REAKTION BOOKS LTD
Unit 32, Waterside
44–48 Wharf Road
London N1 7UX, UK
www.reaktionbooks.co.uk

First published 2023
Copyright © Lottie Whalen 2023

All rights reserved

No part of this publication may be reproduced, stored in a retrieval system,
or transmitted, in any form or by any means, electronic, mechanical,
photocopying, recording or otherwise, without the prior permission
of the publishers

Printed and bound in Great Britain
by TJ Books Ltd, Padstow, Cornwall

A catalogue record for this book is available from the British Library

ISBN 978 1 78914 786 5

CONTENTS

INTRODUCTION

I cannot be the sort of person which my life demands me to be –
so why not try and be my own self.
— GERTRUDE VANDERBILT WHITNEY (1914)

In April 1917, an anonymous artist submitted an upturned porcelain urinal (with 'R. MUTT' scrawled on its side) to the committee of the Society of Independent Artists' First Annual Exhibition and changed art history. The society boldly declared that its exhibition featured no jury, no prizes – in other words, that anyone could exhibit an artwork (for a $6 fee) and all work would be hung alphabetically to ensure there was no sense of hierarchy. The exhibition began in the same month that the United States entered the First World War, heightening its stakes. The artists' vision for a democratic modern American art movement aligned with a national determination to defend and extend democracy across the world.

What many members of the society did not anticipate, however, was that its inclusive, egalitarian approach would be tested to the limit by some of its most avant-garde associates. The mysterious R. Mutt's now infamous submission (called *Fountain*) caused an immediate crisis. Despite their professed commitment to liberalism, the majority of the board members refused to accept a vulgar, commercial object as art: those against it felt that *Fountain* made a mockery of art; those for it (namely arts patron Walter Arensberg and artist Marcel Duchamp) felt that rejecting *Fountain* made a mockery of the society's claim to champion free artistic expression. Arensberg and Duchamp resigned from the board in protest, and the public never got a chance to see the original *Fountain*. Having claimed the work years later, Duchamp authorized replicas of it in 1950 and again in 1963. Until that point, the only public record of *Fountain*'s existence was a striking photograph taken by Alfred Stieglitz, reproduced on a full page of the *Blind Man*, a magazine created by Duchamp, the artist Beatrice Wood and the French writer and art dealer Henri-Pierre Roché to celebrate their avant-garde scene. In addition to the photograph, the magazine contained tongue-in-cheek defences of *Fountain* by Wood and *Rogue* magazine editor Louise Norton, alongside work by other women writers and artists in their circle: a sketch by Clara Tice, a futurist poem by Frances Simpson Stevens and a fragmented prose poem 'compiled' by Mina Loy.

The story of *Fountain* is now an art-history legend but, like any lasting legend, it continues to inspire fresh theories. In recent years, the idea surfaced that *Fountain* was 'stolen' by Duchamp from the one-woman legend Baroness Elsa von Freytag-Loringhoven – known for her uninhibited sexual performances, witty found-object art and scatological wordplay. Art historians Dawn Adès and Alastair Brotchie have robustly rebuffed this still-persistent conspiracy, noting, among other things, that the *Blind Man* circle hardly knew the baroness (who was destitute in Chicago at the time of the scandal), and that, despite her infamously outspoken, domineering demeanour, she never claimed *Fountain*, nor made any reference to it.[1] Those who seek to champion the baroness over Duchamp in an act of feminist recovery risk further obscuring the contribution of other key women who were vital members of the New York avant-garde in the 1910s. Much more compelling evidence leads us to Norton and Wood as provocative co-conspirators.

Yet the determination to credit *Fountain* as the work of one subversive genius seems, in itself, a misguided endeavour. *Fountain* was significant as a statement or an event, rather than an important object in and of itself. It was, in essence, the expression of the radical spirit of a collective of creatives who gravitated to the New York salon of Louise and Walter Arensberg and the vibrant bohemian community in Greenwich Village – many of them talented, influential and now largely forgotten modern women who imbued the New York avant-garde with a defiantly feminist streak.

By referring to these women as radicals and rogues, this book pays tribute to the unique and intertwined mix of serious intent and playful, provocative *joie de vivre* that characterized the scene they created; it celebrates their boldness in creating new ways of living, but also nods to the environment of radical politics in which they worked (fuelled by suffragists and socialist and anarchist activists, such as Emma Goldman, Margaret Sanger and Clara Lemlich). Even artists and writers who claimed to be apolitical (Wood, for example, declared the Arensberg circle to be largely unconcerned by the turbulent politics of their day) were working in this charged atmosphere and responding, in some way, to new theories of organizing society, of understanding the modern self and (for women especially) of being a full citizen in the modern world. 'Rogues' is a tribute to the irreverent little magazine *Rogue* (an experimental periodical aimed at a small coterie readership, unconcerned with public opinion or the commercial market), edited by Norton and her then husband Allen Norton, which set the tone for the New York art scene's irreverent, provocative character; in particular, Norton's idiosyncratic style of fashion commentary (written under her alter ego, Dame Rogue) breezily theorized the link between women's bodily autonomy, their political enfranchisement, fashion and creativity. *Rogue* magazine was short-lived, but a roguish spirit remained and vitalized work created in the decades that followed, from Wood's absurd sketches and ceramics to Florine Stettheimer's camp style.

Radicals and Rogues is an introduction to a group of women whose experiments in life and art set the tone for the rise of New York as the capital of modern culture. In 1910s and '20s New York, women were pushing at the limits of all kinds of boundaries: of bodies, of form, of creative disciplines and of the city itself. They were part of a broader movement that saw women demanding new freedoms and opportunities. Across the divides of class, race and nations, women reimagined the self and fought for the chance to realize their visions – to be equal citizens, to study, to work (and do so in a safe environment), to have bodily autonomy, to rethink approaches to marriage and the family. Against expectations, they opened businesses, were politically active, and flocked to modern metropolises to build independent lives. Some looked for new ways to be wives and mothers, while also cultivating rich, intellectual identities; some eschewed heteronormative expectations for relationships with other women and to build queer communities; some risked their livelihoods to campaign for better working conditions, bodily autonomy, civil rights, voting rights and an end to discrimination on the grounds of race and gender. All were united in harnessing a restless energy that surged through women in the febrile atmosphere of early twentieth-century New York.

The creative arts provided some women with a language to express their experiences of modernity. Through art and poetry, they envisioned a revolution of consciousness and being, seeking to break down the boundaries between art and everyday life. Shockingly unconventional free-verse poetry and provocative new styles of dance became associated with the uninhibited modern woman. Avant-garde little magazines, salons and radical cafés offered spaces for women to collaborate, exchange ideas, stage artistic experiments, earn a living or make a name for themselves. In these sites, the fight for political freedoms and creative free expression merged: for the modern woman, the abilities to think, act, love and dress freely were intimately interconnected.

The creative practitioners who appear in *Radicals and Rogues* disrupted the social order; to varying degrees, they made interventions in feminist politics and efforts to redefine women's roles in modernity. Simply by stepping out in public, raising their voices and making and creating, they challenged gender stereotypes and broke boundaries. Women like Florine Stettheimer, Mina Loy, Clara Tice and Louise Norton shaped modern culture in 1910s and '20s New York in their own image. In some ways, they are foremothers of what Jennifer Cooke calls feminist 'new audacity' contemporary writers, defining audacity as:

a public challenge to conventions, characterised by boldness and a disregard for decorum, protocol, or moral restraints . . . audacity can be oriented towards the future by enacting a step away from the line and the mass of others. To be audacious is to declare that one is striking out with daring in a different direction . . . [it is a] future-facing boldness.[2]

For Cooke, audacious creative expression is inherently political. To emphasize its power, she quotes Chris Kraus's declaration that 'the sheer fact of women talking, being paradoxical, inexplicable, flip, self-destructive, but above all else public is the most revolutionary thing in the world.'[3] For New York's radicals and rogues – emerging from an era of Victorian morality and still battling upholders of conservative values such as Anthony Comstock, head of the New York Society for the Suppression of Vice – this was certainly true.

Yet this book does not seek to claim any of these figures as feminist role models, just as it does not intend to elevate any one of them as an overlooked genius. Heterodoxy, the feminist debating club based in Greenwich Village, sought to help women become 'big, whole human selves', a phrase that implicitly rejects the stereotypically feminine burden of being agreeable and compliant.[4] In a similar vein, American patron of modern art and Heterodoxy member Mabel Dodge's motto, borrowed from Walt Whitman, boldly celebrates contrariness and multiplicity: 'do I contradict myself? Very well then, I contradict myself'; the parenthesis that follows in Whitman's *Leaves of Grass* – '(I am large, I contain multitudes)' – is also applicable to Dodge and her generation of modern women.[5] Whitman's lines echo throughout this book, reminding us that Dodge and her fellow creative modern women were contradictory, flawed figures. Many of them struggled to escape from the repressed, stern environments of their childhoods. Beatrice Wood's fraught relationship with her overbearing, disapproving mother is typical of the conflict that the modern woman was caught up in, pulled back by the old as she flung herself forward into the new. Some, such as Wood, deferred to their male peers and played up to stereotypes of the wide-eyed ingénue, waiting to be corrupted. Like Wood, many of these women came from privileged, wealthy backgrounds and they moved in exclusively white circles. Even Greenwich Village's liberal bohemia reflected the racist, xenophobic and patriarchal society its residents chafed against but were, nevertheless, a part of.

To be sure, *Radicals and Rogues* is the story of *some* of the women who made New York modern. Its scope is limited to women of the New York avant-garde (all of whom were white and from socially privileged backgrounds), whose impact on what became known as New York Dada has been overlooked or diminished in favour of 'great male artist' narratives centred around Duchamp and Man Ray. There are, of course, many other equally significant groups that nurtured cultural innovation and radical experimentation in the early twentieth century. The Harlem Renaissance had an equally vibrant salon culture at its centre, also dominated by radical, restless women. Beauty empire heiress and arts patron A'Lelia Walker opened the doors of her luxury townhouse on Harlem's 108 West 135th Street for glamorous parties, frequented by writers and intellectuals such as Zora Neale Hurston, Langston Hughes, Countee Cullen and W.E.B. Du Bois. Literary editor of *The Crisis* Jessie Redmon Fauset hosted leading Harlem Renaissance writers and artists, including Laura Wheeler Waring, Augusta Savage and Meta Vaux Warwick Fuller, at her apartment on Sunday afternoons. Along with her housemates Ethel Ray and Louella Tucker, librarian Regina M. Anderson also held regular salons at her home in Harlem's Sugar Hill neighbourhood and organized lectures and intellectual gatherings at her branch of the New York Public Library at 135th Street. In these spaces, African American women were at the forefront of cultural innovation and creative revolution.

Communities and groups that were utterly impoverished, eking out precarious lives at the very margins of society, were also vital in building the vibrant cultural life of early twentieth-century New York. Saidiya Hartman's *Wayward Lives, Beautiful Experiments* explores how poor Black women from poor communities, who did not have access to education or elite cultural networks and spaces, engaged in a struggle 'to create autonomous and beautiful lives, to escape the new forms of servitude awaiting them, and to live as if they were free'.[6] The violence of the archive all but erases the traces of dissident lives lived at the margins, but the way that Hartman pieces together an evocative 'intimate history of riotous black girls, troublesome women and queer radicals' demonstrates how vital it is to unpick official histories.

Hartman also shows us that typically privileged, white modern women were not the only trailblazers in 1910s and '20s New York:

> Few, then or now, recognized young black women as sexual modernists, free lovers, radicals and anarchists, or realized that the flapper was a pale imitation of the ghetto girl . . . [they were] radical thinkers who tirelessly imagined other ways to live and never failed to consider how the world might be otherwise.[7]

Wayward Lives powerfully elucidates the many ways that creativity and the pursuit of new ways of living exist outwith sanctioned cultural modes and official archives.

By thinking about gaps in the archive, missteps in the development of artistic practice, institutional barriers, lack of political rights and the rejections and failures that obstruct women's creative paths, we can develop a more nuanced picture of their lives and careers; this picture – and what it tells us about the material realities behind the narrative of the great artistic genius – is often obscured by attempts to fit women into a cultural canon that was built around white Western men. As with efforts to declare the baroness the 'true' creator of *Fountain*, a determination to uncover great female artists risks reinforcing the myth of genius at the expense of a more accurate view of cultural production and women's role within it. Although feminist art historian Linda Nochlin warned against this approach half a decade ago, the temptation to argue the case for certain chosen women remains powerful. The failures of the group of women that this book spotlights (and there were many) attest to the difficulties of sustaining a creative career and challenging the status quo without institutional support, in a society set up to elevate white (straight, cisgender) men to the detriment of all other groups; it also highlights the near impossibility of building a lasting legacy without change on a deep, structural level. In consequence, women and people from marginalized communities are reduced to bit players in the history of twentieth-century art and culture.

By taking a ranging approach to the interconnected web of women who worked to make New York a capital of innovative modern art, *Radicals and Rogues* aims to tell the story not just of individually exceptional women, but of a collective force – a disruptive, feminist force that encompassed new aesthetic and political theories, and pushed for a full-scale revolution of consciousness. As friends and collaborators, this group of women explored new ways of living and being in the modern world. Working together, they created public spaces where new ideas could flourish: from physical sites, including the Arensberg and Stettheimer salons, the Whitney studios, Polly's café and the Sunwise Turn bookshop, to the intellectual spaces of magazines such as *Rogue* and *291*. They were cultural producers, visionaries and trailblazers, all responding to the call of the modern, seeking to change society through experiments in art and living. Together, the radicals and rogues created a rebellious woman-fronted movement that propelled New York to the vanguard of twentieth-century modern culture.

1

THE ARMORY SHOW:
Riot and Rebellion in
New York

Before 17 February 1913, modern art was not on the radar of most Americans. Aspiring young artists – many of them part of a new 'restless', privileged generation who were seeking to experience and express life outside of traditional bourgeois society – made pilgrimages to Europe to experience the radical modernist art forms that were flourishing there, driven by daring innovators like Pablo Picasso, Henri Matisse and F. T. Marinetti. If they were lucky enough to be well connected to intellectual expatriate circles, they might get an invite to the Saturday night salon of Gertrude and Leo Stein in Paris and view the siblings' astonishing art collection; or, if in Florence, they could stop by Mabel Dodge's Villa Curonia, the site of lavish parties where visiting Americans like Carl Van Vechten joined an eclectic mix of European artists, writers and creative practitioners such as Mina Loy, Gordon Craig and Eleonora Duse. In contrast to the United States, which lacked galleries and dealers with interests in modern art, Europe offered American visitors ample opportunities to see new innovations in art at a huge variety of galleries and salons. Across European capitals of modernism, large-scale exhibitions were dedicated to exploring the modern revolution taking place across the arts, including Roger Fry's groundbreaking Post-Impressionist shows in London (in 1910 and 1912), the radical 1912 Sonderbund show in Cologne, the exhibitions of the Neue Künstlervereinigung München in Munich (1909–12) and incredible displays of Cubism at the Salon de la Section d'Or or the annual Salon d'Automne in Paris. Back home in the United States, there were precious few spaces for modern art or supportive networks to promote it. With the notable exception of Alfred Stieglitz's pioneering 291 gallery and Clara Davidge's Madison Art Gallery, modern art and, specifically, young American artists were not a part of America's cultural landscape at the start of the twentieth century.

That all changed in February 1913, when the First Armory Show opened in New York. The Armory Show was the result of years of planning, negotiations and networking across Europe, as the organizing group (the Association of American Painters and Sculptors, or AAPS) set out on a mission to bring the most daring, experimental examples of modern art to the United States for the first time. It was no mean feat, considering the huge distance involved and the fact that the number of artworks borrowed totalled almost 1,300, with two-thirds shipped from Europe – not to mention the careful negotiation of egos and rivalries. The expertise of a core group of influential, enthusiastic supporters was also essential to the show's success. Among them, American painter Walt Kuhn and art critic Walter Pach played a crucial role as European agents, touring across countries to seek out the most exciting artists working in diverse schools and movements, from Impressionism to Fauvism, Cubism to Post-Impressionism. They consulted with key contacts, seeking tips and advice on which artists and sculptors must be included; Picasso's scrawled list of his ten recommendations (including Duchamp, Marie Laurencin and Juan Gris) survives in Kuhn's papers. The intensive work that Pach and Kuhn put in on the ground in Europe played a big part in the Armory show's momentous impact. Through their frenzied and, at times, haphazard forays across Europe's galleries, exhibitions and studios, they secured a truly dazzling array of paintings. Combined, the work they assembled tracked the multifaceted development of modern art and its complex web of influences. By-then-deceased elders such as Van Gogh, Cézanne and Gauguin could be viewed alongside the Cubist and Fauvist artists they had influenced. This democratic approach – privileging no single school or style – reflected the organizers' belief in their message of free artistic expression and would influence the development of exhibitions and groups in New York, including the Society of Independent Artists and the Société Anonyme.

From the outset, the Armory Show was much more than an exhibition. For its logo, Kuhn chose a green pine tree taken from a flag flown during the American Revolution; the Armory Show's motto 'the new spirit' replaces the original phrase 'Appeal to Heaven' (taken from philosopher John Locke's *Two Treatises of Government* (1689), which refuted the divine right of kings and argued that sovereignty was in the hands of the people). This evocative symbol signals the revolutionary aims of the AAPS. The organizers wanted the show to celebrate and affirm individual freedom of expression, radical experimentation and an anti-bourgeois, anti-traditionalist spirit. It would administer a cultural shock that would inspire viewers to embrace the modern and propel American arts forward.

Kuhn felt that the show would be 'the starting point of the new spirit in art' in America, an event that would 'make Americans think'.[1] Writing to Gertrude Stein, Mabel Dodge went further, declaring that it would be 'the most important public event . . . since the signing of the Declaration of Independence . . . There will be a riot and a revolution and things will never be the same afterwards.'[2] The show's organizers and backers sought to place it within the wider context of cultural and sociopolitical ferment that was sweeping the United States as diverse groups agitated for radical change, including the Industrial Workers of the World and other labour movements, the National Association for the Advancement of Colored People, suffrage groups, birth-control activists and anarchists. With different missions and methods, all of these organizations and groups were fighting the conservative forces of an entrenched capitalist, patriarchal, exploitative system that regulated society along gender, race and class lines. By showcasing art that was wilfully subversive and in open defiance of society's traditional moral order, the AAPS was part of a broader wave of disruptive forces.

The Armory Show's huge scope and range show that it was not simply an attempt to create a media scandal; instead, the AAPS wanted to educate and inspire visitors, with the hope of sparking a revolution in American art. A national tour (to Chicago and Boston, spanning a three-month period in total) was also planned to ensure a wide range of Americans would have the opportunity to visit, not just New Yorkers. Kuhn, a skilled PR operator, whipped up a good deal of interest in the press ahead of the show's opening. After the first announcement in

December 1912, the *New York Evening Sun* covered every development with a fevered tone. The reports promised an opportunity for Americans to banish their 'utter ignorance of much of the most talked of work of our time' and encounter modern art directly, rather than relying on 'hearsay or . . . the second-hand work of feeble imitators', according to an article published on 17 December. Although there were plenty of references to the madness of the Futurists and Cubists in the pre-show coverage, there was also a palpable sense of excitement that Americans could finally be part of the dialogue and debates surrounding modern and avant-garde art.

When the Armory Show finally opened in New York, there was – almost as Dodge predicted – a riot in the media. The press and public alike were astounded by the vivid, violent colour palettes, shattered Cubist forms and sheer 'lunacy' that greeted them. Newspaper cartoonists had a field day lampooning Cubist and Futurist works and the baffled responses of visitors. Duchamp's *Nude Descending a Staircase* was a particular source of hilarity and confusion. Few could get their heads around how this fragmented picture plane filled with hard, mechanical shapes related to the nude of its title – not to mention why anyone would distort and degrade the classical nude in such a fashion. The *Nude* became a favourite joke in the press, where it was described as an 'explosion in a shingle factory' and reimagined in a cartoon sketch entitled 'The Rude Descending a Staircase (Rush Hour at the Subway)'.[3] Real ire, however, was reserved for Matisse. If Duchamp was confusing, Matisse was downright offensive: his distorted, vividly coloured portraits were deemed ugly, childlike and primitive, terms that clearly indicated the conservative fear that modern art posed a threat to the 'civilized' moral order. An editorial for the *New York Times* elaborated on this theme in dramatic fashion, declaring:

> This movement is surely a part of the general movement, discernible all over the world, to disrupt and degrade, if not to destroy, not only art, but literature and society, too . . . cubists and futurists are . . . cousins to the anarchists in politics [and] the poets who defy syntax and decency . . . of course, they will not destroy art, supplant literature with ribald nonsense, abolish

economic law, or permanently retard the growth of nations. But we have no present hope that their influence will not grow and produce evil results.[4]

The Armory Show had clearly succeeded in conveying its organizers' revolutionary intent.

Despite the mockery and outrage, the AAPS and its supporters had succeeded in getting the public to pay attention and, in Pach's words, 'to think'. Describing the atmosphere in New York at the time, photographer, critic and man-about-town Carl Van Vechten recalled:

> Everybody went and everybody talked about it. Street-car conductors asked for your opinion of the *Nude Descending the Staircase*, as they asked for your nickel. Elevator boys grinned about Matisse's *La Madras Rouge*, Picabia's *La Danse à la Source*, and Brâncuşi's *Mademoiselle Pogany*, as they lifted you to the twenty-third floor. Ladies you met at dinner found Archipenko's sculpture very amusing, but was it art?[5]

Modern art had spoken to a broad audience and, perhaps surprisingly, caused ordinary people to ponder the fundamental questions that avant-garde artists would continue to explore through most of the century: what constitutes art, and who gets to decide? In a way that was perhaps utterly unique to that moment in time, no academics, art dealers or specialists had the authority to answer them. This vast display of groundbreaking work was unprecedented, and, in the United States, there were no points of reference for it. The art critic was no more an expert than the woman on the street. It was a brief democratic moment, where no academies or institutions exerted power over who could be part of the new modern-art movement. This opened up space for women to get involved on a level they had never been able to reach previously: as artists, collectors, patrons and organizers.

After the Armory Show, modern art also infiltrated everyday life via consumer culture. Department stores, in particular, keyed into the craze for colour, abstract design and – well ahead of museums and galleries – 'became the leading "education centres" for the new aesthetic'.[6]

Gimbel Brothers embraced art with particular enthusiasm: the three brothers who founded and owned it began collecting work by Picasso, Braque and Cézanne and mounting exhibitions in store. Pach noted his surprise that it was businesses, not artists, that 'caught on immediately', with the result that 'the exhibition affected every phase of American life – the apparel of men and women, the stage, automobiles, airplanes, furniture, interior decorations, beauty parlors, advertising and printing.'[7]

This was a new development in art's uneasy but interdependent relationship with capitalism and consumerism. But for ordinary women, it meant they could access modern art as part of their daily routine, both through viewing displays in department stores and by purchasing items with modernist designs. Women were specifically targeted by advertising that playfully referenced Cubist- and Futurist- inspired fashions. An advertisement for Wanamaker's department store proclaimed 'color combinations of the Futurists' and 'Cubist influence in fashions in the new Paris Models for Spring'.[8] Countless other stores echoed this language in their advertising, filling American newspapers and magazines with so-called Cubist styles (a loose term that referred to boxy, baggy-fitting dresses, modernist patterns and bright, clashing colours). This fun, fashionable and provocative face of the avant-garde mirrored the desires of American women for new freedoms and forms of expression.

'Some people think women are the cause of modernism, whatever that is'

As the Armory Show entered the history books, the story became one of pioneering masculine endeavour, the struggles of male genius to enlighten an ignorant public. When women received any recognition for their contribution, it was as passive supporters rather than active contributors. Writing for *Vogue* in 1940, former *Vanity Fair* editor and Armory Show sponsor Frank Crowninshield noted that it was women who 'reacted most spontaneously to the works seen at the Armory' and who 'accorded the modern movement its earliest recognition and patronage'. By focusing on women's reactions, Crowninshield ignores the work that women organizers, financial backers and artists put in during the years leading up to the show. His suggestion that women reacted in a 'spontaneous', almost child-like manner plays to reductive stereotypes that obscure the fact that many women involved with the Armory Show were educated and had direct experience with the European avant-garde while studying, working or travelling overseas. A decade later, Meyer Schapiro's 1952 essay 'Armory Show in Retrospect' echoed Crowninshield's sentiment; Schapiro patronizingly credited women as generous 'friends' of modern art, singling out the 'idealistic wives and daughters of magnates' eager to spend their fortunes.

Both Crowninshield's and Schapiro's comments place women in the role of consumers rather than producers of modern culture in America. This was typical of a broader move to marginalize women's involvement with the development of New York's modern and avant-garde art scene after the 1920s. As male modern artists became firmly established (their art no longer outrageous and obscene, but instead prized possessions of art institutions) and the dazzle of the Roaring Twenties decayed into decades of depression, war and then post-war conservativism, the fortunes of women artists foundered. They lacked support from patrons, critics and institutions, and usually had to balance the demands of family life or, for unmarried women, the need to earn enough money to support themselves. As critics, patrons and organizers, women were marginalized and their efforts overlooked. In the years following the Second World War, the rise of the masculine Abstract Expressionist movement correlated with a wider conservative shift in which women were encouraged to embrace domestic roles as housewives and mothers.[9] The consequence of these shifts meant that women were largely written out of the narrative of American art.

At the end of the 1910s, however, the picture looked very different: women were at the forefront of the modern-art revolution. In 1917, the *New York Evening Sun* informed its readers that 'women were the cause of modernism, whatever that is.'[10] A reporter embarked on a quest across New York to find the ultimate modern woman, a woman who embodied the creative, bohemian spirit sweeping the city (their search ended with Mina Loy, whose 'clothes suggested the smartest shops' but whose avant-garde poetry 'would've puzzled grandma'). In the public consciousness, modern art and poetry became intimately bound up with the popular image of the modern new woman – a sexually liberated, free-thinking, creative provocateur. Beyond this image (which threatened to slip into caricature), women's practical efforts as advisors, financial backers, artists, publicists, gallerists and patrons to foster modern art in America were crucial, both in the build-up to the Armory Show and in the formative years that followed.

Certain histories of the Armory Show fail even to mention the fact that a number of women artists exhibited there. Although women were underrepresented (of the three hundred artists included, fifty were women), several significant women artists from Europe and America appeared. Marie Laurencin (the only woman included on Picasso's list of recommendations) and Jacqueline Marval represented women of the Parisian avant-garde. Mary Cassatt was the most established American woman artist included, but many of her peers were only at the very start of their careers: Frances Simpson Stevens showed a painting she completed under the tutelage of Robert Henri (the following year she moved to Florence and became part of the Futurist movement); Marguerite Zorach, Agnes Pelton and Katharine Rhoades exhibited early work, each just beginning to develop their practice in new, radical directions.

As patrons, women also formed a large part of the financial and practical support system that made the Armory Show possible. In particular, Gertrude Vanderbilt Whitney, Agnes Meyer, Lillie Bliss and Katherine Dreier contributed generously (and bought work for their collections during the show). In an analysis of the data, Jennifer Pfeifer Shircliff reveals that women patrons contributed 48 per cent of the $10,050 that it cost to put on the Armory Show; influential collector Bliss is not included in the financial records because she donated funds anonymously via the show's president, Arthur Davies.[11] If one includes an estimate of Lillie Bliss's total funds, women's financial contribution potentially comes to a huge 88 per cent. Crucially, not all of these women were extravagantly wealthy wives and heiresses: many women of more modest means made relatively small donations of $5. Some were also instrumental in drumming up support from their networks of friends and associates, bringing other wealthy backers to the table.

Clara Davidge was one such key contributor who encouraged other women to make donations. Davidge offers perhaps the most obvious example of the erasure of women's contributions to modern art in New

York.[12] Like Stieglitz, Davidge was a pioneer of the pre-Armory Show New York art scene. Between 1909 and 1912, Davidge owned the Madison Art Gallery, a non-commercial space that promoted the work of young, progressive American artists (virtually the only gallery to do so during this time). Alongside running the gallery, Davidge worked as a successful interior decorator and was part of the Greenwich Village scene. Her large old house at 62 Washington Square served as an informal exhibition space, office and guest house for some of the many writers and painters that Davidge supported.[13] She used her networks and knowledge of the art scene to drum up support for the Armory Show, raising large sums and stoking enthusiasm. Davidge's interior-design skills were also called upon for the design and decoration of the exhibition space. Kuhn gives Davidge scant acknowledgement in his *The Story of the Armory Show* (1938), referring to her only as the owner of a 'small gallery at 305 Madison Avenue', notable simply for being the location where the idea for the Armory Show came to him and two other male artists (Elmer MacRae and Jerome Myers – all three had recently exhibited at the Madison Art Gallery).[14] Davidge was lucky to get a mention at all, as one of only two American women that Kuhn made reference to in his book (the other being Gertrude Vanderbilt Whitney). Davidge's friend, the painter and philanthropist Elizabeth Sage Hare, gave a more accurate assessment of her role in an obituary for *American Art Review*, in which she noted that many people 'closely connected' to the Armory Show viewed Davidge's 'inexhaustible faith and her magical way of securing outside interest at the most critical moment' as essential in bringing it together.[15] Highlighting Davidge's overlooked but crucial work in networking and organizing, Hare adds that 'so many interesting arts ventures have benefited by [Davidge's] optimism and cooperation.'[16]

After the Armory Show, Davidge and Henry Fitch Taylor (the former manager of Madison Art Gallery, whom Davidge married in 1913) provided vital support to many young American artists, including Marguerite and William Zorach. Unlike many of her contemporaries, Davidge was not interested in self-promotion or making a name for herself outside of the circles she moved in; this, in addition to her sudden death in 1921 and the lack of any known surviving archival papers, has further excluded her from the history of the Armory Show and its impact. Although

Davidge's fall into obscurity is extreme, her story is representative of the way women involved in the Armory Show failed to receive recognition in the later 'official' accounts given by male organizers. Without their efforts in providing sustained support for artists and opening up spaces in the city for the development and exhibition of art, it's unlikely that the Armory Show would've been possible and certainly not on such a large scale.

It is worth turning to the influence of five other women who were part of the Armory Show and exploring the spaces they opened up for modern art in the years that followed. As artists, organizers, patrons and supporters, these women formed interconnected networks that challenged patriarchal cultural hierarchies and swept away outdated notions of what American art could and should be. Their efforts in arranging exhibitions, acting as patrons and mentors, hosting salons and get-togethers and creating art ushered in a new era of modern art in America. They reshaped the map of New York City, ensuring it developed a cultural life that could challenge European centres of modernism. The Armory Show posed vital questions: what next for modern art in America? How could the modern movement flourish in New York with so few support systems in place? These women sought to provide answers by daring to dedicate their lives to art. By opening their homes, founding studios and galleries, and starting magazines, they created supportive networks that brought together art, literature and new theories about life in the modern age. Collectively, their efforts put women at the centre of this new arts scene, firmly entwining modern art and modern women in the public consciousness.

Movers and Shakers at Mabel Dodge's Salon, 23 Fifth Avenue

'It seems as though everywhere, in that year of 1913, barriers went down and people reached each other who had never been in touch before.'[17]

Mabel Dodge was a woman in search of a revolution when she arrived in New York from Europe in 1912. The first chill of winter must have felt particularly bitter after seven years spent languishing in the

Mediterranean sun at the grand Villa Curonia, her opulent villa in Florence. It was a bold move, but one she felt compelled to make: although Dodge was well connected in Florence and hosted dazzling parties that attracted visiting artists, writers and intellectuals, Florentine society seemed stuck in the past. Dodge felt far from the centre of things. Her friendship with Gertrude and Leo Stein, in particular, had opened her eyes to new radical forms of modernity that were revolutionizing art and life, sweeping away old inhibitions and traditions in the process. This appealed to Dodge on a deeply personal level; she had gone through an extremely challenging few years, during which she struggled with depressive episodes and attempted suicide twice. Her relationship with her second husband, Edwin Dodge, was at an all-time low (it had always been a practical, rather than romantic, match) and she had become entangled in several tortured love affairs. She was ready for a fresh start and a fresh perspective.

In New York, Dodge hoped for reinvention by submerging herself in the currents of new ideas reshaping understandings of the self, the body, sexuality, art and society. She had already acquired an interest in psychoanalysis (then an emerging field), which led her to conclude that much of the depression, psychological disturbance and difficulty with sexual relationships she experienced stemmed from her upbringing in a wealthy but emotionally cold family. In a new era of free expression, she hoped to find a more balanced, open way of being in the world, connected rather than locked into her own misery; in her memoirs she described her entire life as a series of attempts to escape from the 'separateness and immobility' that characterized her childhood. But at first, she was more miserable and isolated than in Florence. New York appeared relentlessly ugly and devoid of the Florentine warmth and colour that enveloped life in the Villa Curonia. The hectic, grey and grubby streets were a shocking contrast to Italy's classical beauty. Dodge purposefully chose an apartment at 23 Fifth Avenue, north of Washington Square, which could act as a refuge from the chaos of the city. She set about decorating it in European style, with opulent furniture shipped from Italy and all-white walls, rugs and silk drapes – a cleansing palette that recalled the splendour of the Villa Curonia. However, it was not enough to lift her spirits. While Edwin and her son John cheerfully busied themselves with their new American lives, Dodge experienced another serious physical and mental breakdown. After spending months bedridden, Dodge and her doctor came to the agreement that Edwin was the cause of her unhappiness. He was surprisingly accepting of this news and agreed to vacate the apartment to give her space to recover.[18]

Once Dodge had the Fifth Avenue home to herself, her life began to take a new direction. Gertrude Stein had written letters to several of her friends and associates in New York to put in a good word for Dodge. Stein's recommendations proved useful; soon, Dodge's social circle began to swell and exciting new opportunities presented themselves. Carl Van Vechten was bowled over by Dodge's cosmopolitan air and rich appreciation of art and culture. They developed a close, camp friendship characterized by hyperbolic, tongue-in-cheek declarations of love, in which Van Vechten referred to Mabel as 'Mike' or 'Aunt Mike'. Dodge revelled in this half-flirtation, half-mentorship, buoyed by the sense of importance that Van Vechten's admiration bestowed on her. They shared an ambitious streak, as well as the ability to identify (and align themselves with) culturally influential people. During this time, Dodge also became close to Stein's friend Hutchins 'Hutch' Hapgood, in this instance engaging in a more serious flirtation. Hapgood was part of Greenwich Village's bohemian set and in an open marriage with writer Neith Boyce (as was common in Village relationships, Hutch benefited from and therefore embraced the polyamorous approach more enthusiastically than Boyce).

Hutch immediately began opening doors to new worlds. He introduced Dodge to the lively and notorious characters that were influential leaders of New York's radical activist circles and showed her around Greenwich Village. In her memoirs, Dodge describes anxiously accompanying Hutch on a visit to Emma Goldman's apartment, terrified to meet the infamous anarchist who promoted 'direct action' at all costs, even murder: 'these people were not intellectual anarchists like dear Hutch living safely with Neith and the children. They lived under the constant espionage of the police.'[19] When she stepped through the door, Dodge was surprised to find a 'homely, motherly' woman (Goldman) serving a meal to her comrades. Nevertheless, Dodge remained wary of the anarchists' violent tactics; she never affiliated herself with any particular political group or organization, but she remained supportive of certain left-wing causes in the years that followed.

Among the 'radical group' that she met during her first year in New York, birth-control activist Margaret Sanger made perhaps the deepest impression. Dodge's cold, Victorian upbringing as the only child of loveless, bitter parents had impacted on her ability to form fulfilling

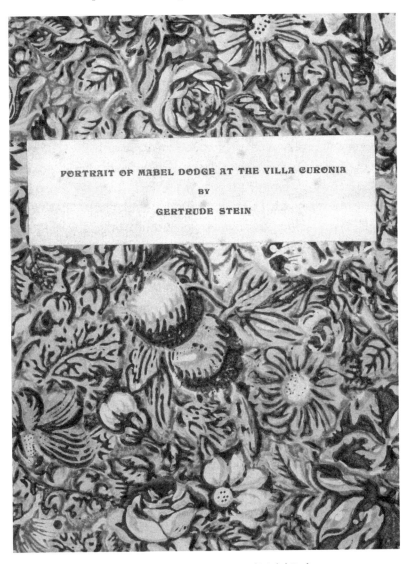

Cover of Gertrude Stein's *Portrait of Mabel Dodge*.

connections, particularly sexual relationships. Sanger opened Dodge's eyes 'not only [to] sex knowledge in regard to conception, but [to] sex knowledge about copulation and its intrinsic importance'; that is, Sanger showed Dodge that women were entitled to – and could achieve – a sex life that was pleasurable, not purely for procreation.[20] Along with psychoanalytic theory, Sanger's ideas offered Dodge new ways of expressing sexuality and imagining relationships, away from the repressed morality enforced by previous generations.

After the boredom that overtook her in Florence, it must have been a revelation for Dodge to find herself at the heart of the intellectual and artistic revolutions unfolding in New York. Life began to make sense, and her apartment was soon to transform from a safe haven against the city to an open house that drew in its eclectic cast of (in Dodge's words) movers and shakers. It was an opportune moment for Dodge to begin making her mark in New York, mere months away from the Armory Show. Seeking to establish herself within the city's flourishing cultural life, Dodge played on her links with the European avant-garde to boost her reputation. During a visit to the Villa Curonia in 1912, Stein had written a poem-portrait of Dodge. Like a Picasso portrait, Stein's portrait in words was experimental and abstract. Stein did not intend to offer a realistic picture of Dodge, but rather capture Dodge's essence and characteristics through fragmented images and impressions. The portrait evokes an atmosphere of intimacy that suggests the pair's warm and flirtatious relationship. In sensuous language, Stein's repetitive breathy lines ('so much breathing') build to a 'climax' of 'looking', 'laughing', 'gliding'.[21]

Dodge was thrilled by the poem and no doubt flattered to have her impression caught in this strikingly experimental style. She became modern through Stein's words. Sensing its importance and potential impact, Dodge had it printed privately and began circulating it widely among her new friends and associates in New York. As she'd anticipated, it caused a flurry of interest and intrigue. Partly as a result of this attention, Dodge was contacted by the organizers of the Armory Show, who invited her to assist with drumming up anticipation and bringing together the final parts of the plan. She joined the organizing committee as a vice president and made a donation of $500. In a display of her

talent for self-promotion, Dodge later claimed ownership of the Armory
Show. Once she joined the committee, she suggested, 'it became, overnight, my own little Revolution. I would upset America . . . [and] the
old world order . . . I was going to dynamite New York and nothing
would stop me.'[22] In reality, Dodge made a comparatively minor contribution to the organization of the show as she joined the committee at
a late stage. Nevertheless, the organizers made a smart choice: by bringing Dodge on board, they secured a publicity boon that would almost
rival the sensation caused by Duchamp and Matisse, thanks to Dodge's
connection with Stein. The experience of the show was, for Dodge, a
personal revolution.

The committee decided to hand out copies of Stein's 'Portrait of
Mabel Dodge' at the Armory Show, making it the only piece of literature that was showcased alongside the works of art. Dodge wrote an
essay to accompany it, in which she attempted to illuminate Stein's
technique and its importance in the modern-art revolution. Confusion
and mockery inevitably ensued, but it also attracted a surge of interest
in Dodge and Stein. A host of other cultural organizations and figures
were eager to feature both works and capitalize on the sensation. Alfred
Stieglitz published 'Portrait of Mabel Dodge' in a special issue of *Camera
Work*, alongside Dodge's essay (entitled 'Speculations'); the two pieces
opened the special issue of June 1913, followed by defences of modern
art and reproductions of work by Cézanne, Picabia, Van Gogh and
Picasso (including his portrait of Stein).

In Dodge's essay, which also appeared in a special Armory Show
issue of *Arts and Decoration* magazine, she drew direct parallels between
Picasso's artistic innovation and Stein's experiments with language:
'Gertrude Stein is doing with words what Picasso is doing with paint
. . . in her impressionistic writing she uses familiar words to create perceptions, conditions, and states of being, never before quite consciously
experienced.'[23] Dodge was the first critic to hail Stein as a genius, a term
that Stein herself went on to eagerly embrace, and situated her not just
within the revolution in art but within popular new philosophical theories, such as those of Henri Bergson. Yet Dodge also warned her reader
that they could only come to a true understanding of Picasso's and
Stein's work through direct personal contact with it; an encounter in

which one must prioritize feeling over rational thought or logic in order to experience their radical expressions of modern consciousness. It was a process, not an easy, immediate moment of comprehension. After all, Dodge reminds readers, 'each time that beauty has been reborn in the world it has needed complete readjustment of sense perceptions . . . If we like St Marks in Venice today, then surely it would have offended us a thousand years ago.'[24]

Through her association with Stein, Dodge skilfully attached her name to a groundbreaking moment in cultural history. In the public imagination, she was at the vanguard of this shocking new movement, along with the likes of Picasso and Duchamp. She was celebrated as one of the prophets of the new phenomenon modernism, blessed (via Stein) with a special insight into what it meant and why it was significant. In Stein's absence (she remained at home in Paris during the show, awaiting news from Dodge and Van Vechten), Dodge stood in as a cipher of sorts, providing a physical connection to the enigmatic expatriate writer who had become a leading figure in the European avant-garde. A sub-heading in *Arts and Decoration* (written by the editor) celebrated the two women on almost equal terms: it declared that the article was 'about the only woman in the world who has put the spirit of post-impressionism into prose [Stein], and written by the only woman in America who fully understands it [Dodge]'.[25]

Such recognition capped off a life-changing year for Dodge, thrusting her from the margins of the modern movement to its centre. Years later, Dodge noted that 'if Gertrude Stein was born at the Armory Show, so was "Mabel Dodge".'[26] Initially, Stein was equally thrilled by Dodge's article and the surrounding publicity: she wrote several enthusiastic letters describing how she was 'proud as punch' and ecstatic when others wrote to tell her that the name Gertrude Stein was being uttered across America in the same breath as Picasso and Matisse (even if these references often took the form of mockery and parody).[27] As time passed, Stein reassessed her position, taking a less favourable view of the way Dodge had (in her view) piggy-backed on Stein's talent.

The fame that Dodge found as a result of the Armory Show enhanced her natural magnetism and charisma. Less than a year after Dodge had designed her apartment as a refuge to keep out the hostile city, she began opening its doors for regular gatherings of artists, writers, activists and intellectuals. Her apartment transformed into a lively salon, where the latest ideas in art, philosophy and politics were hotly debated. In the period immediately after the Armory Show, Dodge's salon provided much-needed space for the exchange of modern thoughts and theories among people eager to enhance the social and cultural life of the United States. Evenings were given over to discussions of the most urgent and contested topics of the day: from modern art to birth control, free-verse poetry to workers' rights, anarchy and direct action (the latter event was called 'Dangerous Characters'), nothing was off limits. Many of her guests experienced revelatory intellectual ideas for the first time, with some speakers bringing strange new theories from across the Atlantic. One of the most significant of Dodge's salon events was the 'Psychoanalysis Evening' in 1915, where A. A. Brill (the first practising psychoanalyst in the United States) lectured on Sigmund Freud, whose work was then little known in the United States.[28]

Among the salons and venues that sprang up in New York through the 1910s, Dodge's was unusual for bringing artists and writers together with political activists – not just 'intellectual anarchists' (as she described Hutch), but people who actively placed their freedom and lives on the line to fight for the causes they believed in, as part of trade unions and political groups. Attempts were also made to expand these conversations beyond the walls of the salon. The most notable example was the Paterson Strike Pageant of 1913, organized to raise funds for striking workers in Paterson, New Jersey. Dodge put together the event, staged at Madison Square Gardens, in collaboration with her then lover the journalist John Reed; artist John Sloan; *The Masses* editor Max Eastman; Bill Haywood, leader of the Industrial Workers of the World; Sanger; and workers involved in the strike (Dodge later remarked 'everybody worked, except me').[29]

Inevitably, Dodge's efforts to bring together artists and radical activists sometimes led to turbulence. During one salon evening, Haywood upbraided the gathered artists (including Marsden Hartley and Francis Picabia) for acting like they were 'special and separate' when, in fact, everyone should have the right to enough free time to make art. Sculptor Janet Scudder, also a political activist from a working-class background, shouted Haywood down. Heated debates mixed with moments of connection and compromise – even radical anarchist Hippolyte Havel was able to embrace Dodge, whom he declared his 'little goddam bourgeois capitalist sister' (he later castigated the left-wing staff of *The Masses* as bourgeois for voting on which poetry to include in the magazine).[30]

In Dodge's opinion, it was fiery disagreements and battles of ideology like these that charged her salon with 'intellectual excitement . . . [and] daring change'.[31] Her guests usually concurred. Journalist Lincoln Steffens pronounced it 'the only successful salon I have ever seen in America. By which I mean that there was conversation and that the conversation developed usually out of one theme and stayed on the floor.'[32] Van Vechten perhaps best captured the salon's electric atmosphere in his autobiographical novel *Peter Whiffle*, describing how 'arguments and discussions floated in the air, were caught and twisted and hauled and tied until the white salon itself was no longer static. There were undercurrents of emotion and sex.'[33] In this way, Dodge's salon channelled all the vital threads energizing New York City at that time. It joined the likes of 291 and Polly's on the post-Armory map of the city's key creative venues.

The New York press also caught on to the events at Dodge's salon, eager to titillate their readers with the latest goings-on of eccentric artists and shocking modern women. A reporter for the *New York Morning Telegraph* attended one of Dodge's packed-out Evenings, where he found Dodge fashionably dressed in a 'shell pink gown and a string of big amber beads', surrounded by 'politicians, painters, sociologists, sexologists, futurists, dramatists, sculptors, editors, writers, anarchists, socialists, and poets'.[34] Dodge herself is described as a 'sphinx' and 'Mona Lisa Mabel Dodge', who sits silently among the whirl of debate. This was a common impression of Dodge that circulated in the press and among later critics and commentators. A cartoon in *New York World* illustrating 'Parlor Socialists and Others at a Wednesday Night Soiree on Fifth' presents Dodge sat like a mannequin among a mostly male crowd, all absorbed in conversation. The idea of Dodge as an enigmatic sphinx seems in direct contrast with the intellectual friendships she cultivated throughout her life (many of which are recorded in letters) and the four-volume memoir that she composed years later. Steffens offered a more nuanced reading of Dodge's quiet skills as a salon host, noting that she would successfully manage a huge number of diverse guests, but 'no one felt that they were managed'; instead, she carefully chose provocative and timely topics, assembling the right mix of guests to ensure that debate flowed.

Communication and free expression were, indeed, vital to Dodge; in many ways, her life was a violent rebellion against the 'mute endurance' that her mother encouraged, 'as though I believed that by ignoring and never speaking of the misery we [Dodge and her parents] caused each other we would thereby blot it out'.[35] Perhaps Dodge's silence at her Evenings can be ascribed to her desire to constantly expand her horizons and keep an open mind to all manifestations of the modern. She provided a platform for others, taking the opportunity to listen and learn rather than putting herself centre stage. Yet the caricature of Dodge as sphinx can also be interpreted as part of wider stereotypes applied to her in her lifetime and over the years since her death. Her commitment to psychoanalysis and the writing of her vast memoirs gave rise to claims that she was self-obsessed and introspective. Her involvement with art and politics has been dismissed as part of a narcissistic vanity project; in other words, a typical stereotype of a wealthy woman who dabbles in the arts without understanding or being truly invested in their aims. There was some truth to this perception of Dodge. Reflecting on the success of her salon, she declared that her hobby was now collecting 'people. Important people', and she clearly revelled in being connected to 'heads of movements, heads of newspapers, heads of all kinds of groups of people'.[36] Mina Loy, at one time a close friend, satirized Dodge in her play *The Pamperers* (written between 1915 and 1917).[37] The action revolves around the ambitions of Diana, a wealthy woman who treats art like a luxury accessory: she has 'Bach [play] for her bath' and Isadora Allen (a thinly veiled Isadora Duncan) 'dance her awake', buys 'a museum to wear at a ball' and, of course, 'collects geniuses' to show off at her salon.[38] Loy's caricature suggests a certain knowingness among those in Dodge's circle regarding her fickle nature and pursuit of prestige via more creatively talented friends and lovers.

Dodge was certainly a woman of many contradictions. She could be notoriously flighty, flippant, entitled and egotistical. Yet she was also generous, supportive of new artists, daring and forward-thinking. She combined an interest in Greenwich Village feminism with an (often destructive) over-dependence on male attention, and supported left-wing political activism while sometimes retreating into her world of privilege, luxury and leisure. This volatile combination of qualities left her perfectly equipped to play a role in the equally volatile world of art, culture and politics that flourished in 1910s New York. Her irrepressible appetite for new ideas brought together wildly opposing groups of people, fostering dynamic exchanges of thoughts across boundaries of class, gender, politics and aesthetics. Dodge's salon was a melting pot for modern New York's ideas and ideals, a place where art and politics collided as artists, activists and thinkers sought new ways both to live modern lives and to make sense of modernity. The Armory Show revealed to Dodge a way of placing her people skills, passion for modernism and privilege in the service of New York's cultural life. In 1916 Dodge left the city to seek new adventures, which would eventually result in her lively literary colony at Taos in New Mexico. The life of her New York salon was brief, but it provided a much-needed home for emerging schools of thought to develop and gave guests access to radical theories that they would not have heard anywhere else in the city.

291 and the Three Graces

Between 1910 and 1914, photographer and painter Edward Steichen worked on *In Exaltation of Flowers*, a richly decorative mural that was intended to hang in the luxurious Park Avenue townhouse of Agnes and Eugene Meyer Jr. Glittering with gold leaf and jewel-coloured tempera, the seven-panel mural evokes an exotic relic from classical antiquity. The Art Nouveau style of the statuesque goddesses who populate the mural, combined with an angular rhythm that runs across each section, locates it firmly in the modern age. The elegant style and poses of each woman bespeak Steichen's work as a pioneering photographer of fashion, which was highly sought after among Parisian fashion journals. Indeed, scenes from the mural would not look out of place in an upmarket magazine. Each panel of *In Exaltation of Flowers* stands

3 metres (10 ft) tall, ensuring its dramatic impact. This was no ordinary commission for elite New Yorkers. The beautiful women depicted in Steichen's mural were (like Steichen) all part of the progressive, creative group that gravitated around Alfred Stieglitz's pioneering 291 gallery. The mural's rich symbolism contains a series of coded allusions to the groups' activities and personalities.

Agnes Meyer commissioned the mural in tribute to the creative trio she was part of, along with artists Katharine Rhoades and Marion Beckett. The women were known as the 'Three Graces', a nickname that alluded to their classical beauty and artistic talent. The luminous Grecian style of Steichen's mural memorializes the three women's role as presiding goddesses of the 291 scene, while the strong colour scheme and linear patterns signal their modern style. Meyer's decision to immortalize their group signifies an act of myth-making that placed Meyer and her friends at the centre of New York's modern movement. Sadly, *In Exaltation of Flowers* never hung at Meyer's home, as the couple were forced to move just before it could be installed. It was exhibited at the Knoedler Gallery in 1915 and then languished in storage until Meyer's death in 1970.[39] The fate of the mural could be said to reflect the marginalization of the 'Three Graces' from the story of 291 and its impact on modernism in America.

Meyer left a strong legacy due to the tireless activism in the fields of civil rights, welfare and education that she dedicated herself to after her husband Eugene purchased the *Washington Post* in 1933. As part of the 291 circle, however, her efforts – and those of other women in the group – were overshadowed as Stieglitz took control of the narrative, which was then further entrenched by later critics. A closer look at the activities of Meyer and Rhoades, in particular, during the 1910s reveals their significance in the networks that allowed modernism to flourish in New York, but it also highlights the many challenges and pressures women faced as part of the 291 scene (and in the broader avant-garde art world), where they were viewed as muses and sexual objects, first and foremost.

Meyer entered the exciting world of 291 through journalism. She was already remarkable and determined, having become the first woman reporter to work for the *New York Evening Sun*. She joined the staff in 1907 after graduating from the prestigious Barnard College of Columbia University, New York City, where she supported herself with a scholarship and part-time jobs (her decision to attend university was strictly against her father's wishes). In the early twentieth century, newspaper journalism was a man's world that very few women broke into, and those that did struggled to be taken seriously. Meyer later suggested that she was hired by *The Sun* as a sort of joke, for the novelty of sending her 'all the places where a man would be thrown out', but nevertheless she revelled in her new role – 'when I landed that job I thought I owned *The Sun*, and the earth and moon, too.'[40]

Meyer's search for new stories led her to the 291 gallery and Stieglitz, who christened her 'the Sun girl'. An interview with Stieglitz turned into a lengthy debate about modern art and, for Meyer, a new world of opportunities: 'I felt that at 291 my sails were filled by the free air I craved,' she recalled many years later in her autobiography.[41] Embracing this sense of freedom that she had found at 291, Meyer left New York the following year to study at the Sorbonne in Paris. Meyer's time in Europe had a profound effect on her, but the time she spent at Gertrude Stein's salon meeting avant-garde artists and writers was more significant than her academic studies at the Sorbonne. When Meyer returned to the United States, she surprised many of the people that knew her by marrying multimillionaire investment banker Eugene Meyer. However, she had no plans to settle into the life of a society wife; instead, she used her newfound wealth to develop and support modern art in New York.

After her experiences in Paris, Meyer rejoined the 291 circle with a deeper understanding of the exciting directions that art was taking. She felt an urge to proactively foster this new art in the United States, and she had both the means and the knowledge to do so. With access to substantial sums of money, she set about making contributions to fund exhibitions at 291 (including the first solo show of Constantin Brâncuşi's work in the country). Eager for a more hands-on experience, she also teamed up with artist Marius de Zayas to open the Modern Gallery in 1915. They navigated a potential conflict of interest with Stieglitz's 291 with great care: de Zayas wrote to Stieglitz informing him that he and Meyer saw the Modern Gallery as 'the business side of 291', while 291 continued as an experimental space, making clear that 'none of us will ever do anything or take any step without the full agreement of those who compose our society [Stieglitz, de Zayas, the Meyers and Francis Picabia]'.[42] Frankly, de Zayas and Meyer sought to move away from the elitism that often defined Steiglitz's manner of handling visitors to 291 and potential buyers of exhibited works. They aimed to interest the public in modern art, in contrast to Stieglitz's focus on educated connoisseurs. After opening the Modern Gallery, Meyer and de Zayas began thinking of other ways to expand the reach and potential of modern art in New York.

A radical little magazine was an obvious way to ensure that the 291 project kept pace with developments in avant-garde culture, both in New York and overseas. With de Zayas and Paul Haviland as co-editors, and Katharine Rhoades as a contributor, Meyer set up *291* the magazine. It would function as an experimental, creative space for art and poetry and also act as a mouthpiece for the 291 circle to express their visions for American culture. Stieglitz was sceptical about backing the magazine, but he acquiesced. His place at the forefront of New York's avant-garde movement became increasingly insecure after the Armory Show: the shock of the show, combined with a proliferation of new spaces for modern art and ideas in the city, meant that the 291 gallery had lost some of its edge. *Camera Work*, Stieglitz's pioneering photography journal, was also losing subscribers and becoming a financial burden. Famously anti-commercial and a passionate believer in the spiritual (over the material) value of art, Stieglitz was struggling to keep his projects going in a market that was much more crowded than it had been five or ten years earlier. Meyer persuaded him to support *291* as a way of showcasing work associated with the gallery and, in the process, bringing in a much-needed funding boost. However, with Meyer and de Zayas controlling the direction of the magazine, it developed a style and character quite distinct from Stieglitz and his 291 gallery. It was a dynamic, avant-garde space that became, in its own right, a work of art – specifically, a work of American art.

Meyer opened the very first issue of *291* with 'How Versus Why', her bold manifesto on the status of art and art criticism in America. Her verdict was damning: she declared art criticism in its traditional form

'OBSOLETE', because 'it measures a new product with old standards and is therefore insidiously pernicious for it clouds the issues and befogs the mind of the public before the work of art has been able to make its own appeal.'[43] As Dodge had attempted in her essay on Stein's Post-Impressionist prose, Meyer made it clear that modern art had swept aside all traditional types of interpretation and understanding in pursuit of forms that conveyed what it meant to be alive in the twentieth century. Meyer appealed for critics of modern art to get past immediate emotional responses (specifically, the uncritical 'like or dislike', which is the 'why' of her title). Instead, they should 'analyze the thought-processes of the artist's mind, the way in which he thinks, how adequately he translates his thoughts into the symbols of his trade and what his relationship is to his fellow artists'.[44] Like Dodge, Meyer urged people to spend time processing new art forms, rather than rushing to judge after a first viewing.

By calling for new understandings of what art is and how we assess it, Meyer's editorial anticipated the *Fountain* scandal of 1917 and the essays that Louise Norton and Beatrice Wood wrote to defend it. She also set the tone for *291*, boldly declaring its aim to change how art was received, discussed and valued in the United States. Where Stieglitz was content to act as a gatekeeper for avant-garde art, Meyer and de Zayas wanted *291* to be part of a new movement that brought the artist and the public in direct contact. They hoped to show a wider public how modern art was part of the fast-paced, sometimes shocking, world they lived in at the start of a new century. It was part of a broader effort to bring forth work that developed directly from the conditions of modern life in the United States (as opposed to work that was derivative of European modernism). This attitude placed *291* at the vanguard of efforts to channel all that was modern and innovative about New York (skyscrapers, sidewalks illuminated by electric lights, billboards, a fast-paced city that was vastly heterogeneous and always in flux) into art and culture, to make a distinctly American art.

Meyer's contributions were an important part of *291*'s unique aesthetic. Branching out from journalism and essays, she collaborated with de Zayas on several dynamic visual poems that responded to life in the city. *Mental Reactions* is a particularly striking example. Its bold mixed-media form is immediately eye-catching, but, beyond this, Meyer's poem is strikingly modern and experimental. Meyer assembled fragments of text to convey a sense of shattered modern selfhood from a woman's perspective. Through snippets of thought, speech, advertisements and observation, Meyer explored the tensions and dilemmas that women faced – split between new possibilities and old-fashioned attitudes, between freedom and expectation. References to the location and views from the window situate the speaker at 291 gallery. Her text is scattered across the page, its form mirroring the flickering 'mental reactions' of thought as the poem's speaker engages in a charged conversation with an unnamed man. As they talk, she gazes out onto snow-covered roofs and thinks on her position as a modern woman, wife and mother.[45] Snippets of text from advertisements for 'cremes and parfums' allude to both the sensory overload of city life and the masks and disguises that women are pressured to adopt. She questions, 'why cannot all the loves of all the world be mine? . . . without the sacrifice of any of those things I think of when I say MYSELF.'[46] Elsewhere, in response to a demand that she 'accept whatever is given [her],' Meyer's speaker asks, 'But is it fair/ to the woman?/ Does it make her/ less – or more?' These questions come loaded with a sense of guilt. Acknowledging the advantages that accompany the compromises of marrying into great wealth, another voice in the speaker's head sneers 'sacrifice? . . . we women, cowards, cheats all of us, who, when our kingdom is offered, stop to calculate the price.'

Motherhood presents another splitting of the self in *Mental Reactions*, represented visually by a separate block of text on the right-hand side of the page. The booming of a clock interrupts the speaker's musings and her conversation with the male figure; it reminds her of 'Their bed-time/ They will want to say good-night./ I must go.' This nagging sense of guilt and divided interests sprang from personal experience. In the same year she began work on *291*, Meyer gave birth to her third child (of a total of five in relatively quick succession) and struggled to balance the domestic and public sides of her life. While nannies cared for her children, 291 gallery offered a retreat for this self-described 'unruly, self-centred, freedom-loving creature'.[47] Despite the demands of motherhood, this section of *Mental Reactions* seems both more

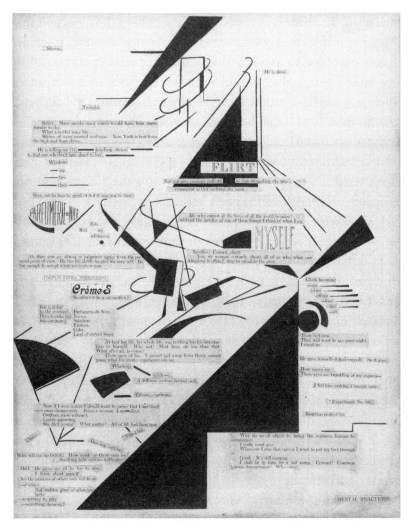

Marius de Zayas and Agnes Meyer, *Mental Reactions*, 1915, brush and pen and black ink with collage of cut-and-pasted texts over graphite on paperboard.

rebellious and less fraught than the others. In this column, the speaker exclaims that 'whenever I pass that canvas I want to put my foot through it' – a surprisingly violent rejection of the work at 291 gallery. The poem concludes with one last rhetorical question that shrugs off the speaker's guilt and uncertainty: 'who cares?'

Ironically, some critics have interpreted *Mental Reactions* as an expression of Meyer's stereotypical sexualized femininity. William Bohn's 1980 analysis of the poem seeks to reinstate the gendered power dynamic that Meyer railed against. For Bohn, Meyer's complex and dynamic exploration of gender is, in fact, simply a poem about eyeing up an 'attractive man at a gathering'.[48] Despite describing the piece as being made up of 'drawings by de Zayas and text by Meyer', he suggests that the word 'FLIRT' was added by de Zayas to call attention to Meyer's coquettish behaviour. Going further, Bohn takes this as proof that 'flirtation was Meyer's secret vice,' something which, he suggests, defines her role in the 291 circle.[49] It is odd to imagine that de Zayas would be moved to meddle with the text in this way, considering that (as Bohn states) Meyer composed the text and de Zayas added the art and design. It also seems troubling that de Zayas, Meyer's friend and collaborator, would imprint a stark denunciation of her behaviour on top of their work (or that Meyer would allow it). Bohn's reading of *Mental Reactions* undermines Meyer's active role in the 291 group and instead relegates her to the role of beautiful femme fatale, the common fate of women artists and patrons. It also misses one of the central points that Meyer makes in the poem: namely, the ways in which men are free to flirt, to give themselves without consequence, whereas women are pulled in many different directions and never fully free. As we shall see in the second chapter, this was a common dilemma faced by avant-garde women on the Greenwich Village scene: they were urged to be modern and embrace free love, while also being left to run the household and raise the children (or, for unmarried women, left alone to deal with the consequences of unplanned pregnancies and the judgement of wider society).

Meyer's close friend Katharine Rhoades also recognized the bind of being a modern woman in the art world. Rhoades was known for her painting, but the poetry she contributed to *291* shows a talent for experimental writing. Her texts were visually startling, featuring erratic typography and scattered stanzas to make a bold impact on the page. Like de Zayas and Meyer in their collaborations, Rhoades sought to convey the fast-paced, fragmented experience of modern life through experimental text. Rhoades's contributions to *291* were sufficiently avant-garde and eye-catching to result in an acknowledgement in Berlin Dadaist Richard Huelsenbeck's *Dada Almanack* (1920), where her name was included in the list of 'Présidents et Présidentes du mouvement Dada' (alongside fellow Americans Mabel Dodge, Louise Norton and Walter Arensberg).

In the pages of *291*, Rhoades became part of a lively exploration of modern art and culture's relation to the self, to gender and to the modern urban experience. In the May 1915 issue, Rhoades's poem 'I Walked into a Moment of Greatness' forms part of a dynamic double-page spread, along with text by Meyer (titled 'Woman') and a bold abstract design by de Zayas. Describing the experience of being at a concert, Rhoades's poem imagines its speaker being swept up in a transcendental swell that merges bodies, time and space. In this moment, the self becomes genderless: 'I was not a woman – I became merely a part of the attunement of the moment – as did all the others . . . we had dropped our little selves.'[50] For Rhoades, art offers hope of moving beyond the boundaries of the self, but the moment is all too brief. The poem ends with the speaker asking, 'if it could have endured – if a climax could have been reached and held for the fraction of a second – would not that instant

Katharine Rhoades,
Standing Nude, 1915,
oil on canvas.

have become infinite? Would it have been death? Or escape – into a quickening of life?'

'I Walked into a Moment of Greatness' reflects some of the concerns that Rhoades was dealing with at this time, as she struggled both to reach her potential as an artist and to wrangle with the expectations placed on her as a woman. A stark image that she created for the second issue of *291* responds to the high stakes women faced, away from art's potential to free the self from the confines of gender. Her sketch of a gun positioned between a sperm and ovum symbolizes the danger encoded in sexual relationships. It was also a direct response to a story in the editorial notices at the front of this issue, under the headline 'Motherhood a Crime', which describes how a young unmarried woman had recently killed herself due to the 'shame' of an illegitimate pregnancy.

During the time Rhoades was involved with *291*, she was all too familiar with the disparities between the image of the liberated modern woman that was popular in the media and the realities of life. The fact that women were playing a huge role in producing and promoting modern art in New York did little to redress the imbalance of power between men and women, in both personal and professional relationships. Unlike Meyer, Rhoades was unmarried and this left her vulnerable to the kind of unwelcome infatuations that all too often accompanied offers of practical, professional support from male artists and patrons. Being part of the 291 circle opened up opportunities for Rhoades, especially the chance to exhibit her paintings at the gallery. However, any sense of success that Rhoades experienced during these years was ultimately tainted by Stieglitz's unwanted and unwelcome advances.

Rhoades's strange and often fraught relationship with Stieglitz highlights the struggles for women artists within their avant-garde networks. It provides a clear example of how the celebrations of free love and sexual experimentation that flourished in New York's creative circles could be used against women and were still charged with gendered power dynamics. When they met, Stieglitz was a leading figure in New York's art world, in his late forties and married with a daughter; Rhoades was 21 years his junior and a little-known artist. She had also been recently bruised by an ill-fated affair with artist Arthur B. Carles, the husband of Rhoades's former friend Mercedes (who informed Rhoades's overbearing mother about the affair, intensifying Rhoades's pain and shame).[51]

Initially, Rhoades's contact with Stieglitz was a source of excitement and opportunity. In their early letters, Rhoades appears thrilled to develop a friendship with the wise, influential and well-connected Stieglitz. She keenly engaged in stimulating intellectual debates that covered the latest ideas about art, life and philosophy, ever eager to learn from a wise founding father of New York's art scene. As the pair became more intimately acquainted, Rhoades realized that Stieglitz did not see himself in a mentor–father role, but rather as a potential lover. In increasingly manipulative and probing letters, he attempted to persuade Rhoades that she could only fully realize her potential as an artist if she had an affair with him. Despite the fact that, at this point, Rhoades was in her late twenties and was not sexually inexperienced, Stieglitz repeatedly infantilized her: he told her that she was his 'wonder-child', who could only transform into his ideal, creatively liberated 'woman-child' if she gave herself to him sexually. She was, from the off, reluctant and uncomfortable, but Stieglitz continued undaunted. He pressured Rhoades using elements of Freudian theory he had heard at the lectures that A. A. Brill delivered at Mabel Dodge's salon; his letters made references to Rhoades's unhappy, repressive childhood, connecting this to what he claimed was her inability to free herself creatively and give herself sexually. Rhoades was caught between not wanting to lose the support of an influential ally in the art world and not wanting to compromise herself in an affair with a married man to whom she was not attracted. Her increasingly tortured responses to his letters show that Rhoades struggled to navigate this difficult position: 'When you wrote to the wonder-child, it was not to me . . . I cannot be the wonder-child. It isn't in me to be it. And so, the question I ask yourself is – not being able to be the wonder-child, can I be the friend?'[52]

It is clear from her letters that Rhoades realized that Stieglitz was projecting his fantasies and desires onto her. Stieglitz had elevated her into a mythical figure that bore no resemblance to her real self – 'it isn't me,' she told him repeatedly, but Stieglitz refused to listen. Frustrated by Rhoades's resolution, Stieglitz piled more and more pressure on her. Her refusal of him was not 'natural', he told her, and would stifle her artistic abilities. Over the few years of their correspondence in the mid-1910s, Stieglitz's manipulative tactics took their toll on Rhoades. She never gave in to his demands, but she began to agree with him that her 'inability' constituted a problem within herself, a failure to be an adventurous modern woman. Inevitably, when another talented young woman came onto his radar, Rhoades lost Stieglitz's attention and his support. As Steiglitz's obsession with his beguiling new protégé – Georgia O'Keeffe – grew, Rhoades's star fell; in a public lecture in the early 1920s, Stieglitz held up Rhoades as an example of a woman artist who had failed to unleash her creative potential.[53] Rhoades converted to Christianity during this decade and destroyed many of her paintings. While newfound religious devotion clearly spurred Rhoades to turn away from her former life as an artist, it is impossible not to suspect that the humiliations and attacks on her creative ability played a part in such a dramatic negation of her past.

Kathleen Pyne suggests that 'Stieglitz's courting of Rhoades as a child and an erotic woman was not simply a seduction strategy' but rather something 'fundamental to the artistic modernism of 291'.[54] Rhoades's experience highlights the extent to which Steiglitz's modernism was intertwined with a patriarchal sense of entitlement and domination, a show of power with which he controlled women artists and indulged his own desires. It was a pattern he would repeat with O'Keeffe, a woman who was in greater need of Stieglitz's financial support and therefore more inclined to risk navigating the kind of compromising relationship he expected. O'Keeffe gave herself to Stieglitz, both as a lover and as a muse, and hugely benefited from his dogged promotion of her as modernism's ultimate woman artist. However, his controlling behaviour and pursuit of other young women caused her continued distress. Over time, O'Keeffe engaged in certain acts of resistance, such as leaving New York to work alone and forbidding Stieglitz to exhibit his nude portraits of her after the early 1920s. In her later years, O'Keeffe's pursuit of a serious, ascetic image and her adamant disavowals of eroticized readings of her work can be seen as further attempts to escape the image of her that Stieglitz created. When

O'Keeffe stopped agreeing to pose naked for him, Stieglitz turned to other young female models, including his teenage niece, Georgia Engelhard; his images of Engelhard, which include nude shots of her (aged fourteen) posing with apples, in an allusion to Eve, highlight the disturbing elements of Stieglitz's obsession with the creative 'woman-child'.[55] Caught up in this patriarchal power play, Rhoades found that modern New York could be a deeply inhospitable place for a woman artist.

The role of 291's 'Three Graces' exemplifies the way that women's contributions to the making of New York's modern-art scene were minimized and erased. Despite being creative, active players in the 291 scene, they become passive, silent muses in the later narrative that was set down by male artists, gallerists, critics and art historians. Rhoades's story, in particular, shows the dark side of modern New York, revealing a patriarchal system of control and influence that would appear again years later, flourishing around the Abstract Expressionist movement. Yet for all of the struggles, Meyer, Rhoades and the other women around 291 helped shape New York's modern-art movement and move it forward in the years that followed the Armory Show. In *291*, Meyer and her collaborators created an 'American journal [that] was unparalleled anywhere in the world as a total work of art': 'in design and content, there was no periodical in America more advanced than *291*.'[56] Thanks to the efforts of Meyer and Rhoades, it is remarkable that such an important modern-art journal not only made space for women's experiences but, in the journal's early issues, made those experiences and perspectives a key part of its avant-garde expression.

At Home with Marguerite Zorach, 123 West Tenth Street

Since no gallery would show our work, we decided to have
little exhibitions in our studio on Tenth Street, and in time it
became a place of interest for people to see. We had decorated
it and there was nothing like it in the country at the time.
Our floors were red lead, our walls lemon yellow. We made
our hall into a little Garden of Eden, with a life-sized Adam
and Eve . . . critics and newspaper writers came around and

wrote about us in the Sunday supplements and on the art pages.
The real miracle was that people came to these exhibitions and
there was sometimes a sale.[57]

Marguerite Thompson Zorach was one of the few Americans who had
a first-hand encounter with European modernism in the days before
the Armory Show. To the horror of her traditional, middle-class parents,
Zorach abandoned a place at Stanford University (she had been one of
the very few women students accepted in 1908) to join her eccentric
Aunt Addie (Harriet Adelaide Harris, an artist) in Paris and study art.
Harris had encouraged her and sent money for the trip after recognizing
her young niece's talent. Zorach's years abroad were truly transformative, thanks largely to her aunt's network of creative friends. When
Harris had moved to Paris years earlier, she was thrilled to discover that
a childhood friend from Christian Science School back in San Francisco
lived there too and hosted a weekly salon for the city's radical young
artists and writers – none other than Gertrude Stein. Aunt Addie's connections ensured that Zorach found herself caught up in the whirlwind
of the Parisian art scene as soon as she arrived from California.

Joining Saturday gatherings at Stein and her partner Alice B. Toklas's
home at 27 rue de Fleurus, Zorach encountered many of the era's already
legendary artists, including Picasso, Matisse and Marie Laurencin.
Despite a busy social calendar, she worked hard on developing her art
practice; during the three years she studied at the progressive Académie
de la Palette, she adopted a Fauvist-inspired style and colour scheme
that would define her work throughout her career. Zorach also made
some important connections of her own among her peers at the acad-
emy. She found a close friend in English artist Jessie Dismorr, who
would become one of only two women in Wyndham Lewis's Vorticist
movement in London. Through Dismorr's associates in London, Zorach
contributed work to the modernist little magazine *Rhythm* (notable
for publishing Katherine Mansfield and D. H. Lawrence). Even more
significantly, however, she met William Finkelstein, the man who was
to become her lifelong creative partner and husband.

William was bowled over by the sophisticated, aesthetically daring
Marguerite. In his autobiography *Art Is My Life*, he recalls going over

Marguerite Zorach, *Scarf*, date unknown, silk batik.

to her easel after a class at la Palette to find her working on a shocking 'pink and yellow nude with a bold blue outline'; he was intrigued and a little outraged, failing to 'understand why such a nice girl would paint such wild pictures'.[58] Unlike William, who lacked experience of the art world, Marguerite was putting into practice styles and ideas she had encountered at Stein's salon. It was not just her art practice that was striking, but also her personal style: Marguerite did not look or 'dress like everyone else. Even then she made her own clothes. She wore a black silk turban on the back of her head with an enormous red rose in the centre . . . she was shy but sure of herself.'[59] Already, in those early years of her life as an artist, she pursued a holistic creative practice that brought art out from the canvas and into everyday life. Marguerite understood art as a way of modern living and free expression of the self. It was not enough to simply paint radical pictures; she also wanted to make clothes and household objects that expressed her creative vision. William quickly learned from this charming and dazzlingly talented young woman, making strides towards a modern style of his own; but, throughout their later partnership, it would be Marguerite's confidence and determination to pursue the life of an artist that kept William going through financial hardship and despair.

When Zorach's training in Paris came to an end, her Aunt Addie was horrified to discover that her niece's friendship with William had blossomed into romance. Although she was fond of William, she feared that marriage would inevitably put an end to her niece's promising career. Hoping that their relationship would peter out with time apart, Aunt Addie insisted that Zorach accompanied her on a world tour, while William glumly returned to New York. She was reluctant to be away from William for so long, but the trip (which included stops in Japan, China, India, Egypt, Myanmar and the Levant) would be incredibly significant to the development of Zorach's art, going beyond the influence of anything she had encountered in the Parisian modernist scene. Her encounters with non-Western art and design (particularly the weavings, carpets and wall hangings she studied during trips to India and the Middle East) brought rich new avenues of exploration. The textile art she created years later in New York continued to reference the artwork she'd seen during this world tour. Zorach's travels also helped to raise her profile back home in the United States. During her years abroad, she wrote regular columns about her experiences for the *Fresno Morning Republican*. When she finally returned to Fresno, California, after her world trip (in mid-1912), she had cultivated enough of a public profile to be invited to show an exhibition of her work and speak at local art schools. Meanwhile, in New York, William had saved the money he earned working in a lithograph shop in anticipation of the couple's eventual reunion and marriage. In other words, Aunt Addie's plan had failed.

Zorach moved from Fresno to New York on 24 December 1912 and married William that same day. Together, they chose to take the surname Zorach, which was originally William's first name (he was born Zorach Gorfinkel in Lithuania in 1889 and renamed William Finkelstein when his family emigrated to the United States five years later). It symbolized the start of a new creative as well as romantic partnership – even if, in practice, the couple would never quite escape the gender biases of both the art world and wider society. Once settled in New York, the Zorachs set about becoming part of the arts scene. It was the start of a whirlwind time of success and struggle. Marguerite's headstrong nature carried both of them through many stretches of extreme financial hardship, her belief in their creative talents never wavering; when William was offered a decent salary to take up a job at a lithography shop, Marguerite forbade him to accept because it would compromise his dedication to art.

The couple sold few paintings in those early years, but they did receive some key acknowledgement. At the start of 1913, both Zorachs found out that their work had been accepted for the Armory Show. This was quite a feat considering they had so recently arrived in New York and were therefore not part of the city's avant-garde circles. At the show, William's work failed to gain any attention, but Marguerite's painting *Study* caught the eye of critics. With its startling Fauvist colour palette and modern subject-matter (an experimental portrait of a woman), *Study* was exactly the style of work that horrified and bemused visitors. Like Matisse's scandalous *Blue Nude* (1907), Marguerite's *Study* represented the so-called insane and barbaric character of modernist artists. Sadly *Study* is now lost, but a critic for the *New York American* described the portrait as showing a lady 'feeling very, very bad. She is portraying her emotions after a day's shopping. The pale yellow eyes and purple lips of her subject indicate that the digestive organs are not functioning properly.' The critic's satirical take on *Study* betrays the latent misogyny and assumptions around the unhealthy, uncivilized nature of modern art that pervaded much of the contemporary discourse around it. In a more ambiguous appraisal, the *New York Times* commented on Zorach's 'extreme modernity'.

Boosted by their inclusion in the groundbreaking Armory Show, the Zorachs were soon at the heart of Greenwich Village's creative scene. Marguerite's striking personal style and talent for fusing modern and applied arts meant that she quickly became one of the Village's much-written-about modern women. Unlike some Villagers who spent more time debating in cafés than they did creating work, the Zorachs threw themselves into helping build up New York's developing art scene. In addition to the couple's valuable experience in Europe, Marguerite's drive and determination were essential at a time when there were few venues for young modern American artists to exhibit. As the

Armory Show had demonstrated, artists and supporters of modern art had to be hands-on and proactive in making space for art in New York. Establishing supportive communities and networks was vital to the development of American modernism. In his autobiography, William describes their efforts to source ad hoc exhibition venues in any abandoned spaces they could find:

> We were active in most of the independent shows that took place after the Armory Show. Some were held in vacant ground-floor stores which we rented, some in the Grand Central Palace, and some on the roof of the old Waldorf-Astoria . . . [The] first ones [were] held on the ground floor of a building on Forty-second street west of Sixth Avenue in about 1915 . . . I decorated a white suit and umbrella in vivid cubistic colours and hired a man to parade up and down Forty-second street in this suit. He was stopped by the police.[60]

Alongside putting together group shows in vacant buildings, the Zorachs opened their own home to fellow artists and avant-garde writers. To preserve what little income they received in these early years, they did not eat and drink at Greenwich Village's cafés (exceptions were occasionally made for balls at Webster Hall and the Liberal Club, when Marguerite made the costumes and decorations); instead, inviting people to their home was a way of networking and being part of the art community without spending money. In the post-Armory landscape, the Zorachs' apartment at 123 West Tenth Street was part of an unconventional map made up of homes, studios, fledgling galleries, cafés, shops and empty buildings, all of which were taken over in the service of modern art.

The Zorachs' home was a vibrant meeting place that played host to small exhibitions, artistic debates and late-night parties. It attracted experimental young poets including Alfred Kreymborg, Marianne Moore and William Carlos Williams, as well as artists, who would gather at the Zorachs' to discuss the future of poetry and develop ideas for new little magazines. Marguerite's creative vision helped set the tone, turning what was a crumbling, run-down apartment into a marvel.

She covered the filthy kitchen walls with murals and batik wall hangings, brightening the dark spaces with vibrant Fauvist colours. The couple salvaged furniture they found abandoned on the city streets or bought pieces cheap at second-hand shops, then restored and painted them. The Zorachs' apartment was a site where art and everyday life merged, in a perfect expression of Marguerite's increasingly holistic creative vision. It was a family home as well as a studio and exhibition space and, as such, there were no boundaries between the domestic and the creative for the Zorachs.

The Zorachs strove to create a progressive marriage of equals and were unusual in that they supported one another's careers throughout their life together. Nevertheless, the arrival of their children inevitably impacted Marguerite's work much more than William's. Reflecting on the birth of their first child, Tessim, in 1915, William claimed: 'I can't

Marguerite Thompson Zorach, *Grapefruit*, c. 1927, lithograph.

even remember that this complicated our life. He slept in a corner of the studio, and when we had all-night parties, he never said a word.'[61] But with the addition of their daughter Dahlov, in 1917, Marguerite felt the burden of domesticity weighing down on her. The couple hired their neighbour Ella Madison (then a down-on-her-luck stage performer who would later star in the first performance of *Porgy and Bess*) to work as a nanny, their 'one extravagance'.[62]

Madison's labour helped ease the load, but Marguerite still struggled to find the large stretches of unbroken time required to paint. Typical of her determined spirit, she explored alternative ways of creating art that would fit around domestic life. Recalling the incredible examples of textile art that she saw during her time in Asia and the Middle East, Marguerite began experimenting with embroidery. In textiles, Marguerite discovered she could achieve heightened versions of scenes she painted, particularly by using richly coloured woollen yarns that were more vibrant and varied than paints. She made bedspreads, hooked rugs, wall hangings, silk scarves and carpets depicting vivid scenes draw from daily life, natural iconography and abstract geometric repeat patterns. The result was a striking mix of formal elements drawn from Islamic and Indian art, traditional American folk art and a modernist aesthetic.

Zorach's textile art was a true achievement of American modernism. She used a traditionally domestic craft to capture modern visions of urban life (for example, in the exquisite *The City of New York in the Year Nineteen Hundred and Twenty*), placing folk art and a modern Fauvist style in dialogue with global art forms. In her lifetime, Zorach's move into textile mediums proved to be both incredibly successful and a financial lifeline for her family. Commissions began to flood in from wealthy families and cultural patrons, including Abby Aldrich Rockefeller (whose tapestry took three years to finish). The money Zorach made from a tapestry for philanthropists Ralph and Selda Jonas in the late 1920s saw her family through the Depression years of the early 1930s. Exhibitions also followed, including a successful 1923 exhibition at the Montross Gallery of Zorach's tapestries, textiles and work in batik (a decorative technique created by applying wax to fabric before dying it, imported from Indonesia, Japan and India); however,

Marguerite Zorach, *The Family*, 1917, plain-weave silk, wool embroidery.

in the long term, the fact that her work was so popular with private collectors had a negative impact on Zorach's reputation, as few pieces were available to exhibit at galleries. Combined with craft's historic association with femininity and domesticity, this led to Marguerite being classed as the lesser artist of the two Zorachs. Despite her being one of the more 'extreme' modernists at the Armory Show, William's profile ultimately overshadowed hers.

The Zorachs' daughter Dahlov Ipcar (a successful artist and illustrator in her own right) remembered her mother as 'independent and outspoken, a feminist ahead of her time. She was anti-establishment, anti-religious, pro-art, pro-creative.'[63] She alludes to her mother's activities in promoting women's art and claiming a space for women in the male-dominated art world. Despite the demands of her own career and domestic life, Zorach found time to represent the interests of women artists. In 1925 she joined with other American women artists who had exhibited at the Armory Show to set up the New York Society of Women Artists (NYSWA), which provided support and arranged exhibitions (Zorach was its first president).[64] Zorach often spoke out in interviews and essays in the 1920s about the challenges that women artists faced. The same year as she became president of the NYSWA, Zorach spoke to women's suffrage magazine *Equal Rights* about the fundamental inequalities that impacted women's success as artists:

> Dealers take men artists under their wing and promote them, push them as a good business proposition, but they refuse to take women artists seriously . . . I started by holding joint exhibitions with my husband. We were a team, and, as such, they were not afraid of me. I am certain that had I not had an artist husband, and had I tried to exhibit on my own, I would have had all the difficulties.[65]

Zorach's comments reveal that being married to an artist had some advantages, in terms of getting a foot in doors that would otherwise have been slammed shut. The couple's creative partnership helped Zorach promote her work and build a public profile. Her comments also allude to the ways that American women artists were doubly impacted by the lack of infrastructure to support modern art in New York. When there were already few galleries and dealers willing to take a risk on avant-garde art, women artists were even less likely to be given exhibitions or sell work.

Zorach's path from the Armory Show was atypical: unlike many women artists who were also wives and mothers, she managed to maintain a relatively prolific output throughout her life, but this also necessitated a move away from painting, into a less respected (and stereotypically 'feminine'-coded) medium. In her lifetime, Zorach was careful to frame her textile work as modern art, referring to it as 'pictures in wool' or 'modern tapestries in colored wools', to anticipate it being assigned to the lesser category of craft.[66] Unfortunately for Zorach's reputation, the boundaries dividing 'masculine' art and 'feminine' craft in the United States only became more deeply entrenched as the century progressed. Only now, more than a century on from the Armory Show, can we begin to appreciate Zorach's contribution to shaping modern art in America – whether through her holistic approach to revolutionizing daily life through art by merging the domestic and creative spheres, or providing support to fellow artists and making space for the modern creative arts to flourish; or in her own innovative handcrafted textile art.

The Whitney Studios, 19 MacDougal Alley

I cannot be the sort of person which my life demands me
to be – so why not try and be my own self . . . say what you
think for a change, be what you are for a change.[67]

In 1916, Gertrude Vanderbilt Whitney commissioned a portrait by the American realist painter Robert Henri, a leading figure in the Ashcan School. The painting shows Whitney reclining on a sofa, staring impassively at the viewer. Her relaxed pose projects an air of confidence and authority befitting her stage of life: at 41 years old, she was a successful artist about to embark on her first solo show and an admired arts patron. Whitney was also extremely privileged, having been born into one of America's wealthiest families (the Vanderbilts) and married into another (the Whitneys). Her vast family wealth enabled her success, but she also created a reputation and a life quite different from that which was expected of a high-society heiress.

Henri's portrait celebrates her transformation into an influential, independent modern woman. Whitney is dressed in a stylish, silky green trouser suit; evoking Léon Bakst's costumes and Paul Poiret's designs, it gives Whitney an androgynous look. Her penchant for trousers was shocking, particularly in the high-society circles she sometimes mixed in: as late as 1932, Whitney's niece Gloria Vanderbilt recalled being shocked at such an eccentricity as a woman in trousers, something she had never seen before.[68] The short hairstyle that Whitney sports in Henri's portrait adds to the sense of androgyny; the jewel tones and rich fabrics evoke an opulence that nods to her wealth and status. The portrait's decadent details do not distract from Whitney herself: draped across the sofa, her body is sensuous but strong, ready to spring into action. The stylized nature of the painting gives Whitney a youthful glow that belies her age. Like Florine Stettheimer, Whitney carefully controlled her image, often subverting gender norms and adopting an ageless appearance (achieved, in photographs, by retouching techniques).

When the portrait was complete, Whitney's husband (businessman and horse breeder Harry Payne Whitney) famously refused to hang it in their Fifth Avenue home because he did not want his friends to see his wife 'in pants'. Nonplussed, Whitney gave it pride of place in her Greenwich Village studio. It was a characteristic statement of boldness from a woman who had long since decided to carve out her own path in life. In autobiographical sketches, Whitney recalls feeling restless and out of place from an early age: at four years old, she cut off her hair because she 'longed to be a boy'; by eleven, she realized, with deep dismay, that her family wealth and status meant she would be famous, talked about and unable to do various things 'simply because I was Miss Vanderbilt'.[69] As a young woman, her activities were closely scrutinized, preparing her for a life upholding the family's name and legacy. Her mother sought to stamp out the romantic relationships Whitney developed with two close female friends (the most significant being Esther Hunt), warning her to beware people who 'chase rich girls'. Chaperones monitored the time spent with young male suitors, which meant that she spent virtually no time alone with Harry before their marriage in 1896.[70] It quickly became clear that the couple had little common ground. When Harry began spending most of his time playing sports, Whitney rejected the role of traditional society wife and resolved to find an occupation of her own. American art soon became something of a vocation, despite her family's disapproval. Whitney's social status made her activities on the arts scene a source of scorn, ridicule and gossip, but her wealth afforded her the luxury of independence and opportunity.

From 1900, Whitney began building her career as a sculptor, starting with lessons at the Art Students League of New York. Her work was traditional and realist in style and often grand in scale. As a result, she began earning commissions for public monuments, including a sculpture for the New York State Building at the 1901 Pan-American Exposition and the Washington Heights–Inwood War Memorial (dedicated to local men killed serving in the First World War, directly inspired by her own experiences working in a field hospital). Alongside creating her own work, Whitney developed links to Greenwich Village via her association with Greenwich House. This innovative institution was set up in 1902 by social reformer Mary Kingsbury Simkhovitch as a place that provided advice, support and training to immigrant families in Greenwich Village. Whitney joined the board of trustees, taught art classes and in 1909 donated the funds for a pottery workshop, which, in turn, led to the establishment of a vibrant arts programme that continues to this day.[71] This was the start of a long relationship with the Village, a place that became Whitney's professional creative home and an escape from the stuffiness and strictures of high society.

After spending her teenage years chafing against the oppressive elite world she grew up in and feeling constantly out of place, it's not surprising that Whitney was drawn to Greenwich Village. Its growing bohemian artist community was ripping up the rules that governed bourgeois society and experimenting with new ways of living and being modern. In 1907, Whitney decided to buy a studio on MacDougal Alley, a mews one block down from Washington Square, right at the heart of the Village. The area was known for being ramshackle and run down but Whitney found the perfect spot: her studio had high ceilings and large windows that let in plenty of light, ideal for an artist. As she anticipated, the press reported this development with amusement; one headline sensationally declared 'Daughter of Cornelius Vanderbilt Will Live in Dingy New York Alley' (in fact, Whitney's official residence was the family's mansion on Fifth Avenue).[72] The other artists who worked in neighbouring studios were more supportive. Fellow sculptor Malvina Hoffman recalled that Whitney 'worked tirelessly but was never too busy to help young sculptors; her generosity was well known to the profession'.[73] Indeed, generosity was the bedrock of Whitney's life as an artist and arts patron. After her death, John Sloan noted that there were 'innumerable artists whose studio rent was paid, or [whose] pictures were purchased just at the right time to keep the wolf from the door, or hospital expenses covered, or a trip to Europe made possible' thanks to Whitney.[74] Henry McBride claimed there was not a single 'contemporary artist of note in America' who hadn't received her help.

For Whitney, Greenwich Village opened up a way of putting her wealth and influence to good use, not just by supporting charitable organizations like Greenwich House but through providing for its growing community of struggling young American artists. As Sloan highlights, she helped fellow artists with a range of professional and personal costs, recognizing that artists needed independence and time to develop their practice. In addition, Whitney identified the dearth of networks and institutional support systems that American artists sorely lacked. She helped out a range of schools, societies and institutions that represented all types of art, from conservative and neoclassical to avant-garde and experimental. Her generosity and enthusiasm for promoting the arts in America led her to be part of some crucial moments in the development of American modernism. When Davidge, Fitch, Kuhn and the other exhibiting artists at the Madison Gallery began discussing ideas for the Armory Show, Davidge turned to Whitney for help and advice. Although Whitney was not a radical artist, she became a staunch supporter of the avant-garde; her funding kept the Society of Independent Artists going, contributed to the printing of the *Blind Man* magazine, and bankrolled the infamous *Brâncuși* v. *The United States* court case, which successfully overturned the import tariff placed on *Bird in Space* (after it had been deemed 'raw material', not art, by customs officials).

Whitney's studio developed into a centre for creativity and collaboration, where artists would gather to show work, discuss ideas and socialize. Through the 1910s, Whitney expanded her influence in the

Village. She bought 8 West Eighth Street, around the corner from her MacDougal Alley studio, to set up two galleries, making it easier to host exhibitions of work by artists she supported. She also purchased other buildings in the area for the purpose of renting out affordable studios and apartments. By 1918, Whitney turned her attentions to creating a social club for artists, which would provide exhibition space, a library and rooms for relaxing and recreation; she was inspired by conversations with young artists and students, which revealed a lack of affordable space to support creativity in the city.

The Whitney Club Studio, as the new venue was named, opened at 147 West Fourth Street opposite the Village's favourite dive bar, the Golden Swan (also known as the Hell Hole). Whitney hired her friend Dorothy Draper, a pioneering interior designer, to decorate the studio. Draper's bright design scheme featured modern silk curtains in jewel tones and was complemented by matching furniture made at Greenwich House. In addition to the galleries and library, a squash court and billiard room were added, enhancing the social nature of the club. Artists could become members for $5 a year, although, in reality, collection of membership fees was not routinely enforced (and no records were kept). It was an incredibly popular venture: in ten years, membership swelled from an initial twenty to over four hundred. In the mid-1920s a shop also opened so that members could sell prints and drawings as a way to make money and attract the attention of collectors. Like all of Whitney's organizations and activities, it was a lifeline for progressive young American artists who had few options for showing or selling art. Her club and studios filled in gaps in New York's post-Armory Show cultural landscape, providing much-needed venues for modern art and artists to flourish.

Whitney's personal generosity, passion and understanding saw her influence expand from a single studio to, ultimately, the Whitney Museum of American Art. However, other commitments took her away from Greenwich Village: she often spent time at her second studio in Paris and she couldn't entirely avoid the expectations that being a member of the Vanderbilt and Whitney families brought. As Whitney's investments in New York's modern art scene grew, she increasingly relied on the indomitable spirit of her indispensible right-hand woman – Juliana Force. Force lived up to her name: she was forthright, irrepressible and intensely charismatic. Her background was very different from the privilege and luxury that Whitney had been born into, but both women shared a refusal to settle for a staid life or conform to expectations.

In later life, Force would affect a wealthy and cultured upbringing, but the reality was a rather more humble childhood in Hoboken, New Jersey. Force was a gifted child with literary ambitions. Recognizing her talent, a teacher insisted that she be allowed to continue her education rather than leave school at twelve and start work as her elder sisters had done. With financial help from the local church congregation, Force was sent to a Christian girls' school, but it proved to be a poor match for her headstrong, independent nature. She dropped out and became a teacher, writing (unsuccessfully) on the side. The course of her life changed when she began a scandalous affair with Willard Force, an older married man. Willard divorced his wife to marry Juliana and the couple made a fresh start in New York, away from gossip. The move was truly transformative: after finding work as the social secretary of Helen Hay Whitney in 1907, Force soon crossed paths with Helen's sister-in-law, Gertrude Vanderbilt Whitney. Like many others, Whitney was drawn into the orbit of the smart, captivating Force and immediately realized the value of her talents. Whitney offered Force a job as her literary agent, tasked with selling a novel that she had written under her pen name, Phyllis Lane. Force accepted the role but failed to find a publisher for the book. Nevertheless, Whitney recognized something of a kindred spirit in Force and offered her work on a broader portfolio.

By the time that the Whitney Studio opened in 1914, Force had become essential to Whitney's mission. Although she initially knew little about art, her quick intellect, combined with her charming social skills, meant that she was soon a respected and savvy player in the New York art world. In many ways, Force's outsider status was an advantage in a scene where rules and traditions had been tossed aside. Her ethos was 'think for yourself', which meant that one must 'face [the artwork] alone' in order to make an independent judgement, paying no attention to art critics or the status of the artist.[75] Force learnt to trust her own taste, while also valuing the input of a small circle of artists whom she knew to be reliable and impartial: Robert Henri and John Sloan were among the group that advised Force as she purchased work by young American artists for the Whitney collection. While Whitney was away in Paris (first supporting the hospital she funded during the First World War and, later, working at her studio there), Force was not just a safe pair of hands, but a driving force in continuing and developing their work in New York. The Whitney Museum's librarian Marie Appleton remembered her as a fascinating self-made woman of 'great ability', always 'ahead of a lot of people', and adept at managing the artists (and Whitney!).[76]

Force was also instrumental in ensuring that the legacy she and Whitney built prevailed through the twentieth century. The question of what would happen to Whitney's collection was fraught with difficulty: in 1929, Whitney offered her collection to the Metropolitan Museum of Art, along with $5 million for a purpose-built wing in her name. Her offer was unceremoniously rejected – the collection was too modern for the conservative Met's tastes. The two women decided to open their own museum, based at one of Whitney's studios in the Village. Force became its first director, overseeing renovations and expanding the collection. From the outset, the museum was designed with a pedagogical mission in mind. It sold and commissioned art books, and had an ambitious educational plan that encompassed lectures, debates and national tours of works from its collection. The Whitney Museum's opening was heralded by *Vogue*'s art editor Helen Appleton Read, who praised the 'generosity and far-sightedness' of Mrs Harry Payne Whitney, which had 'at last . . . given [American art] the recognition and serious consideration it deserved'.[77] Read detailed the support Whitney had given artists in the years after the Armory Show, taking care to credit 'the able and far-seeing direction of Mrs Willard Force', Whitney's right-hand woman. The establishment of the museum was a fitting final step in both Whitney's and Force's commitment to supporting and celebrating modern American art.

Thirteen years after Whitney and Force's failed negotiations with the Met, Whitney died. Initially, her family decided that the museum was a financial burden. Without consulting Force, they approached the Met. In the intervening almost decade and a half, tastes and understandings of American art had shifted. By 1942, the Met was eager to subsume Whitney's eclectic modern collection. But Force had other ideas. She was still furious about the contempt that the Met had showed Whitney and was deeply suspicious of their intentions. Refusing to take a backseat in negotiations, she staunchly defended the Whitney Museum's interests. Even after a diagnosis of cancer that would prove fatal, Force rallied herself to attend every meeting between the two museum groups in order to advocate for the Whitney. Indeed, Force's final contribution to New York's arts and culture scene was to preserve the Whitney Museum: just a few months before her death in August 1948, the merger was called off and the Whitney family resolved to keep the museum open, ensuring a legacy that continues into the present day.

Whitney's huge privilege gave her the means to – quite literally – put her name on the map of New York City. Her wealth gave her an enviable level of independence and autonomy as a woman artist, but her lifelong project encompassed much more than simply her own ambition. Through her studios and galleries, Whitney advocated for young modern artists and gave them space to develop. She was an early supporter of American art at a time when many patrons, collectors, critics and gallerists shunned it in favour of more prestigious European work. With Force by her side, Whitney worked hard to ensure that the opportunities brought about by the Armory Show were not lost, that New York began to treat modern art (and modern American artists) seriously. Like Dodge, Zorach, Meyer and Rhoades, Whitney helped reshape the city's art scene into something dynamic, internationally connected and ambitious in scope. Forming supportive networks with other women who embraced public roles and independent urban lives, they ensured that the riot and revolution sparked by the Armory Show rolled on through the 1910s – and beyond.

2

GREENWICH VILLAGE:
Restless Women of the Smock Colony

It was a bitterly cold night in the middle of a freezing New York winter, 1917. Braving the icy weather, a ragtag group of drunken bohemians made their way through Greenwich Village, armed with wine, snacks and cap pistols. Once they reached the imposing Washington Square Arch, they crept through an open gate that led inside to its steep spiral staircase and hurried up to the top. Once atop, they set up a small party, complete with a picnic and bottles of wine, and decorated the arch with balloons and paper lanterns. Among this mischievous band of Arch Conspirators, as they became known, was Marcel Duchamp – never one to miss out on a booze-fuelled prank – and the painter John Sloan, as well as a few actors from the Provincetown Players theatre collective and the poet Gertrude Drick. Their mission was to declare Greenwich Village a 'Free and Independent Republic' and, in honour of the occasion, Drick recited the republic's nonsensical constitution: a single word – 'whereas' – repeated several times. As dawn neared, the group disbanded, leaving only a trail of red, white and blue balloons fluttering at the top of the arch to mark the symbolic moment.

The Arch Conspiracy was a typical Greenwich Village escapade, but this playful, peaceful mock coup had a serious political message at this particular moment in time, as the United States stood on the brink of entering the First World War. The nationalism and warmongering sweeping the country was completely anathema to Greenwich Village's socialist, pacifist ethos and united both its avant-garde artists and its political activists in disgust. As war encroached into their self-built bohemia, many felt compelled to assert their ideals – to shout them from the top of Washington Square Arch, literally and metaphorically, in protest. The Arch Conspirators were expressing a common sentiment felt by those who made the Village their home in the 1910s. Its growing community was a magnet for artists, intellectuals, activists and anyone eager to free themselves from gender norms and the moral codes enforced by patriarchal, capitalist bourgeois society. Anarchist Hippolyte Havel proclaimed Greenwich Village a 'spiritual zone of the mind' (a phrase that anticipates its later incarnation as the centre of 1960s beat counterculture).[1]

Anna Alice Chapin, one of the first to capitalize on the area's burgeoning tourist industry, echoed Havel's sentiments in her 1920 guidebook, in which she declared that Greenwich Village 'is not only a locality . . . it is a point of view'.[2] The Village became widely known as Bohemia or the 'smock colony' (in reference to the loose-fitting artistic smocks that Village women wore), symbolizing its separation from the rest of the city and its open attitude towards alternative lifestyles. The 'smock colony' best encapsulates the Village's core qualities and quirks: women were absolutely at the forefront of its cultural and political life (something that was unprecedented in America and Europe at this time). Their fashion choices represented a physical liberation from old-fashion corsetry and other restrictive garments that went hand in hand with the many other freedoms that Villagers were seeking. In Village bookshop owner Frank Shay's opinion, 'in all this great United States it is the only place a person can sport a stocking with a hole in the heel, and an idea. Elsewhere both are taboo.'[3] Casting conservative values aside, the Village's residents embarked on experiments in new ways living and creating art. Life itself was a creative practice; to this end, interior decoration, clothing and socializing all became part of collaborative efforts to build modern communities and break free from the past.

At the height of its radical bohemianism in the mid-1910s, Greenwich Village was a space for fantasy, experimentation and subversion. It was underpinned by an interconnected network of artists, intellectuals and activists all working together to revolutionize art, politics and everyday life. Collaborative creative groups thrived in this febrile atmosphere. From political groups like the feminist Heterodoxy club to the

GREENWICH VILLAGE

By

ANNA ALICE CHAPIN

Author of "Wonder Tales from Wagner,"
"Masters of Music," etc.

WITH ILLUSTRATIONS BY
ALLAN GILBERT CRAM

NEW YORK
DODD, MEAD AND COMPANY
1917

Anna Alice Chapin,
Greenwich Village
(1917).

Provincetown Players theatre group, gatherings of radical, visionary people sprang up across the Village. Magazines were one of the Village's most powerful outputs, often providing a platform for new ideas and a range of work, from political essays to avant-garde sketches. *The Masses*, a socialist, anti-militarist magazine that published poetry and art as well as political articles, operated from 91 Greenwich Avenue and featured many of the Village's activists and writers as regular contributors. When writer and activist Max Eastman became editor in 1912, he used his first editorial to declare *The Masses* a cooperatively owned and published magazine, whose 'final policy is to do as it pleases and conciliate nobody, not even its readers'.[4]

Eastman later linked the beginning of *The Masses* (under his editorship) with 'the birth of "Greenwich Village" as a self-conscious entity, an American Bohemia', highlighting how essential such groups and organizations were in the formation of the Village as a centre for radicalism, feminism and avant-garde art.[5] Similarly, the innovative literary magazine the *Little Review* (which combined experimental poetry from the likes of Baroness Elsa von Freytag-Loringhoven and Mina Loy with support for anarchism and feminism) moved its offices to Greenwich Village in 1917 to continue its mission of breaking new ground and 'making no compromise with the public taste'.[6] In the pages of these magazines, avant-garde art and radical politics collided. The Village provided a site on which eclectic groups could map their desires, ideals and experimentations in art, love, life and politics. Webster Hall hosted extravagant costume balls, fundraisers and political rallies, bringing together residents of all factions in acts of subversion and solidarity. However, much of Village life played out in its cafés, tea rooms and restaurants, all of which offered cheap meals in informal surroundings; many, such as Polly's, the Mad Hatter and Romany Marie's were run by women who were also active members of artist and political activist circles. These were spaces of lively camaraderie, where residents would gather each evening to exchange ideas, drink and cut loose. Proprietor Romany Marie described them as 'centers . . . not so much restaurants as centers for people to get off the edge of the ordinary'.[7]

Among the woman-dominated communities in the Village, forms of feminism flourished, but there were also many creative women who would not have defined themselves as feminists, despite seeking independent lives not defined by roles as wives and mothers. The pressures of family and the fact that the struggle for women to win and maintain new rights was still in its early days complicated many of these women's attempts to 'become modern'. Village socialist and feminist activist Crystal Eastman noted in a 1918 essay on 'Birth Control in the Feminist Program', 'Feminism means different things to different people,' ranging from voting rights to 'freedom to enter athletic contests and games', 'social and sex freedom' and 'the freedom to choose one's way of making a living as men do'; for Eastman, 'sex knowledge' (that is, freedom of choice concerning if and when a woman gets pregnant) was essential for all women, whether conscious or – in Eastman's words – unconscious feminists.[8] In the Village, there were many ways of being a modern woman or a feminist, but key issues around bodily autonomy and economic freedom were impossible to avoid.

Visions of the modern, bohemian Village women are deeply inflected by race and class. The (mostly) young women who sought freedom from traditional forms of living in Greenwich Village's studios, salons, cafés and clubs were typically white and of middle- or upper-class backgrounds; their methods of agitating for change and experiences of building unconventional lives offer just one (white and, in the main, financially privileged) perspective on feminism and the modern woman in early twentieth-century New York. There are, of course, many more: not least the 'wayward lives and beautiful experiments' being pursued by young Black women in 1910s and '20s New York, unfolded by Saidiya Hartman.[9] The history of Black women's essential role in fighting for women's rights in the United States – which Martha S. Jones explores in *Vanguard: How Black Women Broke Barriers, Won the Vote, and Insisted on Equality for All* (2020) – largely runs parallel to the activism of white feminists, due to entrenched racism and prejudice within white suffrage movements.

This current book is interested in the ways that Village feminism inflected and merged with innovations in the avant-garde arts scene that centred around Greenwich Village and the salons of Walter and Louise Arensberg and the Stettheimer sisters; an arts scene that ossified into a male-dominated movement in later critical evaluations but which, during its chaotic heyday, was shaped by the influence of a network of restless women. Looking again at the development of modern art in New York through the lens of their (gendered, raced and classed) experiences offers a new perspective on its relationship with broader social and cultural shifts.

This chapter maps out some of the Village's significant feminist radicals and its daring rogues (that is, women artists and writers), revealing how the two groups met, merged and sometimes shot off in different directions. In the Village, New York's emerging modern-art scene blossomed against a backdrop of feminism and socialism; its radical activists

Clara Tice, illustration for *Greenwich Village Inn*.

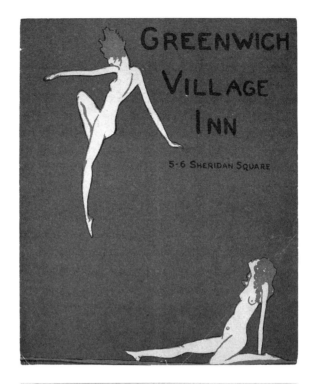

GREENWICH
VILLAGE
INN
5-6 SHERIDAN SQUARE

⚥⚥⚥⚥ DRINK LIST ⚥⚥⚥⚥

	Greenwich Village Inn Cider	Large Pitcher 5.00	Small 2.00
CUPS:	Virginia Dare	Large Pitcher 5.50	Small 2.00
	Chompomme	Large Pitcher 4.00	Small 2.50

COCKTAILS

Clover Leaf	.50
Cherry Blossom	.50
Jack Rose	.50

HIGHBALLS

Grenadine	.50
Loganberry	.50
Grappe de France	.50

PUNCHES
Fruit, Greenwich Village 50

LEMONADES

Plain	.50
Fruit	.50
Grappe de France	.50
Seltzer	.50
Lemon Squash	.50
Grenadine Lemonade	.50
Orangeade	.50
Orange or Lemon Juice	.50

FANCY DRINKS

Creme de Menthe Frappe	.50
Mint Julep, Superior	.50
Grenadine Punch	.50

MINERAL WATERS

White Rock	Split	.50
Apollinaris	Split	.50
Perrier	Split	.60

GINGER ALES

White Rock	Split	.50
C. & C.	Split	.50
Canada Dry	Split	.50
Clicquot sec.	Split	.50
G.V.I. Special	Split	.50

BEVERAGES

Pabst Blue Ribbon	.50
Anheuser-Busch Budweiser	.50
Trommer's White Label	.50
Sarsaparilla	.50
Lemon Soda	.50

Clara Tice, drink menu for *Greenwich Village Inn*.

Arnold Genthe,
Crystal Eastman,
1916, black and
white glass negative.

developed campaigns and theorized new political movements in the same spaces that women created provocative experiments in art and literature. Art and politics collided in the active, independent lives that many Village women carved out for themselves, but the Village's ideals were also pushed to the limit. Free love proved to be less freeing than some might have hoped, and, as the experiences of Baroness Elsa von Freytag-Loringhoven (whom we shall meet later in this chapter) demonstrate, misogyny and ageism lurked close to the surface of what first appeared to be progressive bohemianism. Indeed, women had to constantly ward against the oppressive attitudes they moved to the village to escape. Queer women, in particular, suffered the same kinds of marginalization and harassment within artistic circles as in more ostensibly conservative groups elsewhere. Lillian Faderman describes how 'many bohemian men, if they could take lesbianism seriously at all, resented not only women's ties to each other but their general assertiveness, which in itself may have signified danger.'[10] When poet Edna St Vincent Millay moved to the Village, *The Masses* editor Floyd Dell set about (unsuccessfully) trying to 'rescue' her from lesbianism by pressuring her into a sexual relationship.

By the dawn of the 1920s, the Village heyday was over (until a later generation of bohemians arrived in the 1960s, pursuing their own ideals of free love, free poetry and anti-capitalist activism). It underwent a strange transition from a space of socialist and feminist beliefs, where alternative ways of living were dreamed up and debated, to a tourist hotspot populated by woman-led businesses catering to visiting slummers (as those who came to gawp at bohemia were known). The arrival of the West Side Subway in 1917, which brought the Village in easy reach of Wall Street and Times Square, further fuelled a process of gentrification that priced the artists out. Greenwich Village's early twentieth-century bohemia was short-lived and its shifting community was often in pursuit of contradictory aims and ideals. Nevertheless, the Village offered women the space, freedom and community with which to fashion new identities as artists and writers. Their contributions to modern art and culture have often been marginalized, but their restless

'The Dutch Oven', from Anna Alice Chapin, *Greenwich Village* (1917).

searching for modern forms of self-expression echoes through the century of American art that followed.

Radicals: Feminism in the Village

Restless women were at the heart of Village life: whether agitating for change on picket lines, making avant-garde art in their studios, or dressed in a daring outfit and causing a stir at a café, women were leading active, public lives that defied society's standards and broke the boundaries that previously circumscribed women's lives. Much of the Village's radical energy stemmed from a generation of women who demanded new freedoms and were determined to refashion society. Although the anarchist activism of figures such as Emma Goldman seems, on the surface, far removed from the whimsical art of Clara Tice or the witty commentary of Louise Norton, the fight for women to be equal citizens extended across art, politics, fashion and relationships. The Village's politically charged atmosphere allowed creative women the freedom to express themselves in new ways, via art, clothing and lifestyles that would be branded obscene or improper in wider society. These broad concerns and the disregard for traditional values meant that Greenwich Village feminism was markedly different to many suffrage groups that existed elsewhere in the country.

A vital factor in much of the Village's feminist activity was the combination of socialist politics with the struggle for women's rights. The Village's radical history as a site of collective action and protest preceded (and partly enabled) its incarnation as a bohemian paradise. At the start of the twentieth century, Greenwich Village was home to a large population of working-class immigrant communities, predominantly Italians, whose struggles with dire living and working conditions sparked the growth of organizations and movements to campaign for change. The founding of Greenwich House by Mary Simkhovitch in 1902 provided a focal point for community action. Greenwich House hosted educational classes, health workshops and a neighbourhood association; its mission was to advise tenants on their rights and empower the Village's immigrant population, particularly women and working mothers (by 1919, a Montessori nursery operated on the site).

Jessie Tarbox Beals, *Suffrage Parade*, Greenwich Village, *c.* 1915–18, gelatin silver print.

Many women from the Village's large community of Italian immigrants worked at nearby textile factories, usually in appalling conditions and for low pay. The founding of the International Ladies' Garment Workers' Union in 1900, followed by the Women's Trade Union League in 1903, prompted waves of strike action and unrest led by women, including Goldman and garment workers Rose Schneiderman and Clara Lemlich. Schneiderman and Lemlich, in particular, worked hard through the 1910s to make suffrage movement inclusive of working-class women, convinced that enfranchisement was essential to improving working conditions.

Lemlich joined a high-profile suffrage march in May 1912, which set off from Washington Square. It was a huge event that attracted a reported 10,000 marchers and reflected a growing number of diverse groups of women who supported suffrage in different ways (and to different ends). The *New York Times* described it as 'a parade of contrasts' that featured 'an army of women . . . [led by] women on horseback and carrying in big automobiles only the women who cannot march, the octogenarian suffragists, the grandmothers 80 years old and 90 years old', alongside trade unionists, Quakers, socialists, working and professional women and 'even men'.[11] At the front of the march, sixteen-year-old Mabel Ping-Hua Lee led the procession. Her boldness in leading the march was remarkable because of not only her youth but her status as a Chinese immigrant. The Chinese Exclusion Act of 1882, which declared Chinese nationals ineligible for American citizenship, started a decades-long discriminatory policy against Chinese immigrants. It went hand in hand with rampant violent xenophobia towards Chinese people. Despite the hostile environment, Lee saw it as her duty to join the march. She had been invited by white American suffragists who were eager to

Unknown photographer, *Dr Mabel Lee*, c. 1900.

learn from China's feminist movement, which had been fired up by the 1911 Revolution. Lee agreed, taking the interest of white American suffragettes as an opportunity to draw attention to the prejudices faced by Chinese women in America and to educate them on the intersection of race and gender discrimination; unsurprisingly, she did not find that her support was reciprocated.

Like Lee, Lemlich was also a young woman from an immigrant family who aligned herself with the suffrage movement in an attempt to empower her community. Her family had fled antisemitic violence in Ukraine for a new life in New York, arriving when Lemlich was seventeen. She was already well read, resourceful and politically radical: her conservative father forbade reading and the school in their Ukrainian town banned Jewish pupils, but she carried out tasks for neighbours as a way of earning money to buy books. Shortly after the family settled in New York, Lemlich joined the International Ladies' Garment Workers' Union and became politically active. Agitating for reform in the factories, she was a leader of the 1909 Uprising of the 20,000, a mass strike of garment workers who demanded better pay and safer working conditions. At a meeting, Lemlich took to the stage at Cooper Union's Grand Hall and gave an impassioned speech that ended with a call to strike. She was undaunted by the trade union movement's male-dominated leadership or by the violent treatment she had already suffered at the hands of the enforcers hired by factory owners. The fact that Lemlich was a factory worker herself and spoke Yiddish meant that Jewish women workers trusted in her and readily followed her lead, despite the struggles that came along with taking strike action.

At the march, Lemlich walked with the Fire Battalion League, who held a sombre black banner unadorned but for the words 'We Want the Vote for Protection'. They represented a larger group of missing women, women who had been killed in the 1911 Triangle Shirtwaist factory fire at the Asch Building near Washington Square. A total of 146 people lost their lives in the tragedy, many of them young, poorly paid women from Greenwich Village's Italian and Jewish immigrant communities. Along with labour union leader Rose Schneiderman, Lemlich stepped up her efforts to bring the attention of wealthy, influential suffragist women to the plight of working-class women from immigrant communities.

The same year as the May march from Washington Square, Lemlich wrote an article in *Good Housekeeping*, appealing to the middle-class women who 'buy and wear the beautiful clothes' made in factories like the Triangle Shirtwaist factory. After describing the appalling, unsanitary and exploitative conditions that women were forced to put up with in factories, she set out the reason why the vote was essential for working-class women:

> The manufacturer has a vote; the bosses have votes; the foremen have votes; the inspectors have votes. The working girl has no vote . . . until the men in the Legislature at Albany represent her as well as the bosses and the foremen, she will not get justice; she will not get fair conditions. That is why the working-woman now says that she must have the vote.[12]

The marches from Washington Square demonstrate the often uneasy alliances between women focused on the fight for suffrage (usually white, middle- and upper-class, and conservative) and groups of women who understood that the vote alone was not enough to bring equality, but was just one of many changes needed. Journalist Winnifred Harper Cooley declared that 'all feminists are suffragists, but not all suffragists are feminists.'[13] Although the suffrage movement remained largely divided, the issue of worker's rights was firmly supported by bohemians in the Village, where socialist and feminist ideas entwined. The vibrant social life of the Village provided the ideal environment for the exchange and evolution of ideas. Activists such as Goldman, Margaret Sanger, Max and Crystal Eastman, writer and journalist John Reed and writer Mary Heaton Vorse moved between the Village's working-class and bohemian communities, often working to radicalize the latter and recruit wealthy and/or influential figures to their causes.

In many ways, the socialist elements present in the Village (and specifically in Village feminism) further enforced its separation from the rest of the city and country. June Sochen suggests that the 'commitment to socialism' demonstrated by Village women 'made [them] open to suspicion by outsiders' and 'frightened away' many suffragists, particularly wealthy conservatives.[14] Unlike the suffragists, women in the Village understood that only a much bigger revolution would bring about real change in women's lives and status. In 1920, after the ratification of the Nineteenth Amendment granted women the right to vote, Crystal Eastman spelled out how much was still at stake in an article for *The Liberator*: it was essential, she declared, to 'arrange the world so that women can be human beings', not just housewives and mothers. Eastman clarifies that women who chose the latter should 'have that occupation recognized by the world as work, requiring a definite economic reward'.[15] This meant more access to the professions, raising 'feminist sons' who would share housework, 'voluntary motherhood' and, crucially, 'motherhood endowments . . . the only way we can keep mothers free, at least in a capitalist society'.[16]

Bodily autonomy, birth control and the rights of working mothers were important components of the Village feminists' agenda. Emma Goldman's activism within the immigrant communities on the Lower East Side sparked her belief in the importance of birth control and 'voluntary motherhood'. Her efforts to educate women and smuggle in contraceptive devices to the United States inspired others to join the cause, most notably Margaret Sanger. For Goldman, the anti-birth-control movement was driven by the twin forces of capitalism and militarism, which demand the constant provision of masses of people to be sacrificed in the killing machines of the battlefield and to make up an exploitable, disposable workforce. While living in the Village, Sanger and Goldman each set up journals to promote their visions and political ideals – the *Woman Rebel* and *Mother Earth*, respectively – and were also supported by Max Eastman's *The Masses*. Goldman did not always reciprocate the support of *The Masses*: in 1916 she expressed disappointment that *The Masses* had devoted an issue to 'Votes for Women' (or what she called 'the suffrage disease'), adding 'perhaps *Mother Earth* alone has any faith in women . . . that women are capable and are ready to fight for freedom and revolution'.[17]

The clubs and cafés of Greenwich Village provided vital locations for groups of women to share ideas, build supportive networks and reimagine ways of being women in the modern world. They were open, informal venues where women were free to smoke, drink, dance and

Frontispiece from
*Anarchism and Other
Essays* with a bust
portrait of Emma
Goldman.

debate without judgement. The combination of cheap rents and cheap
meals gave independent young women a chance to leave their family
homes and strike out as artists and writers. Many continued to enjoy
the support of family wealth, but even those of lesser means could
potentially earn a small living by using their creative skills to make
money: journalism, illustration, craft and design all opened up options
for Village women and enabled their pursuit of freedom. By bringing
together artists, performers, activists and writers, the Village's many
cafés and clubs staged unexpected collaborations and exchanges. There
were few barriers between art and politics, avant-garde art and middle-
brow culture. In this atmosphere, dreams of new lives and new ways of
expressing what it meant to be a woman in the modern world entwined.

Heterodoxy: Big, Whole Human Selves

Goldman and Sanger gave several lectures to perhaps one of the most influential networks of feminists in the Village: the Heterodoxy club. Founded by Marie Jenney Howe in 1912, Heterodoxy was a woman-only club where a mix of 'unorthodox women who did things and did them openly' gathered together to debate the pressing sociopolitical, feminist issues of the day.[18] Howe had become a resident of the Village in 1910. Active in suffrage circles and labour-reform movements, she immediately felt at home among its community of radicals and joined its network of progressive, pioneering women. In fact, through her suffrage activism, Howe was already well acquainted with many of the women who would be at the centre of the Village's political life. After becoming chair of the 25th Assembly District division of the New York City Women Suffrage Party in 1910, she became friends with multi-talented intellectual, lawyer and organizer Crystal Eastman, writer and activist Mary Heaton Vorse and teacher Henrietta Rodman; Rodman would shortly become notorious for taking on the New York City Board of Education over their policy of barring married women teachers and for bobbing her hair when, 'far from being the fashion, [it] brought street notoriety to its possessor'.[19]

Howe's move to the Village brought her closer to an emerging radical feminist community that shared concerns with suffrage groups but were engaged with a huge number of other issues that affected women's lives. Eastman and her brother Max, editor of *The Masses*, and Rodman were among her neighbours, as well as psychologist and educational pioneer Elisabeth Antoinette Irwin and her partner, the renowned feminist biographer and social-welfare worker Katharine Anthony. In this febrile atmosphere, Howe identified the need for a dedicated space where women could discuss the many things that fell outside of the often narrow fields of political allegiances and enfranchisement. In response, Howe set up Heterodoxy, an organization that would function as a debating forum and a supportive group.

Heterodoxy reflected the diversity of political beliefs and points of view that existed across women interested in feminism and enfranchisement during the 1910s. Early member Inez Haynes Irwin recalled that it brought together 'Democrats, Republicans, Socialists, anarchists, liberals and radicals of all opinions. They possessed minds startlingly free of prejudice. They were at home with ideas. All could talk; all could argue; all could listen.'[20] It provided a space for diverse ideas to converge – and sometimes, inevitably, clash. Howe was a skilled chairwoman who could keep the peace 'in spite of 59 varieties of temper, temperament and viewpoint'.[21] Unfortunately, we know little about what went on during meetings, beyond recollections in members' autobiographies: Howe ruled that Heterodoxy would keep no records, to ensure privacy for its members, many of whom were active in public life, held potentially controversial political views and/or were in relationships with other women.

In *Radical Feminists of Heterodoxy: Greenwich Village, 1912–1940* (1982), Judith Schwarz suggests that Heterodoxy had a 'surprisingly diverse' membership for the era, with the age group ranging from women in their early twenties to the over-fifties, and many members from immigrant backgrounds. An album of photographs that the members presented to Howe in 1920 shows what an eclectic bunch they were: older veterans of the suffrage movement dressed in conservative attire mix with young bohemians in fashionable outfits. Some members wore striking masculine suits, their hair cut into sleek bobs or close crops. However, with the exception of civil rights activist and arts patron Grace Nail Johnson, all of the members were white.[22] Although its members extended their support across class lines, many white feminists gave little consideration to the struggles of Black women. Heterodoxy's membership was comparatively varied by the standards of the day, but it nevertheless showed the entrenched racism and narrow perspectives that often persisted in feminist movements through the rest of the century.

The social and political mix of women who gathered at Heterodoxy's bi-monthly meetings was reflected in the wide range of topics that they covered. Schwarz suggests that these ranged from the Russian Revolution to infant mortality, 'education of women, Black civil rights, disabled women, the Irish independence movement, free love, psychology, and so much more'.[23] It had an international outlook that recognized a need for a far-reaching revolution in women's rights (beyond simply the issue of the vote in the United States) and was attuned to the plight of women in countries facing huge sociopolitical upheavals. Despite their differences, the women who were drawn to Heterodoxy shared a common belief in women's right to cultivate 'big, whole human selves' – to live full, independent lives, both professional and private.

The right to choose fulfilling relationships and the free expression of sexuality were essential parts of this. At a time when divorce was frowned upon and made particularly difficult for women in the United States, almost a third of Heterodoxy members were divorced. Many rejected traditional gender roles, striving instead to find alternatives to patriarchal family structures. They pursued lives free from the traditional expectations and conventions of wider society, facilitated by the progressive atmosphere that flourished in Greenwich Village and, in most cases, made possible by the privileges of their race and class. Some members embraced the Village bohemian ideal of free love, signalling a rejection of restrictive marriage and the expectations that being a wife and mother brought. Heterodoxy was also welcoming to lesbian and bisexual members, and provided a supportive environment for non-heteronormative families, such as Heterodoxy members and couple Irwin and Anthony, who lived together with their two adopted daughters. Even within the nonconforming, open environment of Greenwich Village, attitudes towards queer women were mixed. As Lillian Faderman highlights, on one hand the Village was one of the 'earliest public manifestations of a non-working-class white American lesbian subculture'; 'on the other hand, among bohemian men (who controlled the mores of the Village, despite their occasional pretence to sexual egalitarianism), sexual love between women was never validated as equal to heterosexual discourse.'[24] Threatened by women's true sexual freedom, these men encouraged a period of bisexuality but expected it to end with a heterosexual relationship. In anarchist activist circles, Goldman noted that her vocal support for gay, lesbian and gender-non-conforming people was 'condemned'.[25]

Heterodoxy's members and supporters made it their mission to raise awareness of what feminism was, how it could change society, and why it was essential for women to become 'big, whole human selves'. Although meetings remained private, Heterodoxy's members made their mission public, working to encourage more women to live bold, unorthodox lives. Howe organized a number of public lectures and debating events to spark public interest in feminism, including 'Twenty-Five Answers to Antis', a lively forum in which 25 speakers were allowed five minutes each to argue against anti-suffrage ideas. In 1914, she arranged two larger events at Cooper Union's People's Institute, with a similar quick-fire format: a mix of leading intellectuals and activists (men and women) were invited to talk about what feminism meant to them in short ten-minute speeches that would hold the audience's attention. In a follow-up session, topics covered a range of issues relating to home and work life, such as the right to be a working mother, to strike, to keep one's maiden name after marriage, and even to 'ignore fashion'. The title – 'What Is Feminism? Come and Find Out' – demonstrated Howe's aim to encourage women (and men) who were outside of traditional suffrage groups to find out more about feminism. The ambitious scope of Heterodoxy's mission shows Greenwich Village feminism at its boldest. Its members blazed a trail, uncompromising in their commitment to living modern, liberated lives and in the mission to encourage other women to do the same.

Polly's: Who's Who in New York's Bohemia

Heterodoxy's unofficial headquarters was Polly's, a lively bohemian restaurant located at 137 MacDougal Street that was the Village's earliest epicentre of radicalism and revelry. Decorated in bright Fauvist colours with green walls and with simple wood tables and chairs, Polly's was the quintessential Village café. Café culture was an essential part of Village life: run by bohemians and radicals, cafés offered cheap meals and an informal atmosphere perfectly suited to long afternoons and evenings spent discussing the latest developments in art, philosophy and politics (not to mention the latest Village gossip). They were places to be seen, where Village fashions flourished and the most fashionably outré Villagers made a name for themselves in the New York press. As the decade progressed, a number of cafés and bars popped up to cater to the bohemian set, each with its own eccentricities and regular characters. Yet despite the competition, Polly's was the undisputed centre of Village life for much of the 1910s – it was, Mabel Dodge later recalled, 'the only restaurant of its kind'.[26]

Radical politics and culture were at the heart of Polly's. Its proprietor, Paula 'Polly' Holladay, was an anarchist and grew up in a creative family. Her mother, Adele, was an actress who had been the protégée of Otis Skinner and a friend of Eugene O'Neill's father, James (also an actor). O'Neill was a close friend of Polly's brother, Louis, a bright but troubled young man with ambitions of being a writer, and the two could often be found at Polly's or drinking at other Village bars and cafés (most notoriously, the Golden Swan).[27] Few records of Holladay's life and the lives of her family survive, beyond references in the letters and autobiographies of better-known Villagers; in the words of writer W. Adolphe Roberts, she was a 'robust young woman . . . a frequenter of rebel balls given by all factions'.[28] O'Neill's wife, Agnes Boulton, recalls a 'tall, dark-eyed, and calm' woman, 'with an interesting and receptive mind . . . [who] gave her place the air of a club'.[29] Polly was also assisted by her lover, Hippolyte Havel, an anarchist activist who gained notoriety after being arrested in connection with the assassination of President William McKinley in 1901 (along with his on–off lover, Emma Goldman). Havel was a true Bohemian (hailing from the former Bohemia, now Czech Republic), one of the Village's most eccentric characters and, according to Hutchins Hapgood, a 'wild little man' always in a 'perpetual state of vituperative excitement'; Havel's characteristic habits of scrounging a dollar off everyone he met and calling even the most radical of his friends 'Goddam Bourgeois' fed into the character of Hugo in O'Neill's *The Iceman Cometh* (1939).[30] Alongside his political work, Havel worked as the chef at Polly's, serving up Czech beef goulash and other hearty meals to sustain the struggling artists, writers and activists.

Polly's was much more than a cheap restaurant. Bohemian poet Harry Kemp felt that Polly's was a creative act in and of itself: 'in the creation of her unique little restaurant [Holladay] had achieved art, had hit upon her right form of expression.'[31] In its first location, Polly's occupied the same building as the Liberal Club, at 137 MacDougal Street, with the two establishments sharing the same clientele of radicals, activists and intellectuals. The Greenwich Village Liberal Club was a new iteration of New York's original Liberal Club, made up of younger left-wing intellectuals who challenged the first club's exclusion of W.E.B. Du Bois (on the grounds of race) and Emma Goldman (for being too radical). Heterodoxy member Henrietta Rodman was a leading voice in the new Liberal Club, after playing a part in the split with the other club: many conservative, genteel members of the original Liberal Club refused to support Rodman when she challenged the New York City Board of Education's policy of firing married women teachers.

In its new home on MacDougal Street, a lively bohemian crowd moved between debates at the Liberal Club and dinner at Polly's, continuing conversations about feminism, socialism, art and fashion across floors. The Liberal Club was set up for the kinds of raucous late-night costume balls that became de rigueur in the Village through the 1910s. Its brightly coloured, Cubist-inspired modern decorative scheme was complemented by a parquet floor, perfect for dancing, and an electric piano. The club's extravagant fundraising balls (known as Pagan Routs) set the tone for similar events at Webster Hall and other Village bars and restaurants that sprang up over the course of the decade. The status of 137 MacDougal Street as the Village's ultimate social and intellectual hub was secured when the next door Washington Square Bookshop knocked through into Polly's, allowing for the free mingling of an eccentric cast of writers, thinkers, artists and activists.

Polly's reputation energized the neighbourhood, drawing a wide range of visitors who were eager to be part of the new scene. Roberts describes the opening of Polly's restaurant as the beginning of the Village's transformation into New York's very own Latin Quarter:

> Polly's had more to do with change at first than the Liberal Club did. Her basement was a big success. Down flocked the anarchists, the more festive of the socialists . . . students, would-be artists recently arrived in New York, and sheer sensation seekers. They crowded together in a thick pall of tobacco smoke, drank red wine or coffee, and argued half the night. An invitation upstairs to dance was a highly regarded privilege. Other restaurants opened in competition, and there was a development to which there has been no end.[32]

Polly's sparked the vital sense of community that sustained Greenwich Village's bohemia through the 1910s. Its popularity led to other similar venues opening, each offering an individual spin on Polly's informal, cheap and cheerful model. Women, in particular, were keen to follow Holladay's lead by becoming proprietors of Village cafés and restaurants; before long, the majority of businesses in the area were run by women sporting the bobbed hair, patterned smock dresses and sandals that became emblematic of Village bohemianism.

The influx of competitors never succeeded in overtaking Polly's as the quintessential Village venue. By the time Anna Alice Chapin wrote her 1917 Greenwich Village guidebook, Polly's was an institution; in Chapin's words, Polly's was 'Greenwich Village in little', a 'fixed, representative, and sacred' space that was indispensable to Village life.[33] Despite growing tourist interest, Polly's remained the key location for a who's who of bohemia on any given evening. Clara Tice might be found dining and gossiping with editor Frank Crowninshield, as Crystal and Max Eastman sat discussing plans for *The Masses*, or Louise Norton would be holding court while Margaret Sanger and Emma Goldman planned campaigns for birth control at the next table.

Rogues

In March 1915 a new little magazine with a distinctive chequerboard front cover began circulating among Greenwich Village's bohemians. Its title, *Rogue* (an obvious pun on *Vogue*), hinted at the magazine's irreverent attitude and satirical pose, and its initial tagline – 'a magazine that believes in the people, and that the people express genius even more than genius itself' – situated the magazine in ongoing debates around the role of art and the artist in modernity, which had begun with the furore of the Armory Show two years earlier and would come to a head during the *Fountain* scandal two years later.[34] The first issue contained strange and exciting experimental poetry by new poets from New York and Europe. The presence of a poem by Gertrude Stein was a particular coup for the editors. Stein's poem 'Aux Galeries Lafayette' was a bold statement of *Rogue*'s intent, aligning the magazine with the radical modern forms of art that caused a scandal at the Armory Show.

When a second issue was published the following month, Mina Loy and Clara Tice had joined *Rogue*'s list of contributors. Like Stein, Tice had a reputation as a modern provocateur: the joyful nude sketches she exhibited at Polly's café in 1914 made her infamous in New York, after moral-purity crusader Anthony Comstock attempted to confiscate the work (Comstock crops up in *Rogue* as one of the many targets of its mockery). The enigmatic Loy was less well known: her poems arrived from Florence, via Carl Van Vechten, who also arranged for Stein's work to be placed in *Rogue*. Loy's mix of futurist forms and feminist thought was a hit with the *Rogue* crowd and she became one of its most frequent contributors. She was joined by a cohort of other young women artists and writers, such as Djuna Barnes and Frances Simpson Stevens, who gave the magazine a distinctly feminist energy that was daring and radical for its time. It was unusual to encounter such a range of women's perspectives on modern life in one place.

One of the most intriguing features in *Rogue* was the monthly 'Philosophic Fashions' essay written by Dame Rogue, alias of Louise Norton. The segment cast a wry eye on contemporary fashions, while also making it clear that fashion was an important, worthy topic of serious contemplation. In her first column, Norton noted that

> fashion may be to some 'fickle, frail and flighty'. But there are those to whom the rise and fall of petticoats is as momentous as the fluctuations of the market. Think of the psychological capitalists who may be behind this song of a [short] skirt, great minds who understand how to turn feminine failings into masculine millions.[35]

Elsewhere, she quotes from a vast range of sources, including Michel de Montaigne, Oscar Wilde, Henry James and Guy de Maupassant, evidence of what she described as her bookish nature. In staking a claim for fashion as philosophy, Norton was ahead of her time; her breezy but shrewd thoughts on clothes and fads were grounded in theories of gender politics and economics, giving fashion criticism a depth that would not be commonly accepted until many decades later.

Rogue, III/3 (December 1915).

Norton's column claimed that fashion was philosophy, but she also argued that fashion was political. In an essay that accompanied Loy's sketch 'Consider Your Grandmother's Stays' (which depicted a woman with modern bobbed hair and a made-up face squeezed into a Victorian-style corset and hoop skirt), Norton deftly demonstrates the ways that women's clothes were linked to their status as citizens and their opportunities in life. Referring to recent efforts to revive the steel corset, Norton reminds her readers that restrictive dress was a tactic to 'keep [women] out of the polls and politics'; she urges them to ask themselves 'can the mind . . . be enfranchised when the body is enslaved? Can the soul take to itself wings and soar out of a solar plexus constantly confined?'[36] In other words, restrictive clothing kept women out of public life. In these columns, Norton presents the views of the Village's socialist feminist activists in her own humorous style. An unpublished essay by Crystal Eastman on 'Short Hair and Short Skirts' sets out some remarkably similar arguments to Norton's; Eastman celebrates the new fashion for bobbed hair and short hemlines as a much-needed break from the past, adding that efforts to bring back conservative fashion 'would be like trying to stop us smoking cigarettes'. For Eastman, short skirts and short hair represent a step towards freedom, not least because that taste of freedom (in personal style) would make a woman want more: watching a 'bobbed haired girl' pull off a hat and shake her head in joy and relief, Eastman notes that 'though perhaps [the girl] doesn't know it, [her] new sense of freedom will always prevent her from willingly going back to the old style.'[37]

Like Eastman, Norton and many of her *Rogue* contributors (Tice and Loy, in particular) understood that enfranchisement extended well beyond the vote: freedoms in everyday life were as important as the freedom to cast a vote. For Norton, fashion could also be a way of imagining a society free from gender norms. In an article on men's trousers, she points out that men's fashion is just as impractical ('are collars more comfortable than corsets?') and even absurdly comical.[38] Norton alludes to the media's mockery of Greenwich Village's bobbed-haired women and long-haired men by welcoming this loss of 'definite definitions'. Once again linking dress to social and political issues, she argues that the whole individual matters much more than one's sex in the modern

Philosophic Fashions

KEEPING OUR WIVES AT HOME

"NEW things are only those which have been forgotten." Does it make today seem less modern than yesterday, or yesterday even post-modern to us to read of Rose Bertin, the Queen's dressmaker, philosophising after the fashion of today to Marie-Antoinette in her boudoir in 1776? The perfume of modernity sprayed over dead years thrills one like a memory, as though we ourselves had been or had the soul to have been of that other era of chiffons akin to our own but seemingly more brilliant because of its reflected values. Mlle. Bertin, like Madame du Barry, rose from the position of milliner's apprentice to royal favors. Jeanne Becu became a king's mistress, but Rose Bertin did a harder thing and became the mistress of a queen— Counsellor of the Clothes Press and, as she was called, Minister of Fashions.

And now that we hear so much of the re-vival of old styles, and see our grand-mothers' gowns in all the windows as well as our great-great and more great-grand-mothers' too, Rose Bertin's epigram is apropos. What can one not wear this Spring? Are you slim, are you long-lined as Récamier? You may wear her gowns and recline all day in a *chaise longue* posing for portraits by—no, Adams is dead, you will change the artist. Have you a *mince taille* (the French to me has even a slimmer sound than our old English slender waist)? Then is the fitted black bodice ready to make you as tiny and dainty as a Dres-den shepherdess. Are you without curves, straight as an arrow, "divinely fair and most divinely tall"? *Moyen âge*, loved of Poiret, is still possible though on the wane. Are your limbs so awkward, to use no grosser word, that tight skirts gossip about them? Cover them up and hide them under boundless billows of material. Any style, all styles, you may wear, and the only law in this world of license that you must obey is, for all styles, skirts *en haut!* Even Ma-dame Récamier, rising from her couch, must rise on long, thin ankles undenied. For the stork and the crane are to be our models this season. There is a fallacy abroad among little women that short skirts make them look shorter. This may be true. It doesn't matter. The point is that if you look *chic* you won't look short. For always the newest thing is noticed. It is a law!

Rogue, 1/2 (April 1915).

age, and, as such, the idea of masculine and feminine style becomes irrelevant: 'trousers . . . I hold to be mere arbitrary symbols of sex which I, for one, think obsolete.'[39] On this issue (as on many others), Norton's 'Philosophic Fashions' column set *Rogue*'s tone: across the magazine's illustrations and written content, it invoked the language and symbols of decadence to evoke subversive sexuality and gender fluidity.

The fact that Norton (as Dame Rogue) set the magazine's agenda indicates the central role she played in its production. Norton's then husband, Allen, a poet, was listed as its editor; Louise Norton's name only ever appears in tiny print on the contents page, listed as the magazine's vice president, secretary and treasurer. But Norton was clearly a major influence on its direction, specifically its focus on the voice and perspective of the modern woman. In *Autobiography of Alice B. Toklas*, Stein writes that 'V. Vechten interested Allen and Louise Norton in her [Stein's] work and induced them to print in the little magazine they founded, the first thing of G. Stein's ever printed in a little magazine.'[40] Norton also made it onto a list of 'male and female dadaists' displayed at the 1920 First International Dada Art Fair in Berlin (along with Mina Lloyd (*sic*), Katharine N. Rhoades and Mabel Dodge – Allen was not listed), which suggests that her reputation extended to the European avant-garde.[41]

Alongside Clara Tice, Norton was the quintessential Greenwich Village woman. Like many Village bohemians, Norton was from a cultured and progressive wealthy family. Her father, John Lindsay McCutcheon, was heir to the Lindsay and McCutcheon iron and steel firm and was also a highly successful lawyer who had studied at Bonn University in Germany, and Harvard and Columbia Law School. A polymath, McCutcheon's obituary in the *Pittsburgh Press* notes that he was 'much devoted to music, art, and the study of chess . . . the composer of several popular musical numbers and was the possessor of a rare collection of paintings by the old masters'.[42] Chess was a big part of McCutcheon's life: he was a member of the American team and even had a variation of the French Defence move named after him, a rare honour for an amateur player. Her father's prowess in the game gave Norton a unique point of connection with the chess-obsessed Marcel Duchamp and Walter Arensberg. The intellectual environment

Philosophic Fashions

The Importance of Being Dressed

THE custom of wearing clothes is one of civilization's contributions to the difficult art of complicating life.

As Wilde said:

"What is interesting about people is the mask that each one of them wears, not the reality that lies behind the mask. The more one analyses people, the more all reasons for analysis disappear. Sooner or later one comes to that dreadful universal thing called human nature."

That is why to me Henry James is so exciting. When I lose the sweet sensation of complexity in my own life I read "The Awkward Age" and taste again the ultra importance of life among the Philistines. Henry James' style is like those Russian nests of dolls; you uncover and uncover and uncover, and you come, at last, to—another doll. Pater, too, is an intoxicant—the very

best wine. When life grows stale I can get drunk on "Imaginary Portraits" and "The Child in the House," and occasionally on "Greek Studies." These two, Walter Pater and Henry James, have the magic touch that magnifies.

Someone once sent me some doggerel by somebody, called, "Thank God for clothes!" I remember part of it went something like this:

"Thank God for dress!

"That through the darkest day can send a gleam

"When some long pondered frock comes home a dream

"That glorifies the marriage rites; and, yes,

"Lends to bereavement craped becomingness,

"That gives us courage to confront our fate—

Rogue, 1/7 (July 1915).

she grew up in also fostered Norton's own passion for learning; she grew up fluent in French and studied at the elite Smith College in Massachusetts, but she dropped out in 1911, a year before she was due to graduate, to marry Allen (she was likely pregnant with her son Michael, born in 1912).[43]

Despite their marriage and young child, the Nortons were determined to pursue an unconventional, bohemian life. Norton's passion for the arts, desire for freedom and zest for life led her to Greenwich Village, where she soon became one of its most influential modern women. She popped up in countless features on the Village scene over the 1910s, her exquisitely stylish outfits making her easy to spot as she flitted between Village hotspots. In Tice's 'Who's Who in Manhattan' sketch (published in *Cartoons* magazine in August 1917), Norton is resplendent in a risqué fitted dress and high heels, her glamorous costume matched only by that of Tice's fellow illustrator and party girl Edith Plummer. Sarah Addington's feature on Village hotspots for a November 1915 issue of the *New York Tribune* includes Norton among the notable clientele at Polly's, standing out from the crowd in a leopard-skin coat and a large, sweeping hat. Norton set the trend for other Villagers to follow. Even the equally fashionable Mina Loy appeared to have taken direction from Norton: when poet Marianne Moore met Loy a few years later, William Carlos Williams recalled that Moore was awestruck by Loy's leopard-skin coat.

Norton's approach to life was as daring as her fashion sense. She was a sexual libertine who embraced the era's spirit of free love. While married to Allen, she took a number of other lovers, including Henri-Pierre Roché and Marcel Duchamp. Beatrice Wood recorded her dislike for Norton in her diary, presumably motivated by jealousy and the inevitable awkwardness caused by these overlapping affairs. Wood was not Norton's only rival. In her biography of her second husband, French composer Edgard Varèse, Norton recalls an incident with Djuna Barnes, who (Norton claims) was an admirer of his: while walking through the Village, Norton and her husband were heckled by Barnes, who shouted 'so you've fallen for Edgard too!'[44] Gossip about Norton's behaviour was rife in Village circles – women who actually practised free love often found themselves the target of criticism, despite the Village's supposed

Unidentified photographer, Louise Varèse, Edgard Varèse, Suzanne Duchamp, Jean Crotti and Mary Reynolds in Paris, 1924, sepia photographic print.

openness and bohemianism. Norton's relationship with Polly Holladay's brother Louis (best friend and drinking partner of Eugene O'Neill) became a particular source of scandal among the bohemians after Louis's death in 1917.

The night that Louis died from a heroin overdose at Romany Marie's café is shrouded in Village myth. Louis had returned from an extended stay in Oregon (at Norton's expense), where he had gone to sober up after getting into trouble with the police. During his time away, Norton fell in love with Varèse and decided to end her affair with Louis. Norton told O'Neill's biographer that she had already written to him to break off the romance, so she did not see Louis when he returned to New York. Agnes Boulton, O'Neill's wife, contradicted this version of events, claiming that Norton reunited with Louis at the Hell Hole and left him distraught after she announced she was involved with another man.[45] In Boulton's version, Louis then purchased heroin in a suicidal state, but others present that evening suggest he took the drug recreationally with a group of friends, including painter Charles Demuth. From Boulton's version of events, we can infer that some among the Village bohemian lay the blame for his death at Norton's door, casting her as a stereotypical femme fatale.

Norton was undaunted by gossip or public opinion. She satirized Village sexual politics and its decadent bohemianism in *Little Wax Candle*, a play published in 1914 by her friend Donald Evans's Claire Marie (a small press that also published Stein's *Tender Buttons* in the same year, thanks to the efforts of Dodge and Van Vechten). Norton's recollection of the early years of her relationship with Varèse also reveal a woman determined to do things her way. Although members of the O'Neill circle claimed that Norton had agreed to marry Holladay but had broken it off after becoming engaged to Varèse, Norton's own recollections paint the late 1910s as a time when she avoided serious, formal affairs. Her relationship with Varèse started casually because Norton was 'enjoying the sensation of being as free as the sparrows of New York'; she broke things off temporarily in 1918 when Varèse attempted to curtail her 'dancing, drinking habits' – Norton 'objected to . . . his assumption that he had the right to dictate to [her]'.[46] Of course, Norton's freedom during these years was a privilege that many other women could not have afforded. Her family's wealth enabled her to live independently after she split from Allen, and her mother took care of her son Michael, leaving Norton free to pursue her own interests.

As a member of the cosmopolitan Arensberg circle, Norton's irreverent wit fed into the atmosphere of iconoclastic provocation and subversive high jinks. She had a close relationship with Duchamp around the time of the *Fountain* scandal and was a co-conspirator in the prank. Norton's address at 110 West 88th Street and phone number were added to the submission label, making it highly likely that this was the female friend Duchamp referred to in a letter to his sister Suzanne, in which he described how this unnamed woman 'adopted the masculine pseudonym Richard Mutt [and] sent in a porcelain urinal as a sculpture'.[47] Norton's comments on *Fountain* were published in the second (and final) issue of the *Blind Man* magazine in May 1917, alongside work by Wood and Loy – her essay 'Buddha of the Bathroom' was printed on the page adjacent to Stieglitz's photograph of *Fountain*, giving it a prominent position in the magazine. 'Buddha of the Bathroom' reads much like one of Dame Rogue's 'Philosophic Fashions' articles and quotes from a typically eclectic range of figures, including Gertrude Stein, Montaigne, Nietzsche and Remy de Gourmont. Her astute defence of the 'decadent plumbers' porcelain' deftly sets out its significance to the question 'what is art?'[48] In Norton's reading of *Fountain*, she shows that an artist can elevate an everyday item by shifting its context; by finding formal beauty in the most prosaic of objects, an artist can help others see their surroundings anew. Norton also riffs on *Rogue*'s signature attitude by proclaiming that Mutt's submission was both serious *and* a joke, reminding readers that the ridiculous and tragic are often intertwined. Norton's nuanced understanding of the subject could only come from one close to the matter.

Norton never spoke of her involvement with *Fountain*. Like Beatrice Wood, she seemed happy to play the role of ingénue to Duchamp's worldly, devilish seductor. In a tribute to Duchamp that she wrote several decades after they first met, Norton acknowledges that she was up to date with the developments in modern art before she knew Duchamp, due to the evenings she spent with the Arensbergs and the impact of the Armory Show. Despite this, she credits Duchamp with opening her eyes to radical modern culture during visits to the 291 gallery and his studio. Deploying a troubling sexual metaphor, Norton casts herself as a virgin passed from Duchamp to Alfred Stieglitz, describing the latter as 'a tireless talker, propagandist, and pedagogue [who] whetted my appetite by all he poured into my virgin ears'.[49] In Duchamp's studio, Norton describes learning 'not verbally but by osmosis, receiving quite a fillip from the Readymades, though I hardly appreciated their paradoxical multiplicity of intent'.[50] But 'Buddha of the Bathroom' makes it clear that Norton did indeed understand the 'multiplicity of intent' at work in the readymades, and, the evidence suggests, had a hand in the creation of the most notorious example.

Norton's deference to Duchamp (and Stieglitz) echoes Wood's and reminds us that, despite being educated, creative and wealthy, women in the New York avant-garde still largely relied on men's permission and approval. Modern women like Norton and Wood faced a huge struggle to unlearn the strict gender roles and moral codes that their parents' generation enforced; they also found that men in bohemian and avant-garde circles supported free love but were less enthusiastic when it came to supporting women as equals in other aspects of life and work. In the avant-garde circles of 1910s New York, it was an unspoken rule that creative and flirtatious young women were charming, but they must remember not to overstep the mark. The myth of male genius remained potent and all-powerful.

After her marriage to Varèse in 1922, Norton began working as a literary translator, creating important editions of works by Arthur Rimbaud, Charles Baudelaire and Marcel Proust, among many others (she also supported her husband's work with the International Composers' Guild). Her pseudonyms – Dame Rogue and, perhaps partly, R. Mutt – obscure the impact she had on Greenwich Village's creative circles and the Arensberg salon group. With her wit, style and skill in bringing together *Rogue*'s woman-led roster, Norton helped push the modern woman to the forefront of New York's cultural life and was a key influence on the feminist nature of its early avant-garde.

Djuna Barnes: Becoming Intimate with the Bohemians

Before the commercialization of Greenwich Village picked up pace and Anna Alice Chapin published her guidebook, Djuna Barnes was bohemia's unofficial, tongue-in-cheek tour guide. In a series of articles for the *New York Morning Telegraph*'s Sunday magazine, she offered tantalizing peeks into the antics of Greenwich Village's bohemian movers and shakers, and evocatively conjured up the heady, decadent atmosphere that prevailed there. In a playful, mocking tone, she guides her readers through a day in the life of a Villager, which starts in the late afternoon and ends in the small hours of the morning, long after 'everything else [in the city] closes up . . . and the lights go out'.[51] Life for the Village bohemian is a whirlwind of 'balls [and] dances at the clubs, dinners at the inns . . . chats in the evenings about art and life', as well as drinks, cigarettes and 'jests at free love'.[52]

Despite gleefully sending up the Village's decadence, Barnes highlights the disparities among its mixed communities. Her article first offers a peek inside an 'opulent' studio belonging to one of the Village's wealthier residents, decorated with tapestries and silver curtains and carefully strewn with cultural artefacts: a copy of *Rogue* 'open at Mina Loy's poems', an Oscar Wilde text 'soiled by socialistic thumbs', three paint brushes arranged in a vase, a box of cigarettes and 'choice wines'.[53] But she then reveals less glamorous spaces, such as a neighbouring 'hall bedroom under the eaves' belonging to an 'underfed' aspiring poet, which is grubby and ragged, brightened only by a single flower stuck in a broken shaving mug and a cheap copy of a print on the wall. Elsewhere, Barnes highlights Italian families in rundown tenements and a 'row of houses whose inhabitants provide the Women's Night Court with half its sensations': 'satin and motorcars on this side, squalor and pushcarts on the other'.[54]

In her Greenwich Village articles, Barnes poked fun at the Village's crowd of artists and writers, caught up in an endless cycle of parties in their bohemian bubble. At the same time, she also teased the general public, whose fascination with the Village led the media to fuel the myth of bohemia. Increasingly, Barnes displayed what Mary Unger refers to as 'her disillusionment with the Village under the influence of mass consumerism', as its radical, avant-garde spaces became tourist sites.[55] In 'Becoming Intimate with the Bohemians', Barnes describes meeting a mother and her two daughters prowling the streets desperately looking for the *authentic* Greenwich Village that they had heard so much about: they chase after a woman 'in a gingham gown with a portfolio under her arm', traipse through Polly's and the Dutch Oven, and ask a red-haired birth-control activist if she is an artist.[56] Barnes names the bejewelled and fur-trimmed woman Madame Bronx, to signal that she is part of the growing tribe of slummers, a slang term given to tourists coming from uptown to slum it in the Village for an evening and observe the scandalous sight of women smoking, dancing and going about without a male chaperone. Bronx, like the slummer Alexis who appears in a subsequent article, ends up disappointed that the Village does not quite live up to its hedonistic, shocking reputation.

Unlike many of the journalists reporting on the neighbourhood's eccentric, artistic community, Barnes was an insider, which placed her in the strange position of wanting to both reveal and protect the Village and its lively cast of characters. Barnes moved to the neighbourhood in 1915, just as she was beginning to make a name for herself as a journalist for various New York-based publications and Greenwich Village was gaining its wild reputation. As well as documenting life in 1910s

New York, Barnes was, in her own right, a part of its dazzling crowd of emerging avant-garde artists and writers. In a 1919 interview, Guido Bruno – who published Barnes's first work of fiction, *The Book of Repulsive Women* (1915) – describes her wearing 'fantastic earrings in her ears, picturesquely dressed, ever ready to live and be merry: that's the real Djuna as she walks down Fifth Avenue, or sips her black coffee, a cigarette in hand, in the Café Lafayette'.[57]

Barnes was an adventurous, creative reporter, skilled at uncovering the city's unconventional characters and its vibrant night culture in her inimitable prose style. Her articles fizz with life as she traverses all corners of New York meeting marginalized and unconventional people, each with fascinating stories to tell. In her journalism, Barnes frequently explored the changing roles and opportunities for modern women. She highlighted the trend for dance halls, spoke to suffragettes, watched aviator Ruth Law Oliver fly a plane at a suffrage aviation meet, and interviewed prizefighters Jack Dempsey and Jess Willard (the latter motivated by a new phenomenon of women attending boxing matches).[58] Although by no means a political reporter, Barnes's articles often touched on women's rights, reflecting her own awareness of and interest in the feminist concerns that were part of Village life. In one shocking report, Barnes agreed to be force-fed so that she could help draw attention to the treatment of suffragettes on hunger strike in British prisons.

Across all her articles, Barnes clearly situates herself on the side of the marginalized. In a similar display of fearlessness in the face of authority, Barnes conducted an interview with NYPD commissioner Richard Enright in which she challenged him on ethical and philosophical policing issues and boldly informed him (twice) that 'some of the nicest people I know are either criminals or potential criminals.'[59] Barnes's defence of people that Enright condemned as criminals was a statement in solidarity with her many Village friends and associates who had fallen foul of the law for their activism, art or sexuality. The war on obscenity led by Anthony Comstock of the Society for the Suppression of Vice had in its sights a range of targets. Goldman and Sanger were frequently persecuted for their birth-control campaigns; similarly Guido Bruno was arrested twice for publishing and distributing so-called obscene materials, and Comstock personally raided the Black Rabbit, a queer dive bar, in 1900. Thomas Heise notes that

> the powerful Committee of Fourteen [an anti-vice citizens' association] and the Society for the Suppression of Vice viewed queer sexuality and prostitution as major cultural disturbances and regularly dispatched agents to cruising areas in the Village – dance halls on Thirteenth Street, cafés on MacDougal, bathhouses on Lafayette – to file reports for Enright's police department.[60]

Working with the Society for Suppression of Vice, the NYPD sought to regulate the disorderly, deviant bodies and lifestyles that made up the Village's bohemia.

Barnes's body of work is full of rich depictions of queerness and unorthodox ways of being, most notably her modernist tour de force *Nightwood* (1936), which follows the love affair of Nora and Robin and their circle of 1920s Paris expatriates, including the gender-nonconforming Dr Matthew O'Connor. Years earlier, while living in and reporting on Greenwich Village in 1915, Barnes wrote and illustrated *The Book of Repulsive Women* (published by Guido Bruno), a mixed-media chapbook that celebrated transgressive, queer urban bodies; surprisingly, it escaped the censors (perhaps because Barnes's decadent register left them baffled). In the illustrations that accompany *The Book of Repulsive Women*'s poems, Barnes depicts women dressed in daring outfits with bold modernist prints, and, in one, an exaggerated version of French fashion designer Paul Poiret's signature lampshade tunic and jupes-culottes (knee-length trousers that looked like a skirt). Barnes's women perform, dance and promenade along Third Avenue, like typical restless Village women. Barnes's references to moving through the city and her use of specific New York streets in the titles of her poems ('From Fifth Avenue Up', 'Seen from the "L"') underscore the relationship between modern women and the city. In both *The Book of Repulsive Women* and her journalism, Barnes centres women's experience of – and influence on – the modern urban environment, showing how New York City's emergence as the twentieth century's key metropolis was interlinked with women's emergence as active participants in public life and creators of modern culture.

Barnes's dispatches from Greenwich Village were snapshots that captured an ephemeral scene: the increasing interest in the Village from tourists like Barnes's caricature Madame Bronx threatened its potential as a space of transgression and transformation. Amid rapid changes, Barnes's journalism offers an insight into a brief, unprecedented moment when women began to occupy public space and play roles in urban, cultural, social and political life. An intrepid urban reporter, Barnes proves her own credentials as a fearless, restless Greenwich Village woman: at a time when reporting on and writing about the city was male-dominated, her queer vision of New York in the 1910s challenged the male gaze and championed alternative urban communities.

The Dada Baroness, Scourge of the Village

Baroness Elsa von Freytag-Loringhoven was one of the most eccentric and truly avant-garde Villagers of the 1910s and early '20s. She was an artist and a poet – and, in her biographer Irene Gammel's words, a 'neurasthenic, kleptomaniac, man-chasing proto-punk' – but perhaps her most striking creation was herself. The baroness pounded the city streets dressed in outlandish costumes made of salvaged rubbish and cast-off household items– 'a wig of purple and gold caught roguishly up with strands from a cable once used to moor importations from far Cathay; [wearing] red trousers'.[61] She transformed christmas baubles, curtain rings, tea strainers and even a canary in a cage into jewellery, the perfect accessories to complement her tin-can bra and bizarre outfits. The baroness was a living work of art, and New York City was both her studio and her stage. The baroness was exactly the sort of character 1910s tourists to the Village hoped to spot, and she was hard to miss. Some members of the city's creative circles were less enthusiastic – rumour had it that the genteel poet Wallace Stevens dared not even step foot south of Fourteenth Street when in Manhattan for fear of meeting her. She was written about, photographed and endlessly discussed by other artists and writers, whose responses ranged from admiration to sheer terror.

Unknown photographer, *Baroness Elsa von Freytag-Loringhoven*, c. 1920–25.

A baroness by marriage (her third husband, swiftly abandoned), she moved to the United States from her native Germany in 1910. She had already developed a taste for an artistic, bohemian lifestyle that was far removed from the middle-class conservatism of her upbringing, having studied art in Berlin, performed at Berlin Central Theatre and been part of Munich's progressive Jugendstil movement. In the United States, however, she found the inspiration and freedom to truly unleash her creative vision. Almost immediately after she arrived, she scandalized the residents of Pittsburgh by walking the streets in a suit while smoking. She was arrested for this act of gender subversion and made the front page of the *New York Times* under the headline 'She Wore Men's Clothes'.[62] The fact that this was both an arrestable offence and front-page news shows the extent to which women's appearance in public was policed at the start of the 1910s. The baroness was undaunted.

Before long, the baroness found her way to Greenwich Village; she satirized life among her 'Starved Lady Studio Neighbour' and 'Illustrator Youth Neighbour' in a circa 1919–22 poem-play 'This is the Life – in Greenwich Village'.[63] Working as an artist's model, the baroness came to know New York's circle of avant-garde artists, including Man Ray and Duchamp. Even among the most radical of these groups, the baroness caused a stir. The strange, discarded objects that she turned into assemblage artworks were unlike anything else, comparable only to Duchamp's readymades. In fact, the Baroness was ahead of Duchamp in turning a found object into an art object: *Enduring Ornament*, a rusted industrial iron ring that she salvaged from the street in 1913, pre-dates Duchamp's *Bottle Rack* by one year. Across her assemblage of art, costumes and poetry, the baroness subverted the gendered nature of art and the artist. Some of her contemporaries in the New York avant-garde scene also highlighted the ways that male artists reproduced society's misogyny and gendered hierarchies (for instance, Mina Loy's critiques of Futurism or Beatrice Wood's satirical sketches) but none were so clear-sighted in their criticism as the baroness.

In 1917, the same year as the *Fountain* scandal, she created *God* (attributed to the baroness and artist Morton Schamberg), an inverted plumbing trap mounted on a mitre box.[64] It reads as a retort to Duchamp:

its twisted, scarred and filthy form a contrast against the cool, gleaming sensuousness of *Fountain*'s curves. Despite its function, the urinal was still an object designed to be part of a bathroom; as Ezra Shales has pointed out, ceramic 'sanitary ware' was marketed as desirable and almost aspirational at this time, as it was part of America's civilized, hygienic and affluent modernity.[65] The plumbing trap, however, is subterranean, purely utilitarian and constantly contaminated by waste. *God* symbolizes the tying of a knot in the phallus of the patriarchy. Its profane symbolism most obviously continues the baroness's attacks

Baroness Elsa von Freytag-Loringhoven and Morton Schamberg,
God, 1917, gelatin silver print.

RADICALS AND ROGUES

on religion and patriarchal Christian beliefs. The baroness draws attention to the waste and squalor that lurk under America's vaunted sanitary systems and, by implication, its self-declared modern, masculine, civilized society. The title might also allude to the god-like figure of the male genius, perhaps Duchamp. When referring to him in her poetry, the baroness often created scatological puns on Duchamp's name, including 'Dushit' and 'M'ars' (or, 'my arse'). In *God*, the baroness alludes to Duchamp and/or the male genius as being full of shit – in other words, just another patriarch.

When the *Little Review,* a little magazine that published experimental modern art and literature, moved to Greenwich Village in 1917, its editors, Jane Heap and Margaret Anderson, quickly identified the baroness as an avant-garde trailblazer. Heap declared in a 1919 editorial that the baroness was the 'only one living anywhere who dresses dada, loves dada, lives dada'.[66] Her obscene and erotic work became a regular feature of the magazine, alongside work by James Joyce, Loy, Demuth, Brâncuşi and Williams. Perhaps even more than Joyce's *Ulysses*, the baroness's art and poetry best expressed the *Little Review*'s mission statement of 'Making No Compromise with the Public Taste'. The baroness's continued presence in the pages of the magazine seemed to signal a riposte to outdated notions of decency and America's vigilant censorship system.

Heap and Anderson fell foul of strict anti-obscenity laws when they published the 'Nausicaa' section of *Ulysses* in 1921, infamous for its allusion to protagonist Leopold Bloom's public masturbation. When Heap and Anderson wrote an editorial to defend their decision, they pointedly selected a photograph of the baroness to open the issue. In the image, she is captured in profile, staring defiantly ahead, her face framed by a geometric bobbed haircut and beaded jewellery. The photographer is Man Ray, but the baroness added a doodle of a crown atop her head, as if to reclaim her image from the male gaze of the photographer. Her spiky signature, graffitied in capitals at the bottom of the photograph, completes the act of reappropriation by completely seizing credit from Man Ray. This portrait confronts the reader with a strikingly assertive woman, fully in control of her own image and defiant in her role as a creator of avant-garde art.

104

As an artist, the baroness pushed the formal limits of art and poetry. As a woman in Greenwich Village's liberated modern-art scene, she similarly broke boundaries, revealing the ways that its progressive attitudes towards sex and gender were still dogged by latent misogyny. She was older than many of the other women artists and writers, with hard features and a solid physique that she would often bare at random in company. In terms of dress, her style was not fashionably artistic but, quite literally, art. Most startling of all, while Villagers discussed free love in a high-minded way, the baroness casually flaunted her irrepressible sexuality at any opportunity. She proclaimed her lust at parties, in poetry and during intense pieces of performance art for which she became notorious. Perhaps the most outré example was an episode at the studio of Louis Bouché, who recalled her standing naked, rubbing herself with an image of *Nude Descending a Staircase* ('missing no part of her anatomy') and chanting 'Marcel, Marcel, I love you like Hell, Marcel', in tribute to Duchamp. The baroness's willingness to name her would-be lovers in her work added to the fear and alarm that surrounded her. She made men her muses, no matter their stature within New York's avant-garde circles or whether they reciprocated her lust. This was not the kind of free love that the Village's male bohemians envisioned.

The baroness addressed her unsatisfactory relationships with the men she pursued in explicit visual, mixed-media poetry. For a woman to write about sex and desire so directly, from the perspective of the pursuer rather than the pursued, was scandalous. One example, 'Graveyard Surrounding Nunnery', is a typically bawdy, comical, intensely somatic expression of unrequited lust.[67] Duchamp features as 'Marcel Dushit' who 'behaved mulish'; he is succeeded by 'chaste . . . Redtopped Robert' and 'yellow . . . Carlos [Williams]', two more unwilling objects of the baroness's lust. A strange sketch dominates the top half of the page, encroaching on the poem's title. Looking something like a black hole, it provocatively imagines the doubly barren 'Graveyard Surrounding Nunnery'. Within the sketch, phallic figures mix with spider-like creatures and tombs, vividly illustrating the death of the baroness's sexual desires in the hands of unsatisfactory men. As with all of her drafts, 'Graveyard Surrounding Nunnery' is handwritten in the baroness's distinctive, angular, all-capitals style.[68] Eschewing the typewriter, her poems situate the body at the centre of their formal composition; her archive reveals that she obsessively drafted and re-drafted poems and correspondence by hand. Her stylized writing creates a strong, jolting visual impression. The bold, expressive lettering grabs the reader's attention and amplifies the poem's brazen message. 'Graveyard Surrounding Nunnery' ends with the baroness's signature, further establishing its status as an art object, while also asserting her presence over and above the weak men listed in the poem's text. The positioning of her initials adds her own name to the list of 'saint – corpse – angel – nun –'. This subverts the poem's closing suggestion that the baroness becomes one (or all) of these figures; alternately, she defies them:

> I go to bed – saint –
> Corpse – angel – nun –
> It ain't E.v.F.L
> (Fun.)[69]

William Carlos Williams was both attracted and repulsed by the baroness. The strength of his feelings remained evident even in his auto-biography, written almost three decades after their strange relationship occurred. His attitude towards her is typical of the latent misogyny that lurked below the Village's outwardly progressive, egalitarian ethos. Williams paints a grotesque portrait of her: repeatedly referring to her age as 'well over fifty' (in fact, she was only 49 when she returned to Europe in 1923), he describes her as masculine, aggressive and a sexual predator.[70] Her terrifying sexual appetite, Williams suggests, led her to physically accost and assault men; he alleges that she once hid naked under the bed of an unnamed Russian painter, before dragging him off to her apartment. Williams is equally disparaging about the baroness's dingy 'slum room', describing ashes 'deep on the miserable hearth' and her two pet dogs 'at it on her dirty bed'.[71] This grotesque image links the baroness's unbridled sexual appetite with the bestial.

By associating her disorderly, ageing, unfeminine body with her dirty apartment, Williams passes judgement on the baroness's lifestyle. Implicit in his comments is the suggestion that living in a garret and pursuing sexual liberation are acceptable lifestyle choices for men, but not for women – and certainly not middle-aged, 'unattractive' women. In Williams's view, her apartment is threateningly undomesticated and stages a disturbing sexual spectacle that symbolizes its resident's depravity. At the same time as his acquaintance with the baroness, Williams harboured an unrequited crush on Mina Loy – a woman who also had a reputation for writing about sex and was, during this time, a divorced mother of two in her late thirties. Despite this, Loy's youthful beauty and elegant style clearly made her more acceptable to Williams and others in the Arensberg circle.

The painter George Biddle (a friend of the baroness's, whom she modelled for) similarly describes her apartment as chaotic, but with a more finely tuned appreciation of her unique aesthetic sensibility:

> [It was] crowded and reeking with the strange relics which she had purloined over a period of years from the New York gutters. Old bits of ironware, automobile tires, gilded vegetables, a dozen starved dogs, celluloid paintings, ash cans, every conceivable horror, which to her tortured, yet highly sensitized perception, became objects of formal beauty.[72]

In Biddle's description, the baroness's apartment is part home, part studio; it is a space of assemblage, creativity and transformation, where the baroness makes art from the detritus of the city streets. Biddle's less biased perspective underscores how the baroness truly merged art and the everyday. Many of her contemporaries in the avant-garde were exploring ways of merging radical lifestyles with creative practice, seeking freedom from gender norms and social rules; but few truly broke down the boundaries between art and life quite like the baroness. Her commitment to unbridled self-expression and disregard for norms of gender, sexuality and public decency far exceeded the boundaries of Greenwich Village bohemianism and the avant-garde movement. Despite the ambivalence of her contemporaries and a decades-long exclusion from the histories of experimental writing and performance (until Gammel's critical act of recovery), the baroness inspired generations of feminist and queer urban artists and performers decades later, from

Carolee Schneemann to Leigh Bowery. Rather than ahead of her time, it might be more appropriate to suggest that the baroness was in a whole different space and time.

Postcards from Bohemia

A dash of Greenwich Village's bohemian atmosphere survives in a series of charming postcards that show intimate scenes of the interiors and exteriors of its eclectic cafés, restaurants, studios and stores: smiling groups gather around unpretentious bare tables and chairs to share bowls of spaghetti; a woman in a long flowing smock and sandals strums a guitar; Edna St Vincent Millay stands bemused beside a scarecrow with a sign that reads 'Poem' around its neck; Louise Allison, in loose tunic and trousers, dyes scarves on a stove, ready to be sold in her homely studio. Many of the images are accompanied by little ditties about the proprietor of the place pictured and what visitors can find there. They offer a fascinating visual insight into the vibrant, feminist character of the area, partly by documenting the many women café and gallery owners, artists and craft-makers and eccentric characters who developed the Village's creative network. All too often, these women faded into obscurity as the Village became more commercialized (and therefore more expensive) in the 1920s and culture moved on in the decades that followed. Each photograph tells a story of a woman in the midst of an adventure, attempting to create a life for herself on her own terms. But the images also indicate how narrow the Village scene was – the people on the postcards are young, white and neatly dressed in the uniform of the Village (patterned smocks, bobbed hair, sandals).

Jessie Tarbox Beals, the woman responsible for these photographic postcards, also faded into obscurity after a remarkable life and career. Many of her negatives and prints were lost after she died in poverty at New York's Bellevue Hospital in 1942, but some were saved by her fellow photographer and Villager Alexander Alland. Her photographs lack the sharp composition and understated drama of fellow Villager Berenice Abbott's New York photography. They are not (nor were they intended to be) avant-garde creations. Instead, Beals created a record of the unique spirit that prevailed in the Village and its unconventional

Jessie Tarbox Beals, *Charlotte Powell the Village Painter*, c. 1905–16,
photograph, gelatin silver print.

community. They show everyday scenes, with subjects smiling for the camera or caught joking among themselves – the kind of photographs that friends and family might take. This informality is striking for the time, when women were more often photographed posing in elegant evening attire or standing stiffly alongside their families. By contrast, Beals's subjects are relaxed, in stylish yet casual outfits.

Location is just as important as style, with most of the women photographed in their places of work. Beals's subjects were women who cast off their traditional roles as wives and mothers, stepped out of the domestic realm and became active in building up Greenwich Village's creative community. In addition to café, craft studio and gift shop owners – including the ukulele-playing Miss Crump of the Crumperie café and Romany Marie, wearing a band in her coiled hair and a long, loose floral gown smiling at the door of her kitchen – Beals's photographs reveal the surprisingly diverse jobs that women took on. Charlotte Powell, the Village decorator, appears with cropped hair and grubby overalls astride a ladder; Sonia selling 'art cigarettes' is elegant in flowing patterned robes and leather sandals; and Adele Kennedy, the Greenwich Village tour guide, chats to a well-dressed group outside the Treasure Box.[73]

Many of these Village bohemians have been lost to the mists of time, leaving little record beyond Beals's portraits or footnotes in the biographies of more successful figures. By assembling these fragments, we can work out that most of the women studio and shop owners were also artists and designers, who set up businesses as a way to make a regular income from their talents. Handcrafted decorative objects and clothes dyed using the then fashionable batik technique were particularly popular choices, allowing women artists to experiment creatively while also capitalizing on the public's fascination with life in Greenwich Village. Craft shops that sold clothes, accessories and homewares were particularly popular with, in Barnes's words, 'the endless crowds of "slummers" looking for painted beads and black tassels'.[74] Ruth Murchison, for example, poses for Beals outside the Little Shop Around the Corner, where she sold decorative homewares. Murchison was also a painter, known for her portraits of women in Dutch folk costumes that appeared on the cover of magazines including *Punch* (18 November

1914). Similarly, Beals captures Edith Haynes Thompson outside 'Her Shop', the bric-a-brac and homeware store she ran alongside her design work (she is listed as the set designer for Provincetown Players performances between 1916 and 1919, including Neith Boyce's *Winter's Night*). Louise Allison, a scarf designer, is photographed dying scarves in her kitchen sink and, in another image, sitting with her dog in her studio at 131 Sheridan Square (Beals's accompanying ditty informs us that this former butcher's shop was transformed by Allison 'into a charming bit of form and color'). Heterodoxy member Ami Mali Hicks also appears in her studio, surrounded by the batik-dyed clothing and handcrafted drapes, rugs and assorted homewares that she made alongside her feminist activism.

The vision of Greenwich Village that emerges from Beals's photographs is strikingly different from the traditional patriarchal society that existed elsewhere. The community of women business owners that feature in her photographs mostly ran their cafés and shops independently, or alongside sisters, partners and friends. Sisters Joan and Lin Schromache ran Jolin, which sold 'jolly gifts' and fashionable soft-fitting underwear by C/B a la Spirite Corsets; the whimsical underwear advertisements in the background of their portraits appear to be hand-painted, in a style reminiscent of Clara Tice. Little else is known about the sisters, but they pop up in other group scenes photographed by Beals (including at Polly's), which suggests that they were active members in Village circles. At the Mad Hatter Tearoom (a popular basement café that shared patrons with the adjacent dive bar the Golden Swan), Beals took several portraits of its androgynous owner, Jimmie Criswell, wearing her characteristic loose smock, necktie and pageboy haircut.

Jimmie's story is fairly typical of the women that flocked to the Village in the 1910s in search of the freedom to experiment with their style and identity. After graduating from Bryn Mawr College in Pennsylvania in 1904, Jimmie met her partner Mathilda Spence and moved to the Village with her. She immediately cropped her hair, noting in an interview that she 'could hardly wait to come to Manhattan and have it done', and began wearing smocks (switching to tailored suits on special occasions).[75] The couple bought the Mad Hatter in 1917 from the sculptor Edith Unger and ran it together for a couple of years, until Spence

Jessie Tarbox Beals, *Lin in Her shop, c.* 1916–20, gelatin silver print.

left the country for unknown reasons. Jimmie continued to run the Mad Hatter into the 1920s and, like many Villagers, combined the café business with creative outlets: her archive contains a draft of a play, as well as copies of *The Mad Hatter Mutterings*, a small magazine of creative writing, news and gossip from the Village, in the style of *Bruno's Weekly.* Jimmie's archive survives thanks to the somewhat surprising turn her life took in 1920, when she embarked on a turbulent marriage with esteemed journalist and historian Hendrick Willem van Loon.[76]

In one Village photograph, Beals turns the camera on herself. She smiles awkwardly, as if uncomfortable in front of the lens, and poses outside the Village Art Gallery, 68 Sheridan Square. Beals set up the gallery in 1917 after divorcing her husband. She used the space to host small exhibitions and as a shop to sell postcards of her Village photography, cannily capitalizing on the area's thriving tourist industry. The Village Art Gallery also functioned as an ad hoc tea room, where guests could dine 'à la Paris' (meaning al fresco) at makeshift tables and benches.

This self-consciously European phrasing shows how Beals was appealing to Village slummers who were looking to experience its cosmopolitan atmosphere. Similarly, her postcards were intended to be commercial items with cultural currency: slummers on a day trip to the Village could purchase an image of Polly's or Louise Allison's studio to show off to their friends, signalling that they were 'in the know'. Beals's postcards were portable pieces of bohemia, designed to infiltrate distant corners of America with eccentric images of the much-talked-of phenomenon, the modern woman and her milieu.

Beals occupies a complex position in the history of the Village. On the one hand, she created a unique archive of life in 1910s Greenwich Village and the people that turned it into a bohemian bastion of creativity and freedom. Beals also lived the life of a modern, liberated woman. She was the first published female photojournalist in the United States, a fearless photographer who dragged her huge 22-kilogram (50 lb) camera wherever it was needed to get the best shot.[77] After her divorce, she supported herself and her daughter with her photography business. On the other hand, Beals's commercial work was part of the commodification of the Village. Her photographs create a relatively sanitized view of the Village scene; they depict some androgynous Villagers (such as Jimmie Criswell) but Beals's cheery captions gloss over the subversive aspects of Village life. Removed from the broader context of their lives, the women in Beals's photographs are eccentric but unthreatening. With her photojournalist's eye, Beals recognized the Village's public appeal and saw a way to turn its bohemian atmosphere into a mass-produced product.

Ironically, Beals became a victim of the Village's changing status when, in 1919, her building was purchased by the Corn Exchange Bank and demolished. The crowds of tourist slummers had certainly impacted on the Village's spirit of freedom and community. They intruded in the spaces that artists and writers had carved out specifically to get away from bourgeois, staid society. In an article about Greenwich Village that appeared in a March 1920 issue of the *Ladies' Home Journal*, Jimmie Criswell bemoaned the fact that 'Lady Slummers who read the *Ladies' Home Journal* are swamping us,' with 'quartets of old ladies [infesting the] front room'.[78] However, Beals's situation highlights that, by the turn of the 1920s, the Village was under threat from more than just 'Lady Slummers'. The opening of the Seventh Avenue subway extension in the summer of 1919 linked the Village to Wall Street by a ten-minute train ride. This development reshaped the landscape of the Village and caused property prices to skyrocket.

Two years later, an article in the *New York Tribune* told a story of gentrification that is all too familiar to twenty-first-century residents of New York, London and many other major cities across the world. Asking 'Where Is the Artist Who Is Rich Enough to Rent a Studio [in Greenwich Village]?', it notes the rise in rents: in the early 1910s, the best apartment in Washington Square South could be had for $45 a month and a private room for as little as $5; by 1921, a basic apartment in the Village cost well over $75, and a private room without a bath could not be found for less than $60.[79] Perhaps unfairly, the article attributes some blame to Gertrude Vanderbilt Whitney (named only as a 'wealthy amateur artist'), who 'unwittingly' made MacDougal Alley respectable, her presence encouraging nearby landlords to raise rents. Suggesting that this problem will follow artists around New York City and beyond, the writer worries about what will become of 'America's contribution to art' if artists lack a community. He shows less concern for New York's Black and immigrant communities, which had already been marginalized in the original bohemian takeover of the Village. Suggesting that artists should 'invade' Minetta Lane, an area of the South Village with a large Black community, the writer draws attention to the level of privilege that white bohemian artists enjoyed, despite financial precarity, and anticipates later cycles of gentrification in the city.

In fact, many of the Village's radicals and rogues left New York and the United States in the 1920s. Some, like Djuna Barnes, headed to Europe, seeking new communities and fresh opportunities for inspiration. Others, such as Emma Goldman, were forcibly deported in crackdowns against radicalism and obscenity. As Europe re-emerged from the ruins of the First World War, the Left Bank in Paris drew women from New York and other avant-garde hotspots, offering a new opportunity to build a woman-led creative community. Most women who left for Paris carried the ideals of Greenwich Village with them, continuing to escape conventional modes of living and thinking through creative experiments and alternative communities. This is not to say that there was no longer a home for radicalism in the Village. Despite the huge shifts that took place there between 1910 and the beginning of the 1920s, the Village continued to draw women who were seeking new ideas and lives outside of patriarchal norms through the latter decade. Future first lady Eleanor Roosevelt was among those women; her experiences at the intellectual salon of her close friends Esther Lape and Elizabeth Read, an influential queer couple active in feminist socio-political circles, were formative for both her personal drive and political vision.[80]

Through the twentieth century, Greenwich Village would have many reinventions, shifting to reflect the radicalism of each decade. It continued to be a locus of artistic fervour and political ferment: in the 1960s, it was the epicentre of that decade's counterculture and the site where the Stonewall riots started in 1969. The spirit of this mid-century protest and radicalism owes something to that first wave of bohemians. The restless Village women expressed themselves through creative experiments and political activism, showing how the pursuit of freedom and independence was interwoven with the very fabric of daily life. By stepping out into the city, opening shops and cafés, designing clothes, editing magazines and making art, these women refused to be bound by old-fashioned morals and duties. They might have failed to spark a full-scale revolution, but the tremors of their actions can be felt over the course of the century that followed.

Photographer unknown, Clara Tice, date unknown.

3

CLARA TICE:
Belle of the Ball,
Bohemian Queen

'Who is Clara Tice?'
Haven't you been struck lately by the odd and insistent way
in which this question keeps cropping up in drawing-room
conversations, in theatrical bureaus, in newspaper offices, at
Bohemian studio parties, in Fifth Avenue clubs, and in the smarter
waffle-emporiums of Greenwich Village . . . How, you will ask, has
this diminutive young lady succeeded in so strongly impressing
her personality on the artistic life of New York?
FRANK CROWNINSHIELD, 'Who Is Clara Tice?'[1]

At the peak of Greenwich Village's 1910s heyday, Clara Tice was its undisputed queen. She cut a striking figure as she dashed from Polly's restaurant to one of the Village's nightly parties, often accompanied by her enormous Russian wolfhound: her outfits consisted of shockingly short dresses (usually her own design) or riding costumes complete with thigh-high boots, and she was infamous for being the first woman in the Village to bob her hair. Tice would have been instantly recognizable to anyone familiar with New York newspapers. Her name was a byword for Village eccentricity and she represented a paradigm of the chic, shocking new women who made the area their home. Consequently, her photograph was usually chosen to accompany stories about the latest bohemian scandals and high jinks, whether she was involved or not.

As an artist, Tice similarly captured the spirit of the age and her work was in high demand both from popular, fashionable publications such as *Vogue* and *Vanity Fair*, and from experimental little magazines. She effortlessly collapsed the boundary between highbrow and middle-brow culture, with sketches that expressed the exuberant and exhilarating experiences of modernity: from Edgard Varèse's avant-garde compositions and Sergei Diaghilev's radical ballet to ragtime dances at public dance halls and shopping on Fifth Avenue. Tice's sketches reveal the eclectic environment in which modern art and literature emerged in New York, inextricably linked with shifts in women's lives and opportunities.

Tice was a born and bred New Yorker, giving her a special insight into the city's fast-paced, ever-changing character. Unlike many women of her generation, she was supported in her creative ambitions by liberal parents. In a short article for the *St Louis Star and Times*, she recalls that 'being encouraged by fond parents in my work, the usual obstacles placed in the path of aspirants for an artistic career [particularly girls] were practically unknown to me'.[2] As a result, she took art classes with Robert Henri of the Ashcan School movement. Henri immediately identified Tice's unique ability to convey feeling and action in her art and became an important early supporter and mentor. Although he was by no means radical as an artist, he staunchly rejected old-fashioned academicism in favour of a bold, realist style. Eschewing sentimentality, Henri's portraits use light, bright colours and expressive, loose brushstrokes to capture the character of ordinary people and young women in fashionable modern dress (such as his 1916 portrait of Gertrude Vanderbilt Whitney). Tice would go on to develop a very different style to Henri and favour illustration over painting. However, some sense of her tutor's commitment to capturing the vitality and freshness of his subjects rubbed off on Tice's own development as an artist. Henri also gave Tice her first opportunity to exhibit work, at the 1910 Exhibition of Independent Artists (an egalitarian but less experimental forerunner of the Society of Independent Artists exhibition of 1917). Her work hung alongside that of future Armory Show organizers Walt Kuhn and Arthur B. Davies; Tice was one of five artists to make a sale at the exhibition.

The fact that Henri had no visible influence on her methods and practices is a testament to Tice's confidence and unique vision. She took little time finding her signature style, quickly abandoning experimentations with oil paints and chalk for dynamic sketches in black ink. By 1915, Tice's work had become synonymous with the youthful, permissive atmosphere that defined life in New York's bohemia. Her whimsical line drawings of lithe female nudes seem tame by today's standards, but, in the 1910s and '20s, they symbolized Greenwich Village's radical feminist spirit. In her sketches, Tice created a visual language that explored the ways women's bodies increasingly sat at the nexus between modernity, sexuality, fashion and culture, as, variously, aspirational embodiments of modernity and/or obscene and disruptive threats to society's moral order. Tice's stylish modern women dance, drive and play sport with shameless *joie de vivre*. Through these active portraits, Tice celebrated women's right to live independent, public lives. She represented women who had broken free of the home and boldly staked a claim on the city – whether through dancing at one of New York's public dance halls, cutting a dash on Fifth Avenue, or talking art and politics in a late-night café. Her sketches sang with the exhilarating, unbound sense of freedom that a modern metropolis like New York promised young women during this decade. Sexual freedom was also part of modern living, and Tice's playful eroticism defied old-fashioned puritanism to publicly celebrate this too.

Tice's popularity in this period stems not only from the joyous way she captured the spirit of the moment, but from the fact that she appealed to both highbrow and middlebrow audiences. Tice's work was equally at home among the avant-garde as it was in popular mainstream media. In the wake of the Armory Show, modern art and poetry had excited enough interest and fashionable appeal to be in demand by newspapers and magazines like *Vogue*; but Tice, in particular, skilfully broke down the boundaries between art, sports, fashion and everyday life. Her sketches perfectly aligned with New York Dada's witty, irreverent and erotic ethos, while also speaking to a wider audience that was fascinated by all things modern.

Tice herself caught the public's imagination as much as her sketches. With her petite frame, bobbed hair and stylish fashion sense, she looked like she had sprung from one of her own illustrations. Her outfits were daring, artistic and unconventional, without being too strangely outlandish (as in the manner of Baroness Elsa von Freytag-Loringhoven). Tice lived the life of a modern woman, in defiance of traditional expectations and assumptions about women's lives. She partied until dawn at the Village's almost nightly costume balls, breakfasting with her artist friends at the Hotel Brevoort. Like many other creative Greenwich Village women, Tice rejected the role of wife and mother. Through her 1910s heyday, she had a brief engagement to Village troubadour Bobby Edwards and had affairs with several avant-garde artists in the Arensberg circle, but she shunned marriage.[3]

In 1919, Tice gave up her single life to marry the printer and aspiring artist Harry Cunningham. However, true to her principles, Tice only committed to a lifelong partnership with a man who was devoted to supporting her artwork over and above his own ambitions. Upending stereotypical gender roles, Cunningham set aside his own artistic career to assist Tice, taking on the role of printmaker. The couple formed one of the more successful, egalitarian domestic set-ups to come from the Village's era of feminism and free love. Cunningham managed many household chores, particularly grocery shopping and cooking, leaving Tice time for her art and illustration commissions. In her unpublished autobiography, 'My Model World', Tice acknowledges that it must have 'appeared curious to people for Harry to have done all the shopping, marketing and cooking. But then he did it ever so much better than I could have!'[4]

Queen of Greenwich Village

Tice's reputation as the queen of Greenwich Village was sealed after a headline-grabbing scandal in 1915, five years after Tice's debut at the American Exhibition of Independent Artists. Her relative success at the exhibition (in being one of the few artists who sold any work) failed to turn into anything larger and, during the excitement of the Armory Show, her profile was low. Tice worked hard on her technique in the intervening years. By 1915, she had refined the art of creating deceptively simple line drawings that fizzed with zest and modern elan. Portraits of energetic, athletic nude young women were her signature style; their lithe bodies leap and cartwheel gracefully across the page, each elegant black line conveying rhythm and motion. When she depicted dressed women, Tice clothed her figures in the style of daring outfits that were fashionable in the Village, such as short dresses, harem trousers and feathered headdresses. Her sketches celebrate the youth and autonomy of a new generation of women eager to live full, active lives outside of the home.

The subversive, playful and free-spirited tone of Tice's work expressed the currents of thought that were flourishing in early 1910s bohemian circles. Her skill in capturing this spirit led to an invitation to exhibit at radical Village hotspot Polly's in 1915. That same year, the *New York Evening Sun* featured a tour of the Village, which centred around an evening at Polly's. Sarah Addington described a typical evening there, among a bohemian 'who's who' featuring Louise Norton, Crystal Eastman, artist and militant suffragist Peggy Baird Johns, *Vogue* editor Edna Woolman Chase and poet and anarchist Sadakichi Hartmann. Tice is at the centre of this scene: 'lean, little, sharp-featured Clara Tice, with her uneven bangs and her six-inch pantalettes, talking in her naïve husky little voice to the curly-haired boy from "Harper's Bazar"'.[5] A caption that accompanies a sketch of Tice describes her as 'she of the panties, black cats and Comstockian nudes'. The adjective that Addington coined to describe Tice's nudes ('Comstockian') provides the clue to her notoriety.

Addington's feature on Polly's was published eight months after Tice's exhibition there. During this time, Tice had gone from unknown artist to art world sensation thanks to the intervention of Anthony Comstock, the anti-vice crusader who forced the shutdown of her show at Polly's. Comstock cast a dark shadow over 1910s Greenwich Village and the work of artists and writers in Tice's circle. He embodied everything that Greenwich Village's liberated new women were fighting against: he was a puritanical patriarch who sought to drag outdated Victorian morality into the twentieth century. He waged a lifelong 'war on vice' and worked tirelessly to ban the distribution of so-called obscene materials. Born in 1844 and a veteran of the Civil War, Comstock must have seemed like a spectre from another world to the generation of modern young Villagers who were dreaming up new ways of living, loving and making art. Yet his actions served to remind its resident artists, writers, activists and bohemians of how little had changed outside of their progressive circles and how vulnerable their queer, feminist spaces were to conservative forces.

Comstock's work began in 1866 with the Young Men's Christian Association, which campaigned against New York City's vices (gambling, alcohol and sex). His early efforts to arrest New York booksellers for stocking obscene literature soon grew into a national campaign, which culminated in the passing of the 1873 Comstock Act. The Act was built on a previous law prohibiting the distribution of obscene literature, but it specifically legislated against sending contraceptives, abortifacient drugs or information about birth control through the post. Fighting against birth control became Comstock's key cause; his rise to prominence coincided with widespread anxiety surrounding a declining birth rate, growing demands for women's rights and the development of doctoring as a profession (in opposition to traditional midwives and 'doctoresses') – all of which fuelled a crackdown on women's reproductive rights.[6] After the Act passed, Comstock's supporters in New York assisted in setting up the Society for the Suppression of Vice and Comstock was granted a charter that gave him the power to make arrests. Even in the 1880s, Comstock was ridiculed in some quarters for his anti-art attitude (an 1888 sketch in *Life* magazine depicts him arresting an artist for painting a bathing woman, chastising: 'Don't you suppose I can't imagine what is under the water?'), but he continued to wield influence well into the twentieth century.

Comstock's crusade against birth control and sex education brought him into frequent conflict with Greenwich Village feminists. He had a history of targeting Village activists and writers in the years before he shut down Tice's exhibition. Both Margaret Sanger and Emma Goldman were prosecuted under the Comstock Act for campaigning on the issues of contraception and sex education. Sanger, charged with violating postal obscenity laws after being caught sending out copies of her magazine the *Woman Rebel*, fled the United States in 1914 to avoid standing trial. During her absence, her estranged husband Bill was arrested for distributing Sanger's pamphlet *Family Limitation* and imprisoned for thirty days. Goldman was arrested for violating the Comstock Act in 1916 after addressing a lecture on 'The Social Aspects of Birth Control' to a crowd of garment workers; she subsequently spent two weeks in a prison workhouse. Comstock was equally fervent in his pursuit of art and literature that he deemed to be promoting licentious behaviour. Guido Bruno, publisher and Village eccentric, had a number of run-ins with Comstock for publishing material that defended the rights of sex workers, as well as Alfred Kreymborg's short story 'Edna: The Girl of the Street' (1919).

When Comstock turned his attention to Tice's exhibition in early 1915, he unwittingly transformed her into a sensation. His actions were eagerly reported on in the newspapers and the story made front-page news in the *New York Tribune* with the headline 'Comstock's Ban Brings Art Buyer'. According to their report, Comstock attempted a raid on Polly's but was thwarted by Louise Norton's then husband, Allen Norton (editor of *Rogue*), who purchased all of Tice's sketches ahead of Comstock's arrival. The media furore ensured that the story grew into Greenwich Village legend. In her unpublished autobiography, Tice notes that she was haunted by a persistent version of the story (written by Frank Harris for *Pearson's Magazine* in 1916) that cast her as an embarrassed, naive girl forced to apologize to Comstock, who confiscated her best drawings. In fact, Tice never met Comstock and he didn't take any of her work. More importantly, she was utterly shameless and unrepentant. In fact, Tice expressed an ironic gratitude to Comstock for propelling her to success. After the scandal hit the newspapers, Tice's sketches sold out and other New York galleries began offering her shows. Comstock fared less well: Tice recalls, 'poor old man. It was his last raid. It couldn't have been only coincidence that he died shortly after.'[7]

It is not clear how Tice's exhibition at Polly's came to Comstock's attention. A *New York Tribune* reporter blamed 'somebody who was neither cubist, futurist nor any other kind of an *ist*, unless, perhaps, modest' for alerting him.[8] As a site of radical activism, Polly's was clearly on Comstock's radar and its reputation likely played a large part in his decision to investigate it. The venue certainly added an additional layer of meaning and significance to Tice's sketches. Seen through the lens of Polly's feminism and rejection of patriarchal, heteronormative society, Tice's nudes become more potently political. By aligning herself and her work with Polly's and its radical milieu, Tice linked the joyful bodily freedoms portrayed in her sketches with the wider fight for bodily autonomy that some feminists were engaged in. Her sketches show women living active, public lives, in defiance of old-fashioned moralizers like Comstock who sought to confine them to lives of domesticity. In this way, Tice's art was part of a network of ideas centred around Greenwich Village, which connected women's freedom to bob their hair, wear short skirts and modern underwear, smoke and play sport with their right to use birth control, to vote and to work after marriage.

After the Polly's scandal, Tice became the artist who best represented and recorded the lifestyles of Village women. Her sketch 'Who's Who in Manhattan' celebrated the Village's most fashionable, creative women working in the arts. Most of them were part of the avant-garde group that circulated between Greenwich Village and the Arensberg salon – including Mina Loy, Frances Stevens, Aileen Dresser (a painter and Beatrice Wood's landlady), Lou Arensberg, Louise Norton and actress Fania Marinoff (married to Carl Van Vechten). The sketch appeared in *Cartoons Magazine* in August 1917 as part of Tice's regular series, which usually featured satirical takes on the impact of the First World War on women's fashion; this change in focus shows the extent to which New York's daring and stylish modern women captured public imagination, despite the troubling times.

In 'Who's Who in Manhattan', Tice symbolizes each woman's style and personality: she captures Mina Loy's intense, enigmatic gaze, presenting her at a quizzical angle, accessorized with a top hat and dangling earrings. Lou Arensberg appears in profile, her face half hidden by a large scarf, alluding to her private, withdrawn nature. Writer Louise Norton and illustrator Ethel Plummer occupy the most space on the page, each drawn in elaborate costumes befitting their status as fashion icons and Village 'It girls'. The Village's culture of women-owned arty shops and cafés is represented by Daisy Thompson, owner of the Shop of Beautiful Things and a Heterodoxy member, sketched with chic bobbed hair. Tice plays on her public role as 'queen of Greenwich Village' to entertain readers with insider knowledge, celebrating her friends in the process. From 1916 onwards, Tice was established as the go-to artist to represent city life from the perspective of the modern woman, working across a broad range of magazines.

Queen of Magazines, Gossip Pages and Fashion

The Comstock scandal gave Tice's profile a huge boost, but there were other factors at play in her rise to prominence as the queen of Greenwich Village. No other artist or writer managed to encapsulate the mood of the city quite like Tice, through both her art and her life. Her work keyed into radical politics, but it was also humorous and a little risqué, giving it broad appeal. The notes for her unpublished autobiography offer an insight into Tice's voluble, lively character. Just like the women she sketched, Tice appears full of life, witty and spirited. As Frank Crowninshield wrote in a 1922 catalogue of her work, Tice is 'unlike most American artists [in that] she not only paints life, but feels it; feels it intensely and poignantly; especially its happiness, its humor, and its fantastic gaiety'.[9] Her charm made her a popular guest at parties, and she became, quite literally, the poster girl for Greenwich Village's costume balls. Her elaborate illustrated advertisements for events including the Bal Primitif in October 1917 and the Insect Frolic of February 1923 (both held at Webster Hall) evoked the bohemian decadence of these occasions; her design for the Bal Primitif features a naked Eve, holding up a fig leaf, on shimmering gold-leaf background. Her handmade costumes usually matched her poster designs for creativity and wit.

Tice's notoriety meant that she was in high demand among magazine editors. It is unclear whether Allen Norton truly purchased all the sketches Tice exhibited at Polly's to save them from Comstock, or whether this was part of Village mythology. Either way, Tice caught the Nortons' attention. They published one of her sketches in the second issue of *Rogue* magazine, a nude woman lounging on a bed while being showered by flowers blowing in through an open window. It marked *Rogue*'s ironic 'Booklover's Contest', alongside a caption that asked: 'What Book Does This Picture NOT Represent?'. Mina Loy made her *Rogue* debut in the same issue with 'Sketch of a Man on a Platform', a poem that enacts a satirical critique of Futurist masculinity. The two women became regular *Rogue* contributors, and, despite differences in their backgrounds (the cosmopolitan Loy was, at that point, in Florence, whereas New Yorker Tice had never left the United States), both women symbolized the fashionable, intellectual, youthful mode of feminism that *Rogue* espoused.

In another issue later that year, the Nortons placed one of Tice's sketches in dialogue with Loy's poem 'Virgins Plus Curtains Minus Dots' on a double-page spread. Tice's sketch, *Virgins Minus Verse*, depicts a sylphlike young woman in a soft-fitting corselette. The corselette was much less restrictive than old-fashioned stiff corsets; it was designed to enhance a modern, sleek silhouette and allowed wearers the freedom to take part in energetic modern dances or play sport. Tice's *Virgins Minus Verse* playfully reworks the title and theme of Loy's poem, which focused on the physical and mental restrictions placed on young

Clara Tice, *Invitation to the Flamingo Dance*, after 1919, lithograph.

women by the conservative Italian marriage market. Her sketch draws parallels between bodily freedom and the modern free-verse form of poetry that Loy – and many other avant-garde women writers – worked with ('minus verse' being a pun on free verse). In a following issue, Loy continued their dialogue with her own sketch, 'Consider Your Grandmother's Stays', which mimicked Tice's decadent, black pen-and-ink style and also mocked restrictive corsets. Their creative conversation continued off the page, when Loy moved to New York in 1917. In an interview with Loy's biographer many years later, Louise Varèse (formerly Norton) recalled that Tice was 'always at Mina's feet – she worshipped Mina'.[10] Both women knew what it was like to challenge traditional standards of morality with their art, and to face a backlash from reactionary elements in society that were not ready for women to express desire, sexual agency and an independent creative spirit.

Tice's association with *Rogue* and its experimental contributors was a boost to her profile: in the same way that her exhibition at Polly's had positioned her work in the context of the café's radical feminist politics, *Rogue* magazine framed her sketches within the context of a feminist avant-garde aesthetic. Tice was astute in placing her sketches in forums that lent them cultural weight and avant-garde credibility, without compromising on the whimsical elan that made them accessible and entertaining. Despite her growing commercial success, she continued her association with the avant-garde through the 1910s, notably appearing as a contributor in the second issue of the *Blind Man* (the magazine edited by the members of the Arensberg circle that defended R. Mutt and *Fountain*). Avant-garde publications similarly benefited from their proximity to Tice. The notoriety that surrounded her following the Comstock scandal lent them an edge and helped a small, limited magazine like *Rogue* get attention outside of elite avant-garde circles.

Along with *Rogue* and the Nortons, Guido Bruno and his magazine *Bruno's Weekly* played a role in helping Tice build up her reputation. As a fellow nemesis of Comstock and the Village's most infamous publicist, Bruno clearly saw in Tice's scandal at Polly's an opportunity to capitalize on public interest. Undaunted by a previous obscenity charge that was near ruinous, he arranged an exhibition of Tice's work at his Washington Square garret almost immediately after the show at Polly's closed. The invitation, designed by Tice, was deliberately provocative: it shows the back view of a nude woman – her long hair protecting her modesty from behind – stepping out onto a stage followed by a black cat. The image reads as a nod to Tice's own feelings of being made vulnerable on a very public stage in the wake of the Comstock scandal. Yet it also poked fun at her reputation and tempted the public to see the scandalous sketches for themselves. The advertisement promised that 258 drawings would be on display showing 'the follies and frolics of her contemporaries (male and female)'.[11] Tice and Bruno correctly banked on publicity: a front-page review in the *New York Times* proclaimed 'Clara Tice Lights Guido Bruno Garret', with subheadings noting 'PURPLE HAIR ON ONE GIRL' and 'Not All the Works Are Nudes – Some Show Arabian Nights Scenes'.[12] Remarkably, this exhibition received no attention from Comstock's New York Society for the Suppression of Vice.

Bruno followed this up with several further exhibitions of Tice's work and a mock trial, which poked fun at the Comstock scandal by acquitting Tice of 'unspeakable black atrocities on white paper, abusing slender bodies of girls, cats, peacocks and butterflies'.[13] She also contributed illustrations to his magazine *Bruno's Weekly*, which showcased the work of Greenwich Village artists and writers and was popular among the growing band of tourists that Bruno (among others) encouraged. Tice's association with Bruno (who declared himself Greenwich Village's mayor) secured her place at the centre of Village life. By frequently exhibiting at his Washington Square garret (located in the centre of the Village), Tice put herself squarely on the map, particularly in the minds of slumming tourists eager to experience its bohemian world.

Around the same time that Tice became a Greenwich Village icon, the area itself took off in the public imagination. Magazine and newspaper journalists revelled in recounting the latest goings-on in the bohemian artist colony that had emerged as America's cultural capital. Greenwich Village bohemianism was a byword for exactly the kind of outré, taboo-breaking behaviour and shockingly modern fashions that made perfect tabloid fodder. As a result, Tice became a figurehead for the latest trends and a key part of the Village myth. In Tice's own words, she was 'good copy' and so:

Clara Tice, *Illustration for 5th Ave Club*, 1926, offset lithograph.

My bobbed hair – long before Irene Castle – five-foot, hundred-pound figure, my working costume of riding breeches and boots, became a familiar spot in the papers every time something unusual happened in Greenwich Village and a picture was needed in a hurry.[14]

Tice's trend-setting bobbed hairstyle was her signature. When the *New York Times* reported on the craze for bobbed hair in June 1920 (which, they reported, had spread from the Village to schoolteachers

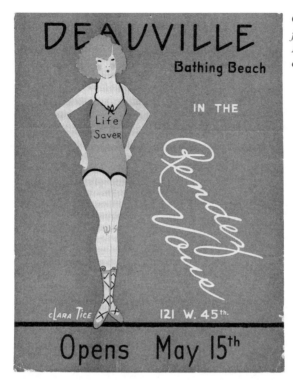

Clara Tice, *Illustration for Deauville Bathing Beach*, 1922, lithograph on paper.

and *even* society women), the article noted that Tice and her friend Francis Gifford began the trend in 1908, inspired by Russian revolutionaries.[15] It was not just the New York Press that reported eagerly on Tice's style. She was mentioned in several of O. O. McIntyre's updates from New York, 'New York Day by Day', a daily column that ran in 508 newspapers across the United States through the 1910s and '20s. McIntyre made reference to Tice's trendsetting styles, crediting her as the inspiration behind the new fashion for 'batik waists'. Tice joined a dazzling line-up of celebrities whose names peppered McIntyre's column, from Amelia Earhart to Charlie Chaplin, which gestures to her fame and influence at this time. By 1921, Tice was well known enough to warrant a large feature in the *St Louis Star and Times* to mark her visit to the city. Lively self-portraits of Tice horse-riding alongside her beloved wolfhound appeared under the headline 'She Set the Fashion for Bobbed Hair'. In an accompanying article, Tice praises short skirts and rolled stockings because they are 'healthy and comfortable', taking care to note that she does not approve of 'imitation beauty' such as false eyelashes – 'beauty is not a woman's best asset,' rather 'brains [and] the ability to do things' are more attractive characteristics.[16]

During the First World War, Tice offered similarly light-hearted but provocative commentary on women's style for *Cartoons Magazine*, an unusual and largely forgotten Chicago-based publication that regularly featured illustrations by Tice and fellow Greenwich Village It girl Ethel Plummer. As the USA entered the war in 1917, Tice appeared in *Cartoons* with a set of satirical sketches showing the latest hat trends. Most display military-themed designs, such as 'La Baionnette',

The Quill (October 1919), cover by Clara Tice.

a small pill-box hat with blades protruding from the back, and the warship-inspired 'Monitor', complete with smoking guns that match the wearer's cigarette. The illustrations were clearly intended to raise a smile during a troubling time, but they also highlight the ways that women's fashion reflected life in wartime; in the same issue, Tice's editorial image titled 'Privations of War' shows a man and woman discussing the fact that the government have not issued hat-rationing cards, with the woman declaring them unnecessary because 'they're so small now that it doesn't matter.'[17]

Tice continued to consider war's impact on women's lives and styles for *Cartoons* for its duration. In 'Wartime Fads for Women', she mixes comical military flourishes like 'swagger sticks', 'military leggings', 'patriotic vests' and 'cartridge belts for cigarettes', with more serious images of women working as nurses and knitting for the Red Cross. In her characteristically whimsical style, Tice highlighted how war was causing upheaval in everyday society from a woman's perspective. Both sets of images also encode sly mockery of the militaristic, jingoistic fervour that accompanied the United States' entry into the war; Tice's sketches suggested a link between the nationalist enthusiasm for war sweeping the country and fashion fads, as if support for war was something that could be put on and later discarded. The undertone of scepticism that ran through Tice's war sketches aligned with the anti-war sentiment that prevailed in Greenwich Village: members of its community wrote protest pieces for *The Masses* and held peace marches in Washington Square, often at personal risk (the U.S. government passed the 1917 Espionage Act to monitor and punish dissent).[18] In this context, Tice's comical images of war costumes can be read as a subversive critique of militarism, designed to go under the radar. These wartime sketches also underline the ways that the politics of fashion (and of women's lives more generally) was a key influence on Tice's work of the 1910s and early 1920s.

Follies and Frolics in *Vanity Fair*

When Frank Crowninshield took the helm of *Vanity Fair*, he was a well-known, well-connected and cultured New York dandy. Unlike Greenwich Village's Guido Bruno, Crowninshield came from a wealthy, distinguished old-world New England family. He spent part of his child-hood in Europe, while his father (Frederic, a respected landscape and mural painter and art teacher) studied. A cosmopolitan upbringing shaped Crowninshield and instilled in him a lifelong passion for the arts. He was well known for his impeccable dress sense and outgoing personality, and was remembered, in his *New York Times* obituary, for being a trailblazing 'prophet of modern art'.[19] In 1913, Crowninshield (then arts editor of the *Century Magazine*) served on the organizing committee of the Armory Show; the following year, his friend Condé Nast invited him to edit Nast's failing *Dress and Vanity Fair* and drag it into the twentieth century.

Inspired by his vibrant New York social life, Crowninshield imme-diately set about remaking the magazine to reflect the 'things people talked about – parties, the arts, sport, theatre, humor, and so on'.[20] Under Crowninshield's direction, the magazine reflected modern New York and effortlessly blended a witty, urbane spirit with intellectual content. To distinguish *Vanity Fair* from *Vogue*, he cut the fashion pages and began building a coterie of avant-garde writers and artists whose work would ensure that *Vanity Fair* had a cultural edge on its competitors. As a patron of Village hotspots like Polly's, Crowninshield was attuned to the feminist spirit of the moment. Almost immedi-ately, Tice became his go-to illustrator for *Vanity Fair*. She was joined by Ethel Plummer and writer Dorothy Parker (then known as Roths-child) as regular contributors, who helped shape *Vanity Fair*'s modern, irreverent tone.

Vanity Fair courted a reputation for the risqué, most obviously via its staff's notoriety: like Tice, whose brush with Comstock made her name synonymous with nudes and eroticism, Dorothy Parker was known for her suggestive writing during her time at *Vogue* (where she worked before joining the staff of *Vanity Fair* in 1918). *Vanity Fair* played on its contributors' public profiles in witty and jocular sketches that func-tioned as in-jokes for regular readers. Invariably, these features centred on the antics of the Greenwich Village set, particularly the 'four Bohemian ladies who . . . [are] the queens of [*Vanity Fair*]' and their 'revels in Washington Square': namely Tice, Plummer, Myrtle Held and Thelma Cudlipp.[21] In 'The Smock Colony in Washington Square', for example,

Vanity Fair celebrates the all-night costume balls that took place 'every single night of the year' in the 'art village of Washington Square'.[22] In the article, Tice offered readers advice on appropriate costumes: 'a nice girl needs ... [only] a domino for yourself and a sailor suit for your social secretary. A pierrot suit is also very useful.'[23] Ethel Plummer, a friend of Tice, was singled out as ringleader of the late-night revellers:

> Old Tom, the man who rakes the so-called grass in Washington Square, recently confided to *Vanity Fair* that he has become so accustomed to meeting Ethel Plummer and her friends, along about eight in the morning, on their way home from a fancy dress party, that he no longer pays the slightest attention to them. Monsieur Elie, the manager of the Brevoort Hotel, certainly rendered a great service to Greenwich Village when he opened a special breakfast room – reserved from 7 o'clock on – for guests still clad in dominos, masks, and fancy dress costumes. Thank you, Elie.[24]

The gossip and celebration of Greenwich Village women's hectic life-styles were not simply aimed at a coterie readership; Crowninshield correctly anticipated that the taboo-breaking fashions that started in the Village would spread to middle- and upper-class women. *Vanity Fair* (and Tice's illustrations) track the spread of new trends in fashion, dance, music and sport from the quintessential Greenwich Village modern woman to society women into the 1920s.

The bulk of Tice's work for *Vanity Fair* revolved around illustrating articles about youthful, active young women and the new craze for sports, which linked to the fashion for loose-fitting clothes and masculine styles. In May 1916, Tice provided the illustrations for a tongue-in-cheek feature on the 'Fashions of 1920' that celebrated Vanity Fair's innovative eye for style ('any fashion magazine can forecast the mode for next summer ... Take *Vogue*, for instance,' but forecasting the fashions of 1920 is 'a tough job – only *Vanity Fair* can do it').[25] The article focused heavily on sportswear, such as form-fitting bathing suits guaranteed to shock high-society matrons. Tice also included a sketch of a woman with bobbed hair on horseback, kitted out in chic 'riding togs', including knee-high black riding boots with matching gauntlets and shorts. It was likely a self-portrait, as Tice was also a horse-riding fan known for wearing riding breeches and boots out and about in the Village. By suggesting that the women of 1920 will look like her, Tice slyly celebrates her role as a trendsetter.

Tice's work for *Vanity Fair* also reveals the spread of Greenwich Village fashion to high society. Tice was sent to illustrate the activities of the smart set holidaying at Bailey's Beach in Newport in 1916 (an elite private beach popular with the likes of the Vanderbilt and Astor families), for an article that lampoons the enthusiasm with which society women had taken up sports and daring physical activities: the image of one Miss Gwendolyn Livingstone '[dropping] down from her Japanese lacquer hydroplane – designed by Elsie de Wolfe' to smoke a cigarette with her beau on the beach is pure *Vanity Fair* parody.[26] Similarly, a trio of bathers that Tice depicts wearing swimming costumes inspired by the Ballets Russes' costume designer, Léon Bakst, playfully mocks the movement of modern art and culture from avant-garde to high-society fashion. Tice was still riding high as the queen of Greenwich Village, but this article offers a wry commentary on the changes in fashion as the styles of the artistic modern woman filtered into the mainstream, losing their radical edge.

Those Naughty, Naughty Dances

The Comstock scandal ensured that Tice was best known for her nudes, but her true skill was in capturing rhythm and movement. In every sketch Tice made, she conveyed the graceful motion and elegant athleticism that were an aspirational aspect of modern women's more liberated lifestyles. In the pages of *Vanity Fair*, Tice's dynamic images of dancing figures and sprightly sportswomen captured changing trends in physical activity, as women began leading more public, active lifestyles and embraced relaxed styles of dress, including soft-fitting underwear and trousers. Dance trends, in particular, were changing to both reflect and enforce more permissive attitudes in matters of morality and public decency. Through the 1910s and '20s, Tice's sketches offer insight into the ways that developments in dance reflected new freedoms sought by women and celebrated queer expressions of sexuality that subverted gender norms. The visual language of Tice's dance sketches highlights dance's key role in the development of modernity and modern ways of living in the city; bursting with vibrancy, sensuousness and wild abandon, Tice's dancers channel a *joie de vivre* that defied repressive, conservative forces and the devastation of war that overshadowed the era. Tice's work for *Vanity Fair* also highlights the spread of dance trends across race and socio-economic class lines; she depicted both the stylized, expressive movements developed by dancers of the avant-garde Ballets Russes company, and also the inhibited dances that were taking hold in dance halls and were popular with working-class groups.

Tice's dynamic style was an obvious match with the ecstatic, animalistic forms that became the signature of Sergei Diaghilev's Ballets Russes. In her unpublished autobiography, she recalls with obvious pride that 'M. De Diagileff [*sic*] saw some of my sketches and made me official artist for the Russian Ballet, [providing] unique opportunities to sketch Nijinsky and Pavlowa.'[27] No evidence of this exchange survives, but Tice did illustrate the performances of the Ballets Russes many times throughout the 1910s and '20s. In November 1915, Tice's sketches of Vaslav Nijinsky appeared in *Vanity Fair*. Her line drawings evoke his sensuous movement, capturing the graceful curve of limbs and the toned strength of the dancer's body. Tice conveys Nijinsky's way of playing with gender identity and his subversive sexuality, emphasizing the dual softness and strength of his body. The year after her sketches of Nijinsky appeared in *Vanity Fair*, Tice painted a portrait showing him performing in *The Afternoon of a Faun* (first performed in 1912). This was the first ballet that Nijinsky choreographed for the Ballets Russes, with assistance from Diaghilev, Léon Bakst and Jean Cocteau. It was as provocative a work as 1913's *The Rite of Spring* and its premier performance was attacked on the front page of *Le Figaro*. Decades later, writer Stephen Birmingham described Nijinsky's performance of sexuality, bodily inhibition and defiant artistic independence as a forerunner of Dada.[28]

The scenario that features in *The Afternoon of a Faun* – a flirtation between a faun and a nymph – was taken from classical antiquity, but the combination of stylized modern dance and explicit male sexuality ensured it was met with scandal. The dancers' animalistic movements climax, quite literally, with the faun (Nijinsky's character) simulating masturbation on the scarf of his lover. Penny Farfan describes the performance as 'one of the most iconic instances' of 'queer modernist performance', one that brought to the 'foreground a dissident male sexuality that disrupted conventional expectations of heterosexual narrative resolution'.[29] Nijinsky's performance made the physicality and sensuousness of the body a spectacle. Through her portraits of Nijinsky, which were made at the height of his notoriety, Tice aligned herself with both the queer, erotic sensibility and the commitment to radical modernist expression that defined Diaghilev's Ballets Russes.

Away from the theatre, working-class people were also developing daring new forms of dance in popular public dance halls that were springing up all over the city. Ragtime dances emerged in Black communities and were then embraced by young white people keen to break with the stuffy traditions and formalities of their parents' generation. The new dance crazes usually had names that referenced animals – the turkey trot, the grizzly bear, the bunny hug, the camel walk – indicating their informal, expressive styles of rhythm and movement. This enthusiasm for dancing went hand in hand with emergence of the modern woman: energetic dances demanded fashions that were less restrictive (shorter hemlines, loose undergarments, sturdy shoes) and dance halls also provided spaces in the city where women could go, without chaperones, to cut loose. For young women of all classes, dancing and dance halls symbolized freedom.

For the older generation, modern dance styles were seen as a threat to public order and decency. Ragtime dances encouraged a physical closeness between dance partners and could be sexually suggestive, leaving conservative white society aghast at what they perceived as displays of obscenity and vulgarity. Social reformers feared that young women would be corrupted by alcohol and bad company, or that working-class people would fall into lazy habits and criminality. White middle- and upper-class people were appalled to think that dance styles developed in Black communities were being adopted by their children; their criticisms of modern dance were couched in racist stereotypes, using the language of white supremacy that dehumanized and sexualized Black bodies. A nationwide moral panic ensued, during which the then president-elect Woodrow Wilson cancelled his 1913 inaugural ball for fear that guests might break out in scandalous ragtime dances; across the country, signs appeared at dances declaring 'No Turkey Trotting Allowed'. A ditty in a 1912 issue of the *Tacoma Times* warned:

When you're in Walla Walla, friends,
You must not 'bunny hug'
Or 'turkey trot', or likeas not
They'll slam you in the jug;
And girls, don't romp with 'Texas Tom';
To do so's taking chances,
For the cops have put the kibosh on
Those naughty, naughty dances.[30]

Tice was drawn to dance because the same rhythm ran through her artwork, in the expressive black lines that she shaped into joyful, vibrant forms. Her sketched bodies sing with boundless energy, leaping across the page with abandon. The frequent nudity we find in her work symbolizes the sensuality and physical freedom that the era of the animal dance ushered in. Tice's nude sketches of the 1910s are not typically erotic (unlike her later work for the Pierre Louÿs society); instead, her nudes convey simple pleasure in their bodies. Tice sketched her own variation of an animal dance for a 1915 issue of *Bruno's Weekly*, or rather an insect dance. In *Butterfly Dance*, a long-limbed nude woman leaps and glides through the air accompanied by a butterfly that flutters beside her. Her hair spreads out like the butterfly's wings as she progresses through a sequence of moves. The butterfly represents the beauty and spirit of Tice's bare modern women, but also introduces a sense of ephemerality; a reminder, perhaps, of the transience of youth, joy and beauty.

My Model World

Butterflies appear often in Tice's nude sketches, carrying a preoccupation with fragility and impermanence through her early work. In a later reflection on her artistic inspiration, Tice noted that 'loved ones change

. . . beauty becomes dumb, men impotent, women sterile', but 'my pictures can always bring back to me the original exaltation of creation, the freshness and aliveness my models as I saw them in the perfection of movement.'[31] Similarly, she notes, sketches of her beloved pets grant their spirits immortality. Tice sought to make permanent the fleeting moment of a body in motion, capturing the vitality of her age on the page and preserving it for posterity.

Tice explained the motivation behind her artwork in a draft of 'My Model World' (unpublished, written circa 1930s), an unconventional and unfinished autobiography of sorts, told through explorations of her favourite models (human and animal). Like Tice's art, it is a mix of whimsy and serious intent. Her imagined 'model world' offers an antidote to the failed promises of 'political statesmen [who] have had their tries at "free worlds", "new orders" and "perfect utopias" long enough'.[32] Yet Tice offers little in the way of a serious manifesto; after all, she admits to 'no knowledge of economics and sociology and whatever related fields are necessary'. Instead, Tice's incomplete and rambling text reaches towards a fantastical, ageless world where everyone and everything that gives her joy lives forever. Beyond personal pleasure, Tice also celebrates qualities she found in her beloved Greenwich Village. Some of the characters that appear in her writing embody the liberated sexuality, gender fluidity and relaxed attitudes towards the body that prevailed in the Village: in particular, the intriguingly enigmatic Sully, an 'around-the-world sexpert' with links to Magnus Hirschfeld's Institute of Sex Research in Berlin, and Grace, Tice's favourite (human) model, with a love of 'tomboy activities' and 'no shame of her body, [who] was never embarrassed or irked by conventionalities'.[33] The attributes that Tice admires in her models and friends offer an insight into the qualities she strove for in her work.

Unsurprisingly, Tice's 'model world' is a lot like Greenwich Village of the 1910s. She describes the latter as a 'literal dream world, where anything could happen and almost always did'. Attempting to explain the Village's notoriety, Tice places the 'wide publicity for the Comstock raid on my exhibition at Polly's' at the top of the list. She also includes 'the splurge of bobbed hair, the intimate theatre groups, the tea shops, the many antiquarian bookshops and the well-publicized Greenwich

Village balls'. There is a note of melancholy in Tice's text, particularly when she suggests that her memory of these times is patchy and unreliable (the half-finished text itself reflects the gaps in her memory): 'some events of long ago seem to have happened yesterday; some as if they could never have happened'. Writing in the years following the Great Depression, as fascism was on the rise and the world inched closer to a second war, it is little surprise that the heady days of bohemia felt like a distant dream. Tice's eccentric autobiography rails against the passing of time, attempting to preserve the vibrant spirit of Greenwich Village life, art and politics in words, just as her sketches crystallized the rhythms of modern dance and modern lifestyles. However, her failure to complete the text suggests that this was an impossible task – Tice was unable to recreate (in words) the sense of possibility, carefree creativity and joy that characterized the Village in the 1910s.

As an artist, Tice became a victim of both a change in fashion and the ephemeral nature of her work (magazines, for example, would be lost or thrown out, and posters for costume balls were similarly liable to disappear or degrade). In the 1920s, Tice took on new projects, but these works were also ephemeral in form or destined for private collections (rather than museums or archives). In the mid-1920s, the Pierre Louÿs Society commissioned her to create opulent, sensuous illustrations for its series of erotic texts; these exquisitely produced books were released in limited runs and became sought-after items that passed between private collectors. In her work for the society, Tice developed her nude sketches into scenes of queer sensuality, with groups of women bathing together and delighting in each other's bodies.

Around the same time as she was working on her erotic illustrations, Tice also turned her attention to mural painting. Nightclub impresario Billy Rose hired her to create a mural of ethereal nymphs (and an illustrated menu) for his upmarket speakeasy the Fifth Avenue Club, and she created another mural depicting New York's cultural elite for Club Rendezvous at 45th Street.[34] Tice had ambitious plans for her 1920s mural work. Helen Appleton Read, at this time an art critic, profiled Tice for an article in the *Brooklyn Eagle* in December 1923, in which she described the 'gifted and original' Tice as 'the most discussed artist north of Washington Square and south as well, since she has moved to Brooklyn

Heights'.[35] Read goes on to offer a tantalizing glimpse into Tice's latest project: turning a Brooklyn brownstone into a 'showroom for her work', where each room of the house would be decorated with a stunning mural. It was a joy, Read suggested, to see a 'new note in interior decoration' that differed from the styles popularized by influential tastemaker and decorator Elsie de Wolfe and 'standardized by the department store'. Conjuring comparisons with Florine Stettheimer, Read declared that Tice was 'a Twentieth Century rebirth of the Rococo', mixing technical skill with knowing humour. Unfortunately, no other documents of this fascinating interior-design installation exist, but Read's description suggests that it was one of Tice's many efforts to bring her vision of a utopian 'model world' to life.

Tice swapped urban life for rural retreat in the 1930s, moving to a Connecticut farmhouse with Cunningham, where they could live surrounded by her beloved animals. But when Cunningham died in 1947, Tice headed back to the city. Post-war New York was much changed and the heyday of the modern woman had been swept away by a wave of conservatism. In the art world, a new avant-garde was pushing through in the form of the Abstract Expressionists, whose large-scale, bold gestural paintings made Tice's work seem decidedly twee. Dogged by ill health, Tice gave up creating art in the final decades of her life. She died unknown and destitute in 1973.

From a contemporary perspective, it's challenging to understand how Tice's sketches were once considered shocking, obscene even. The subversive power of this work is only revealed through an exploration of the social, political and artistic shifts that Tice, and other modern women, navigated. Tice's celebration of women's joy, in the face of obscenity laws, captures just how precious their freedoms were (and how fleeting). Her body of work forms an ode to the simple but essential pleasures of life – sex and sensuality, dance and friendship, art and nature. Tice was the quintessential queen of Greenwich Village not simply because she was the best dressed or the first to bob her hair, but because she captured the dreams, desires and demands of so many women – in Greenwich Village, New York City and across the United States – who were daring to imagine new ways of living and new forms in which to express their modern, restless selves.

Charles Sheeler, *Interior of the Arensberg Apartment*, 1919, casein silver print.

4

THE ARENSBERG SALON:
Home of American Dada

I n the early hours of 26 May 1917, down a quiet street in the Upper West Side, a rowdy bunch of revellers was disturbing the peace. They were dressed in strange costumes, chattering in a mixture of English and French, and – careful observers might have realized – their faces were vaguely familiar from the pages of the *New York Evening Sun*. Indeed, the drunken group stumbling into the gothic Atelier Building at 33 West 67th Street was no ordinary gathering of New Yorkers, but rather members of a 'motley international band' that 'turned night into day' and lived 'an inconceivable orgy of sexuality, jazz, and alcohol', centred around Walter and Louise Arensberg's salon at the address in question.[1] On this May night, the group (consisting of Marcel Duchamp, Mina Loy, Beatrice Wood and Charles Demuth) had come from a night of Dada decadence at the Blind Man's Ball at Greenwich Village's Webster Hall and were eager to continue the festivities. They returned to the Arensberg salon, knowing they would find refreshments in the wealthy couple's well-stocked pantry. After a meal of scrambled eggs and wine, all four decided to retire to Duchamp's studio (which was situated two stories above the Arensbergs') and pile into bed together. Wood memorialized the occasion with a sketch entitled *Lit de Marcel 6.30, Après Webster's Hall*, which depicted their jumbled bodies collapsed on Duchamp's bed. Although the excitement of the Blind Man's Ball added an extra flourish to the evening, this was, in many ways, a typical evening at the Arensbergs' apartment – a vibrant artistic salon, where New York's most progressive artists, writers and intellectuals gravitated to discuss art and philosophy, flirt, drink, dance and play all-night games of chess. It was also the incubator of some of modern art's great scandals and triumphs.

'Walter Arensberg is quite mad.
Mrs. Arensberg is mad, too.'

Both Walter and Louise came from wealthy families and enjoyed privileged, cultured upbringings. After graduating in English and philosophy at Harvard University, Walter spent two years travelling around Europe before returning to Harvard for a postgraduate course, which he quickly abandoned to become a journalist. Louise was also well travelled, well educated and intelligent. She was fluent in German, Russian and French, but her great passion was music: having studied music at a finishing school in Dresden, she was a highly accomplished pianist and, during the couple's New York soirées, she often took to the piano to serenade guests, sometimes singing too.[2] Although the couple both came from wealthy families, it was Louise's vast inheritance from her father's textile business that allowed the couple to maintain their lifestyle; more importantly, it would also enable them to build their art collection long after Walter had used up his own bequest. In the years between their marriage in 1907 and the Armory Show in 1913, the couple lived a quiet, isolated life in Cambridge, Massachusetts. During this time, it was poetry, rather than art, that Walter pursued with a passion. In this, his taste was modern but in no way radical: he was inspired by *fin de siècle* French Symbolism and Decadence and wrote his own work in a pastiche of those styles. The couple's encounter with modern art, however, was to change the course of their lives, as well as that of Western art history.

Like many Americans, the Arensbergs were first introduced to European modern art at the Armory Show. Although there had been small shows in New York, most notably at Alfred Stieglitz's 291 gallery, the Arensbergs' life in Cambridge kept them at a distance from radical cultural happenings. The media furore around the Armory Show piqued their interest enough to compel them to visit New York and catch the exhibition in its final days there. On first impression, the couple were fascinated but a little bewildered. Louise, in particular, was initially taken aback by the shock of the new, describing the paintings in the exhibition as 'weird and grotesque'. Walter was more immediately enthusiastic and keen to buy work. With their first purchases, the couple played it safe; in any case, much of the headline-grabbing work had already sold to savvy, more established collectors such as Arthur Jerome Eddy (who purchased two paintings by Duchamp) and John Quinn. The Arensbergs were particularly drawn to Duchamp's by then infamous *Nude Descending a Staircase, No. 2* (1912), but were disappointed to find that it had already been sold to lawyer Frederick C. Torrey.[3] They settled for one lithograph by Édouard Vuillard but were soon eager for more. When the Armory Show moved to Boston, the Arensbergs returned ready to make more serious purchases. Walter exchanged their Vuillard lithograph for two others – Cézanne's *Bathers* (c. 1898) and Gauguin's *Project for a Plate* (1889) – and they also bought *Sketch for 'Puteaux'* (1912) by Jacques Villon, who was then a relatively young and little-known French artist.

Villon's small abstract painting was a risky acquisition for the couple, in comparison to the purchase of work by the well-established Gauguin and Cézanne. It was an early sign of their commitment to avant-garde art and it marked the start of their relationship with Armory Show co-organizer Walter Pach. Pach quickly turned into one of the Arensbergs' most trusted advisors in their early collecting days. He had developed authority and expertise in modern and avant-garde art in Paris, where he moved in 1908 to pursue painting. Soon, he was mixing with Gertrude and Leo Stein's circle; these connections allowed Pach to build up an extensive network of influential European cultural figures, which, crucially, included art dealers such as Ambroise Vollard and Daniel-Henry Kahnweiler. His links to both artists and art dealers proved vital once plans for the Armory Show were set in motion. Through his contacts, Pach secured loans of art that would go on to be the exhibition's most experimental – and headline-grabbing – pieces, including Duchamp's *Nude Descending a Staircase, No. 2*. Pach formed a solid friendship with Duchamp while in Paris, which deepened after the critical and financial success of the latter's work at the Armory Show.

With Pach guiding them, the Arensbergs quickly made up for their caution at the Armory Show by snapping up radical European artwork that was exhibited in New York (an increasing occurrence thanks to the wave of interest and excitement that the Armory Show incited). They purchased Henri Matisse's *Mademoiselle Yvonne Landsberg* (1914) during Matisse's solo exhibition at New York's Montross Gallery in 1915 (organized by Pach). This portrait signified a radical departure for Matisse – eschewing vivid colours, he created a sombre, brooding portrait of Landsberg with an expressionless, mask-like face, her hands clasped anxiously on her lap. Lines of motion arc into the dark space around her, evoking a sense that her form was expanding beyond its limits, and even beyond the limits of the painting. Matisse sought to capture Landsberg's inner self, rather than create a realistic impression of her physical being. This startling experimental portrait contributed to the baffled reception that greeted the Montross show. *American Art News* went so far as to christen Matisse 'The Apostle of the Ugly' for rendering 'the ugly in an ugly way' in work that 'violates the essential canons of art . . . [and lack] educational or art value'.[4] The Arensbergs' decision to purchase one of the exhibition's most radical – and, according to *American Art News*, most ugly – paintings was a bold move. Undaunted by the still-conservative attitudes of many art critics, they were on a mission to support avant-garde art and nurture its growth in New York.

From the outset, collecting alone was not enough for the Arensbergs. Instead, they wanted to intervene directly in the art world, something that would not be possible in their sleepy, isolated Cambridge neighbourhood. Their experiences at the Armory Show made them completely re-evaluate their lifestyle. In 1914, the Arensbergs packed up and headed for New York, where myriad opportunities to immerse themselves in the vibrant new art scene awaited. Although Greenwich Village was the city's radical epicentre it was, perhaps, a little shabby for their tastes; instead, they settled on the Upper West Side, a neighbourhood close to Central Park which was more affluent and refined than the Village, but still had its own artistic and intellectual atmosphere. The apartment they purchased was part of the Atelier at 33 West 67th Street. This gothic building had been built in 1905 as part of a cooperative project to provide studios suitable for artists in Manhattan – conservative, relatively well-to-do artists who moved in very different circles to those based in the Village. As a result, the apartments were designed to be airy and spacious, with double-height ceilings and windows that let in lots of light. It was the perfect space to showcase the Arensbergs' growing art collection. This careful choice of apartment suggests that, even in their early days as art collectors and patrons, the Arensbergs were specifically building their new life in New York around modern art.

Once the Arensbergs moved into their new apartment, they began to fill it with modern art, demonstrating a particular enthusiasm for Cubism. Building their collection was the new focus in their lives, but Walter continued to write poetry and maintained his enthusiasm for literature. He had a keen understanding of the fact that experimentation in modern art went hand in hand with radical new literature being produced by experimental poets; in other words, that modernism was a revolution of art, culture and life itself, not limited to any single art form. The Arensbergs were keen to expand their reach and broaden their support of modern culture. To that end, they decided to fund small avant-garde magazines. In 1915, they provided financial backing to Allen and Louise Norton for *Rogue*, and to Alfred Kreymborg for the literary magazine *Others: A Magazine of the New Verse*.

Before stepping into the Arensbergs' New York salon and exploring its dizzying mix of avant-garde art and artists, it is important to first take a closer look at the salon's enigmatic hosts. As collectors and people not inclined to seek the limelight, the Arensbergs have been in the background of the story of modern art, despite their profound impact. Louise's profile, in particular, has been eclipsed by that of her husband. This is partly because Louise (always Lou to friends) was quiet and shy, in contrast to her husband's gregarious, outgoing personality. The fact that she did not drink alcohol further relegated her to the sidelines during the often raucous, booze-fuelled parties that raged until dawn in the couple's salon. References to Louise by her friends and guests emphasize her reticent nature. In her sketch of Manhattan's most influential modern women, 'Who's Who in Manhattan', Clara Tice depicts Louise with a face half buried in a voluminous scarf and a hat pulled low over her forehead.[5] The feather in her hat is coiled almost in the shape of a question mark, suggesting its subject's inscrutability. *Rogue* editor Allen Norton's poem 'Walter's Room' alludes to the contradictory role Louise played, as both the host '[holding] court' and a reserved woman who 'disowned' the salon as an 'unnatural child'.[6] Adding that she asserts 'her ownership at the piano', Norton suggests that the piano was where Louise felt most comfortable, accompanying her guests' intellectual chatter with a recent composition by Arnold Schoenberg. Despite her reserved nature, she did develop close friendships with several of the artists who frequented the salon, particularly Beatrice Wood, with whom she formed a lifelong bond. Francis Naumann – pre-eminent Duchamp scholar and a friend of Wood's in the later years of her life – notes that Louise revealed a 'delightfully dry and rare wit' to those she felt at ease with.[7] Violinist Louis Kaufman, who knew the couple in their later years in California, similarly remarked upon Louise's 'quiet wit', as well as her 'great charm [and] excellent taste'.[8]

The gendered assumptions of many art critics and historians over the course of the twentieth century played a large part in the way that Louise is portrayed. Critics often mention her in passing as simply the retiring Mrs Arensberg, who bankrolled the couple's activities but contributed little else. However, in the memoirs of pioneering curator and art historian Katharine Kuh, Kuh emphasizes that the Arensbergs were a formidable, interdependent couple. Kuh came to know them decades after they had left New York and their lively years as salon hosts for a quieter life in Hollywood. As the curator of the first public exhibition of their collection at the Institute of Chicago in 1949, she spent time with them haphazardly cataloguing the vast array of paintings and sculptures that packed every room of their home – even, fittingly, Duchamps in the bathroom. Kuh was drawn to the charming Walter, whom she remembered fondly as 'a remarkable man, a mercurial character who outwitted one [art] institution after another'; she found Louise to be 'an equally strong character, but less volatile. She impressed as withdrawn and tense. It was Walter who braved the public, yet, as a couple, they were always a closely integrated team.'[9] In a 1987 interview with *Archives of American Art*, Kuh was less generous toward Louise, describing her as 'thin, very intelligent, extremely strong-minded, but she covered it up with a kind of well-bred femininity', although 'she was probably hard as nails.'[10] This air of cold 'well-bred femininity' perhaps speaks to the style of uptight, Victorian parenting that Louise's contemporaries Beatrice Wood and Mina Loy struggled to escape. We might also interpret her formal, feminine facade as the front of a shy, guarded person, keen to maintain a sense of privacy and integrity as public interest gathered in their collection.

Walter's own version of events highlights Louise's input in their collection. In an interview given to *Art Digest*'s Arthur Miller to mark the Philadelphia Museum of Art's acquisition of the complete Arensberg collection, Walter pays tribute to the role Louise played in building it. Her 'discrimination', he suggests, 'is keener than mine', adding that 'in all the years since 1914 when we bought our first modern work . . . we have only differed over two pictures . . . our shared interests have been a wonderful bond.'[11] Frustratingly cryptic and brief sentences written by Louise (now contained in the Arensberg archive at the Philadelphia Museum of Art) hint at her private engagement with art; these scraps of paper suggest that Louise made notes to sketch out her understanding of certain artists and their work. On one piece, underneath where Louise has written 'Chagall le Poète', another hand has added '(found in Mrs a's dresser after her death)'; in the same envelope, there are, perhaps, scribbled lines for a poem – 'Everyday the same thing. My cursed tongue is trembling. To you now I pray for help.'[12] In another note, Louise muses on the topic of 'modern art' and the 'idiom . . . [of] the art of our period'.[13] Typical of Louise's reserved nature, she clearly did not seek to have her thoughts published, but nevertheless it was important to her to record them in some way. Sadly, it is impossible to gain a deeper insight into Louise's character, but these notes gesture towards the rich inner world of a woman who dedicated her life, home and marriage to modern art.

Duchamp and Home of New York Dada

Allen Norton's poem 'Walter's Room' paints an evocative picture of the Arensberg salon's collaborative spirit and febrile atmosphere:

The *** room
Which Walter conceived one day
Instead of walking with Pitts in the Park

Or celebrating Sex on the Avenue
Where people who lived in glass houses
Threw stones connubially at one another;
And the super picture on the walls
Had intercourse with the poems that were never written
Where Lou held court[14]

The salon sets the stage for seduction and flirtation, a place where both the artists and their art are promiscuously entwined: Louise Norton and Jean Crotti perform an erotic modern dance, accompanied by Louise Arensberg playing Stravinsky or Schoenberg on the piano, while the paintings on the wall have 'intercourse with the poems that were never written'. The salon is a crucible, where new experimentations in living, loving and making art are forged. By making 'Walter's room' (or 'the *** room', with asterisks implying obscenity) the subject of his poem, Norton signals just how important the space and the art collection were in creating a permissive, stimulating atmosphere.

Many other accounts attest to the the unique experience of visiting the Arensbergs' apartment. In the post-Armory Show years in New York, there were still very few galleries where one could see modern art. This meant that a trip to the Arensbergs' offered an unparalleled encounter with European avant-garde art, alarmingly up close and personal. Charles Sheeler's photographs of the apartment (sadly empty of guests), taken between 1918 and 1919, show the walls covered with paintings, hung close together in a very different style to the careful curation of white-cube galleries that we are used to today. Seen in an intimate domestic setting, the paintings and sculptures in the Arensbergs' collection must have come to life in a powerful way, their dizzying forms and vivid colours providing an overwhelming visual sensation.

Unsurprisingly, close contact with the Arensbergs' remarkable display of art made a deep impression on many guests, some of whom spoke, years later, of being changed by what they saw there – perhaps none more so than Beatrice Wood. Wood experienced 'head-spinning disbelief' and disorientation during her first trip to the Arensbergs', which left her suppressing a giggling fit as she sat staring at 'the most hideous things I had ever seen' (that is, their collection).[15] Wood was bewildered by everything she saw (works by Brâncuşi, Picasso, Gleizes, Braque, Sheeler and Duchamp) but it was Matisse's then infamous *Mademoiselle Yvonne Landsberg* that really alarmed her. In her memoir, she describes her initial impression of the painting as depicting 'an outlandish woman with white streaks – like daggers – surrounding her entire body', echoing the *American Art News* critic who also found it utterly ugly.[16] Despite her shock at the Arensbergs' art collection, Wood continued to engage with the salon because 'these beloved people thought the paintings had merit, and the artists whom they entertained spoke about them in hushed voices, [so] the least [she] could do was try to enter their world of understanding.'[17]

Wood's recollection of this episode, written many years later in her autobiography, shows just how formative the Arensberg salon was for many artists, particularly young Americans. However, not everyone could be convinced. Henry McBride described a trip to the Arensbergs' 'exclusively modern' salon in a July 1920 profile for *The Dial*. At this point, McBride had been the *New York Evening Sun*'s art critic for seven years and was a man of progressive taste, so he was no stranger to modern art's shattered forms, vivid colours and distorted perspectives; the unnamed friend who accompanied McBride on this visit was 'reason-able and educated' but clearly unprepared to confront the avant-garde. Like Wood, McBride's friend was deeply disturbed by Matisse's por-trait of Mademoiselle Yvonne Landsberg and the 'violent' paintings and sculptures that surrounded it. Unlike Wood, McBride's friend was not interested in opening his mind to other possibilities: McBride quotes him as declaring, 'Walter Arensberg is quite mad. Mrs. Arensberg is mad, too,' which 'ended [the] conversation. There was a finality about [his statement] that would have ended any conversation.'[18]

The Arensbergs' staggering collection of avant-garde art was obvi-ously a vital part of their salon's reputation; but its mix of guests ensured that it became a hotspot for raucous parties, all-night chess games and anarchic art pranks. Before the summer of 1915, the Arens-bergs' circle of friends centred on long-standing connections of Walter's, such as former Harvard classmate Wallace Stevens, and a mix of young American poets and artists, including Marsden Hartley, Morton Schamberg and Charles Demuth. It was a lively group, but something was lacking and the apartment was not yet the vibrant salon it would become. The catalyst came from Paris on ss *Rochambeau* in June 1915, in the form of an enigmatic 27-year-old Frenchman with a gaunt face and – in Beatrice Wood's words – 'all the charm of an angel who spoke *slang*': Marcel Duchamp.[19]

Duchamp crossed the Atlantic both to flee the war and to re-energize his creative practice, after becoming bored and disillusioned with painting and the Paris art scene. Walter Pach was on hand to meet Duchamp off the boat and eager to introduce him to wealthy American friends who could support his new experiments at the boundaries of art. The pair headed directly to 33 West 67th Street. The Arensbergs were no doubt thrilled to meet the artist behind *Nude Descending a Staircase, No. 2*, a painting they still coveted. Duchamp and Walter soon found that they shared a love of French Symbolist poets (particularly Stéphane Mallarmé), wordplay and chess – three things that would play as vital a role as art in their lifelong friendship. After hitting it off, the Arensbergs agreed to allow Duchamp to stay and work in their apartment while they took a planned summer vacation to Connecticut. Upon their return, they made Duchamp an appealing offer: they would cover the rent for a small studio apartment in the Atelier building (one floor above their own) in exchange for the intriguing new piece of art that Duchamp was working on. Duchamp agreed.

It would take another eight years before Duchamp declared the Arensbergs' chosen work – *The Bride Stripped Bare by Her Bachelors, Even*, usually known as the *Large Glass* – 'definitively unfinished'. They were able to get their hands on a version of *Nude Descending a Staircase, No. 2* more quickly. In an unusual request, Walter asked Duchamp to create a replica of his own work and Duchamp obliged. The result, titled *Nude Descending a Staircase, No. 3*, was not, in fact, an exact copy. Instead, Duchamp arranged for a full-sized photographic reproduction of the original to be printed, which he then retouched using ink and pencil. In this way, the third *Nude* became a distinct, independent artwork and a Duchampian experiment in the authenticity of art objects. When the Arensbergs finally got hold of the original in 1919, they hung both versions on their walls, no doubt delighting in the subversive Dada trickery of the sibling artworks.

Duchamp's arrival at the Arensbergs' was pivotal not only for the development of their art collection, but for the birth of their salon. In New York, he was sought out by his European artist friends and associates who had also moved to the city or were just passing through. Duchamp and his cosmopolitan crowd were soon at the centre of the Arensbergs' nightly soirées, with friends including Francis Picabia and Gabrielle Buffet-Picabia, Albert Gleizes and Juliette Roche, Jean and Yvonne Croti, Edgard Varèse and diplomat and art collector Henri-Pierre Roché becoming key salon guests. This was a reunion, of sorts, for a network of experimental French artists who had been at the forefront of Cubism in Paris a couple of years earlier. In New York, they once again formed a close-knit group and could often be found breakfasting at the infamous Brevoort Hotel in Greenwich Village after long nights of drinking, dancing and debating art. Gabrielle Buffet-Picabia described being immediately swept up into this 'international motley band' as soon as she arrived in New York with her husband Francis in 1915, on what was supposed to be a brief stopover en route to Cuba. Buffet-Picabia had been close to Duchamp in Paris, so she was surprised at how quickly the otherwise frugal, ascetic Duchamp had taken to cocktails and whisky. Duchamp himself would similarly comment on the raucous atmosphere, describing whisky-fuelled nights that were 'sometimes real drinking bouts'; he added, however, that this was not always the case, and that the Arensbergs hosted a 'truly artistic salon, [and a] rather amusing one at that'.[20]

In addition to Duchamp's Parisian friends and associates, other radical talents arrived at the Arensbergs' door, drawn into his orbit. Poet and artist Mina Loy was a little late to the party (she arrived in New York from Florence in winter 1916), but she soon threw herself into the salon's high jinks. The iconoclast Dada poet, boxer and provocateur Arthur Cravan also arrived earlier that year, dodging the draft in Europe and trailing chaos and scandal – Walter ended up bailing him out of jail in 1917 after he drunkenly stripped naked and tried to start fights with the audience, while he was supposed to be lecturing on modern art. The legendary modern dancer Isadora Duncan was also regularly in attendance at the Arensbergs', until she drunkenly dragged Walter to the floor and knocked out his front teeth. Duncan and Cravan had a rival for most shocking salon attendee, however, in the form of the outrageous, sexually voracious Baroness Elsa von Freytag-Loringhoven. The arrival of Duchamp lured her to the Arensberg salon, where she formed unrequited obsessions first with the nonplussed Duchamp, and then with the less worldly American poet William Carlos Williams, who was attracted and repulsed in equal measure. Williams was, perhaps, one of the salon's less enthusiastic attendees: in his autobiography, he recalled with still obvious resentment an episode when he complimented one of Duchamp's paintings, only to be greeted by a drunken Duchamp's characteristic nonchalance ('do you?'). 'Humiliated' by his inability to 'carry a witty conversation in French', visits to the salon left him feeling like a 'yokel, narrow-eyed, feeling my own inadequacies'.[21] It was not only in matters of art that Williams felt unsophisticated: besotted by the beautiful and cerebral Mina Loy, the staid Williams could only watch her flirt with Duchamp and Cravan (in 'witty' French, no doubt) while he fended off the aggressive attention of the baroness.

End of the Party

In 1921, the party ended. The Arensbergs decided to leave their apartment on 33 West 67th Street for a dramatic change of scene, swapping the hustle and bustle of New York for Hollywood. The salon had already begun to break up before their move. Duchamp moved to Buenos Aires in 1918, then returned to Paris in 1919. Mina Loy followed Arthur Cravan to Mexico, where he would go missing in November 1918 (later presumed dead), leaving Loy pregnant and impoverished. For many of the other salon guests, post-First World War Paris proved an irresistible draw, luring many Americans (including Man Ray and Djuna Barnes) across the Atlantic, along with returning European artists such as Francis Picabia and Gabrielle Buffet-Picabia and Juliette Roche and Albert Gleizes. The Arensbergs were not interested in joining the newly revived Parisian scene. Instead, they sought a break after a whirlwind half-decade that left them financially and emotionally drained.

When discussing the reasons for the Arensbergs' move to California, Kuh asserts that Louise 'tore Walter away' from New York to 'rescue him from his hard drinking, philandering and late-night lifestyle, but she succeeded only in destroying him'.[22] This interpretation overlooks a key fact: shortly before they left New York, Louise had been involved in an intense affair with Duchamp's friend and Wood's lover, Henri-Pierre Roché. Roché had a number of lovers, but the relationship with Louise appears to have been particularly intense. In *Victor*, Roché's semi-fictionalized account of his time in New York, he includes a scene in which Alice (Louise Arensberg) informs Pierre (Roché) that 'if we get married one day, you won't have to earn a living to support me, just yourself, with your writing.'[23] Walter was clearly rattled by the serious-ness of the affair and threatened to attempt suicide if Louise left him. Ultimately, she opted to stay, but she was exhausted by the trail of bad debts and financial mismanagement that Walter had embroiled the couple in. A break from New York was the only way forward.

The Arensbergs' life in Hollywood was markedly different. Wood also moved to California in the late 1920s and remained a close friend of the couple. She remarked on how dull their life seemed initially, compared to the late-night parties and social whirlwind their New York salon hosted. It livened up a little when they moved into a 'surprisingly conventional' house (in Wood's opinion) on Hillside Avenue and had their art collection on display once more, but the atmosphere was very different. As in New York, the Arensbergs were committed to opening their collection to anyone who wanted to see it; in California, how-ever, this attracted a much more highbrow, serious crowd, and Louise found it a chore. Again, Wood provides a fascinating insight into the atmosphere of parties at the Arensbergs:

There was an excitement and enjoyment to the Arensbergs' Los Angeles evenings, but missing was the wild exuberance and youthful sense of revolt that had protested the evils of the jury system or celebrated the originality of Brâncuși or pondered the mysteries of chess. It was not the same freedom of thought that helped us escape from the horrors of the First World War; if those Los Angeles residents could not tolerate [painter and art dealer] Galka Scheyer's outbursts, they would never have stood for the outlandish gestures of Mina Loy and Arthur Cravan![24]

Despite the fact that their Hollywood home was not as lively as 33 West 67th Street, it functioned as the venue for several large events, most notably the reception for the typically surreal double wedding of Max Ernst and Dorothea Tanning and Man Ray and Juliet Browner in 1946. The Arensbergs' continued friendship with avant-garde artists, particularly Wood and Duchamp, also ensured that their life was far from conventional.

Finding a secure permanent home for their collection was a focus for the Arensbergs in the Hollywood years.[25] In order to secure its legacy and that of the artists they had collected, it was essential to maintain the integrity of the collection in a suitable gallery. These efforts also symbolized a final gesture of support and friendship to Duchamp, who was incredibly anxious to see his body of work collected together in a 'coherent whole'. After protracted discussions with a number of institutions (not to mention an attempt at starting a gallery in Los Angeles with the help of actor Vincent Price), the Arensbergs eventually reached an agreement with the Philadelphia Museum of Art in 1950. As Kuh and others noted, Louise became increasingly frail during this time. She died of cancer on 25 November 1953 and a distraught Walter suffered a fatal heart attack mere months later, on 29 January 1954. Their collection opened at the Philadelphia Museum of Art in October 1954, preserved for future generations.

Looking back on the reactions and recollections of the extraordinary few years when the Arensberg salon was at the heart of New York's avant-garde offers us a tantalizing glimpse into a vibrant, unique space where groundbreaking ideas, attitudes and art experiments emerged. It was a place where art was not to be revered in solemn silence, but instead to be experienced amid the whirl of life. Beyond that, recollections of the Arensberg salon also serve as a reminder of just how daring Louise and Walter were in supporting young artists who were practising radical forms of art, whose work was little understood even by those privileged enough to have had an education in the arts. Critics that trivialize Louise as the mere financial backer of her more cultured and worldly husband take for granted the passion she too must have felt to have invested so much of her life and wealth in modern art – against the grain of the media and many established voices in the art world.

Afterlife of the Arensberg Salon: The *Blind Man* and *The Fountain* Alter Art History

On a hot summer's night in 1916, with the party in full swing at the Arensberg salon, conversation turned to the state of modern art in America. The Armory Show had been a revelation but, in the intervening three years, there had been too little progress. New York still lacked the galleries, patrons, art schools and societies to support and develop new innovative art. The city felt ultra-modern in so many ways – its skyscrapers, its electric lighting, its bridges – but when it came to art and culture, it was lacking. There was a clear sense of frustration among America's young artists and intellectuals. How could New York ever compete with Paris as a capital of culture? How would American artists reach the awesome heights of their European counterparts without the support, investment and audiences that came along with a network of galleries and regular exhibitions? In response to this dire situation, the artists assembled at the Arensberg salon in the summer of 1916 agreed upon the need for an annual exhibition that would bring together modern artists and the public. Spurred into action, they established the Society of Independent Artists, an association with a mission to host regular shows of modern art that were intended to be completely accessible and inclusive.

The society's board of governors brought together a who's who of New York's fledgling modern-art scene: Walter Arensberg was the managing director, with Walter Pach acting as treasurer and artist and arts patron Katherine Dreier on the organizing committee. Many of the women whose support was indispensable to the arts in the decades following the Armory Show were listed as guarantors, including Gertrude Vanderbilt Whitney, Louise Arensberg, Dreier and the glamorous socialite Rita de Acosta Lydig. The $10,000 sum that the guarantors pledged would be called on in March 1917, when the society's account was in deficit following the first exhibition's financial failure. In terms of artists, its board of directors combined traditional painters, such as John Sloan, Mary Rogers and William Glackens, with experimental avant-garde artists Man Ray, Marcel Duchamp and Morton Schamberg. Their aim was to 'represent every important tendency in contemporary art' so that each school of art, 'from the most conservative to the most radical', could be presented to the public without bias.

The founders set out their intentions for the society in a statement included in the catalogue of their First Annual Exhibition in spring 1917. It would function as an American alternative to the French Société des Artistes Indépendants that had been established in Paris in 1884 in rejection of the old-fashioned formality of the government-sponsored Salon. Like its French counterpart, the society declared its intention to have 'no judge, no prize', but it took this democratic ethos one step further by pledging to hang work in alphabetical order. This decision, made by Duchamp, meant that no one artist would be given prominence or special treatment, but also that forms and themes were mixed together. In this way, the exhibition could stage surprising dialogues across mediums and schools of art; there would also be no bias or special treatment for 'star' artists. Each exhibiting artist was required to sign up as a member at a cost of just $5 per annum. It was an opportunity for artists who were fed up with the formalism and traditions of American art to find an outlet for experimentation and a new community of like-minded creative people. The society also proclaimed that its annual fee would give each artist a vote at its meetings and, crucially, the right to 'exhibit whatever he wishes'. However, by the time of the first exhibition, this statement was already out of date: the submission of an upturned urinal with 'R. Mutt, 1917' scrawled on it had rocked the society to its core.

Fountain was submitted for the society's inaugural exhibiton under the mysterious pseudonym Richard Mutt, to the consternation of most of the directors. Many of them could not accept a mass-produced object as art and some were disgusted by its 'vulgarity'. After an emergency meeting to discuss whether or not they should accept it, the majority of the society's board members voted to reject *Fountain*. Pach suggested that this move was driven by fears of a serious public backlash. A statement released the day after the exhibition opened declared that *Fountain* was a 'useful object in its place' but it was 'by no definition a work of art', suggesting that this was a matter of aesthetics as much as of morality. Despite the panel's commitment to innovative and progressive art, many of them felt that *Fountain* was a step too far. In response, Duchamp and Arensberg immediately resigned from the board.

Speculation was rife as to the artist's real identity but, shortly after the scandal, it was commonly accepted that Duchamp was behind this subversive act. In later years, he spoke openly about it and claimed that the idea for *Fountain* came about during conversations with Walter Arensberg and Joseph Stella. Yet questions and inconsistencies remained, particularly regarding the identity of the woman that Duchamp referred to in a letter to his sister Suzanne in 1917, in which he suggested that one of his female friends submitted the work using a male alias. Recently, some critics have looked to Baroness Elsa von Freytag-Loringhoven as the 'true' creator of the work. While it is true that there are crossovers between the baroness's shocking performance art and scatological aesthetic and *Fountain*, the theory is ultimately unconvincing. The baroness was certainly no shrinking violet (and not afraid of speaking out against male posturing within the New York avant-garde), so what could explain the fact that she never once claimed the piece or made any reference to it at all? The baroness wasn't in New York at the time and, furthermore, she made no contribution to the *Blind Man* magazine, a forum for members of the Arensberg salon who were in on the *Fountain* scandal to defend it. In fact, the identity of one of Duchamp's likely co-conspirators was hiding in plain sight.

In early April 1917, Charles Demuth (a member of the Arensberg salon) wrote to art critic Henry McBride to let him know about the amusing affair, suggesting that it would make good copy for McBride's weekly column in the *New York Evening Sun*. Demuth informed him that the rebels were considering setting up 'a show called "The Super Independents" – a Salon des Refusés' in an act of defiance against the Society of Independent Artists' betrayal of its supposedly democratic values; he added the postscript 'If you wish any more information please "phone Marcel Duchamp, 4225 Columbus, or Richard Mutt, 9255 Schuyler".'[26] This addition is intriguing: if Duchamp was Mutt, why did Demuth provide a different telephone number for his pseudonym? Even more intriguing is that the owner of 9255 Schuyler was Louise Norton. On the photograph of *Fountain* taken by Alfred Stieglitz, its submission tag (with the name Richard Mutt and an address) is still attached and just about visible. Mutt's address (110 West 88th Street) also led to Norton. Although many outside of the Arensberg circle were in the dark regarding *Fountain*, Demuth (a contributor to the *Blind Man*) was most certainly in the know; the references to Duchamp and Mutt as separate figures across their circle of collaborators, confidants and friendship groups suggest that Norton had a clear role in the escapade. Just as she critiqued style, aesthetics and art as Dame Rogue in the pages of *Rogue* magazine, Norton once again played the part of provocateur and displayed her sly wit from behind a mask of anonymity.

In many ways, it is misleading and unproductive to focus on the idea that any single person was behind *Fountain*. Its radical rejection of the artist as a god-like genius reflects the febrile atmosphere of the Arensberg salon: *Fountain* sprang from all-night conversations about the place of art in a fast-paced world that promised life-changing freedoms, connections and innovations, but had also brought about death and destruction on a terrifying, mechanized level in the form of the First World War. It responded to cross-media experimentation, as painters, poets, photographers, sculptors and designers exchanged ideas and came together to explore new modes of making art. *Fountain* also gestured to the spirit of gender fluidity and sexual freedoms pursued by Greenwich Villagers and the Arensberg salon circle. Although it is hard to completely appreciate from a contemporary post-postmodernist perspective, *Fountain* was a profoundly disruptive artwork: it made a troubling intervention in the exhibition space and subverted the boundaries between art and the everyday. It queered the subject/object dynamic and challenged the spectator's assumptions about art, beauty and commercial objects; in this way, it is irreducible and open to multiple coexisting interpretations. As an inherently queer artwork, *Fountain* encapsulated the decadent, sensuous and subversive aesthetic that defined the New York avant-garde.

If you try to visualize *Fountain* today, the image you most likely have in mind is one of a number of reproductions held in museum collections across the world. Until Duchamp authorized replicas in the 1950s and '60s, the work survived only as a photograph in the *Blind Man*. The second issue contained an eclectic mix of responses to – and defences of – *Fountain*, alongside work by writers and artists including Frances Simpson Stevens, Gabrielle Buffet-Picabia, Clara Tice and Mina Loy. In the *Blind Man*, as in *Rogue*, women artists and writers were well represented and their work was crucial in shaping the magazine's tone and vision. Beatrice Wood's and Louise Norton's comments on *Fountain* were critical in the reception and framing of the work; both women added a vital contribution to the conversations around *Fountain*'s relationship with artistic production.

Before exploring those works, we must first pause to explore *Fountain* captured in all its glory by photographer and gallerist Alfred Stieglitz. Stieglitz's striking photograph is, in and of itself, a significant cultural artefact and piece of artistic composition. Stieglitz's photograph

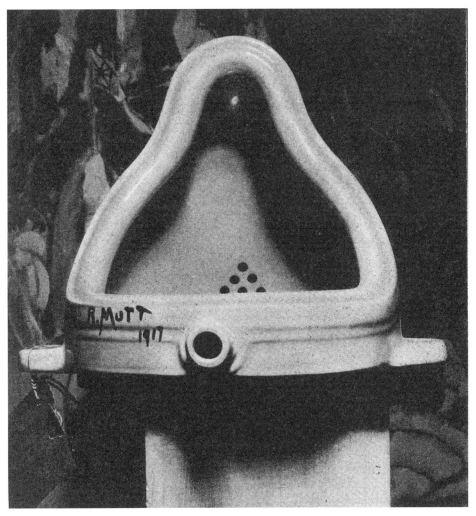

Alfred Stieglitz, '*Fountain* by R. Mutt', *The Blind Man*, no. 2 (May 1917).

intervenes in the complex process through which *Fountain* acquired the meaning it carries today. The page on which it appears in the *Blind Man* gives Stieglitz's name equal prominence with 'R. Mutt': 'Photograph by Alfred Stieglitz' sits alongside '*Fountain* by R. Mutt' atop the image. A caption below boldly reminds the reader that this is 'THE EXHIBIT REFUSED BY THE INDEPENDENTS'. Turning to the image itself, it is fascinating to note the many ways that Stieglitz's composition draws out *Fountain*'s subversive aesthetic. Stieglitz's careful framing of the work emphasizes the qualities that the board of the Society of Independent Artists missed. *Fountain* is shot close-up and cropped, giving an uncanny sense that it is staring back at you from the page. This angle further decontextualizes the piece, forcing us to look at the object anew. The skilful manner in which Stieglitz captures the play of light and shade exaggerates *Fountain*'s curved form and gleaming surface. In this photograph, the object is truly transformed from a piece of plumbing into an intriguing play of undulating shapes and sensuous lines.

The backdrop is also significant: rather than a plain, uncluttered one, Stieglitz chose to shoot *Fountain* against *The Warriors*, a painting by Marsden Hartley that depicts German soldiers parading on horseback. Hartley created this piece as part of a series while living in Germany between 1913 and 1915. By including symbols of German militarism in the photograph, Stieglitz encodes a reference to the First World War, which America had entered in April 1917 (the same month as the Society of Independents Exhibition). The war's incoherent brutality and devastating destruction had fuelled the Dada art movement in Berlin and Zurich; through their innovative, anarchic work, Dada artists like Hannah Höch and poet Hugo Ball questioned the meaning of art and culture in a time of rampant nationalist aggression and senseless mass slaughter. Although New York Dada was less political and ideologically driven than its European counterparts, it increasingly responded to the social upheavals and mechanized warfare that were wreaking havoc across the Atlantic.

Despite its military subject-matter, *The Warriors* is also a highly sensual image. Hartley's German paintings key into the fraught debates surrounding homosexuality and the military in Germany in the wake of the Eulenburg affair (1906–9); this scandal was brought about by journalist Maximilian Harden over the influence of a so-called 'homosexual clique' on Kaiser Wilhelm II. In pre-war Berlin, a macho cult of masculinity became intrinsically linked with militarism and gay culture. During the Eulenburg affair, homophobia was weaponized against Wilhelm and it fuelled concerns about the masculinity of the nation. On a more personal level, the homoerotic overtones of Hartley's war work reference Hartley's partner Lieutenant Karl von Freyburg, whom he first met on his European travels in 1912. Hartley moved to Germany to be with Freyburg but he was left devastated when Freyburg was killed in the first weeks of the war. In this way, *The Warriors* frames *Fountain* in the context of an absurd, senseless war. The painting's homoerotic elements also chime with aspects of *Fountain*'s queer eroticism, specifically its association with public bathrooms, sites of queer sexual encounters, where gay men could meet anonymously. This link highlights the ways that *Fountain* blurs the boundaries between public and private, intimacy and spectacle.

The curved lines of Hartley's painting echo and emphasize *Fountain*'s own fluid curves, drawing the eye to its surprisingly sensual form. By exaggerating the smooth fluidity of *Fountain*'s form, Hartley's painting magnifies its disruption of gendered boundaries. A masculine-coded object becomes a 'uterine-like' shape, with a title that connotes the source of life, and therefore the feminine and maternal. *Fountain* makes a playful and, for its time, obscene association between the flow of urine and pipe waste and water's more spiritual, life-giving properties. In a letter to Georgia O'Keeffe, Stieglitz boasted that his photograph is 'quite a wonder . . . it has an oriental look about it – a cross between a Buddha & a veiled woman'.[27] Steiglitz's comments highlight the avant-garde's Orientalist appropriation of Eastern aesthetics to signify sexuality and promiscuity. It aligns *Fountain* (and Stieglitz's framing of it through his photographic composition) with the popularity of Paul Poiret-style harem trousers among fashionable modern women.

Fountain's 'Buddha-like' qualities also draw attention to the pure formal beauty, even a sense of the sublime, that can be found in everyday objects. It is, perhaps, unsurprising that Louise Norton draws these qualities out further in her essay 'Buddha of the Bathroom'.[28] Placed opposite Stieglitz's photograph of *Fountain* and below Beatrice Wood's editorial 'The Richard Mutt Case', Norton's essay frames the object's reception and enhances the public's understanding of its cultural significance. Whereas Wood emphasizes the importance of integrating art and everyday life and valorizes concept over craft, Norton takes aim at the reactionary attitudes that undermined modern culture's professed commitment to 'Progress, Speed and Efficiency'. Instead of progress, society becomes like 'a little dog chasing after his own wagging tail that has dazzled him'. Her tone is characteristically droll, but it conceals a fierce reproach towards the critics who rejected *Fountain*. Modern people, she suggested, are like 'those philosophers whom Dante placed in his Inferno with their heads set the wrong way on their shoulders. We walk forward looking backward, each with more of his predecessors' personality than his own. Our eyes are not ours.'[29]

Norton clearly felt that moral puritanism and ignorance were behind the society's decision, because they could not get over their 'atavistic minds' that associated *Fountain* with 'a certain natural function of a secretive sort'; far from being independent and progressive, the society's board members betrayed their ideals by acting more like a 'Board of Censors sitting upon the ambiguous question, What is ART?'. 'Buddha of the Bathroom' is key to understanding *Fountain* partly because Norton invokes the irreverent attitude of *Rogue* magazine to point out that it does not matter if 'R. Mutt' is serious or joking – 'perhaps he is both! Is it not possible?' It reminds us of the collaborative community spirit that fed into *Fountain*. 'Perhaps' is a crucial word for Norton in that it symbolizes an indeterminate space, a point of slippage between style and substance, seriousness and jest, absurdity and profundity, art and life; it is, she claims, the 'most profound word in language' and the one which she chooses to end her defence of *Fountain* with.

In the editorial, Beatrice Wood also takes aim at the suggestion of immorality, arguing that the *Fountain* is no more immoral 'than a bathtub'.[30] By highlighting the everyday nature of the urinal – 'it is a fixture that you see every day in plumbers' show windows' – Wood's editorial alludes to the avant-garde's mission to merge art and life. The anti-immorality argument would be fought repeatedly in the early years of modernism, most notoriously with the publication of James Joyce's *Ulysses* in 1922, which portrayed excretion, sex and masturbation as

THE BLIND MAN

The Richard Mutt Case

They say any artist paying six dollars may exhibit.

Mr. Richard Mutt sent in a fountain. Without discussion this article disappeared and never was exhibited.

What were the grounds for refusing Mr. Mutt's fountain:—

1. *Some contended it was immoral, vulgar.*

2. *Others, it was plagiarism, a plain piece of plumbing.*

Now Mr. Mutt's fountain is not immoral, that is absurd, no more than a bath tub is immoral. It is a fixture that you see every day in plumbers' show windows.

Whether Mr. Mutt with his own hands made the fountain or not has no importance. He CHOSE it. He took an ordinary article of life, placed it so that its useful significance disappeared under the new title and point of view—created a new thought for that object.

As for plumbing, that is absurd. The only works of art America has given are her plumbing and her bridges.

"Buddha of the Bathroom"

I suppose monkeys hated to lose their tail. Necessary, useful and an ornament, monkey imagination could not stretch to a tailless existence (and frankly, do you see the biological beauty of our loss of them?), yet now that we are used to it, we get on pretty well without them. But evolution is not pleasing to the monkey race; "there is a death in every change" and we monkeys do not love death as we should. We are like those philosophers whom Dante placed in his Inferno with their heads set the wrong way on their shoulders. We walk forward looking backward, each with more of his predecessors' personality than his own. Our eyes are not ours.

The ideas that our ancestors have joined together let no man put asunder! In *La Dissociation des Idees,* Remy de Gourmont, quietly analytic, shows how sacred is the marriage of ideas. At least one charm-ing thing about our human institution is that although a man marry he can never be *only* a husband. Besides being a money-making device and the *one* man that *one* woman can sleep with in legal purity without sin he may even be as well some other woman's very personification of her abstract idea. Sin, while to his employees he is nothing but their "Boss," to his children only their "Father," and to himself certainly something more complex.

But with objects and ideas it is different. Recently we have had a chance to observe their meticulous monogomy.

When the jurors of *The Society of Independent Artists* fairly rushed to remove the bit of sculpture called the *Fountain* sent in by Richard Mutt, because the object was irrevocably associated in their atavistic minds with a certain natural function of a secretive sort. Yet to any "innocent" eye ordinary aspects of the human experience. Along with Clara Tice's decadent nudes, *Fountain* was a forerunner in this backlash against outdated, Victorian prudish attitudes. Yet there were inevitable risks associated with challenges to societal norms (as the American publishers of excerpts from *Ulysses* Margaret Anderson and Jane Heap would find out in a 1921 anti-obscenity trial). Wood's bourgeois father was disgusted by her involvement with the *Blind Man* and feared she would go to jail if it was sent out by post. Although she cared little for her father's opinion, Wood, alongside Roché and Duchamp, was worried about the impact a legal trial would have on the magazine's financial backers; to minimize the risk, they resolved to distribute the magazine by hand.

Wood's brief but forthright editorial is intriguing in the ways it makes use of arguments that anticipate the rise of conceptual art. She tells her reader that it is not important whether or not Mutt made *Fountain* 'with his own hands'; rather, the artistry lies in taking an object out of its ordinary context and shifting the viewer's perspective of it – creating 'a new thought for that object'.[31] In other words, ideas that shocked viewers out of their complacency and challenged their suppositions were more important than craft. The editorial's final line – 'the only works of art America has given are her plumbing and her bridges' – gesture towards a new layer of meaning to *Fountain*. Ezra Shales reveals that Wood played on the language used in trade publications for the commercial pottery trade, which touted expensive new bathroom sets as aspirational, luxury items. Louise Norton's reference to 'decadent plumber's porcelain' also appears to have been lifted straight from one of these advertisements; indeed, Shales points out that 'luxurious porcelain fixtures were a selling point for New York skyscrapers', a mark of modern sophistication.[32] Toilets and 'sanitaryware' even appeared in exhibitions, most notably 'New Jersey Clay Products' (1915) at the Newark Museum Association (a favourite spot of Alfred Stieglitz). Rather than simply a mass-produced object, the ceramic urinal was produced through a process of craftsmanship that required skill and artistic ability. Understanding the cultural and material history of sanitaryware in the 1910s therefore opens up new avenues of interpretation. Perhaps an elitist criticism of American industry's efforts to promote its role in modern culture was embedded in *Fountain*; but it is equally possible that the object was also a celebration of industry's commitment to innovation, which was more attuned to modern life than the so-called progressive artists attached to the Society of Independent Artists. Mina Loy would later express her own admiration for Henry Ford, another pioneer of American industry, describing him as her greatest hero.

Charles Demuth's short poem 'For Richard Mutt', which appears below 'Buddha of the Bathroom', undercuts Norton's deliberately ambiguous conclusion. In spite of its brevity, the poem is a sharp riposte to the Society of Independent Artists and vindicates the 'true' artist's limitless progress. Demuth contrasts Mutt's momentum with the inertia of 'most' people who 'stop or get a style'. Stopping is creative death: 'when they stop they make/ a convention./ That is their end'.[33] In other words, Demuth makes clear the fact that there is no progress to be made when adhering to the conventional. For 'the going' (by which Demuth means artists), 'every thing has a value', and thus they demonstrate an advanced perception that allows them to find aesthetic worth in the everyday. Those that cannot see this value, it is implied, suffer from a failure of imagination. The poem's final two lines predict that the critics cannot hinder progress and, in fact, matter little to the artist. It is a defiant riposte to *Fountain*'s critics (several of whom were artists) and draws a sharp line between those with a truly modern aesthetic sensibility and those who are stuck in the past. As if to underscore Demuth's message, Clara Tice's abstract portrait of the experimental composer Edgard Varèse appears on the opposite page. Varèse was also a radical, uncompromising innovator whose work shocked critics and audiences alike; as such, this image celebrates innovation across the arts, placing *Fountain* in a wider cross-disciplinary movement. Having also had a notorious brush with censorship, Tice's appearance in the magazine further reinforces the transgressive tone; more than simply a defence of *Fountain*, the *Blind Man* appears to put forward an artistic manifesto that centres a collaborative, liberated, queer approach to modern art and modern life.

The second page of the *Blind Man* magazine offered its readers an invitation to the Blind Man's Ball on Friday, 25 May. The venue was 'Prehistoric, ultra-Bohemian Webster Hall' (in Greenwich Village), a legendary site of activism and social protest as well as the location of

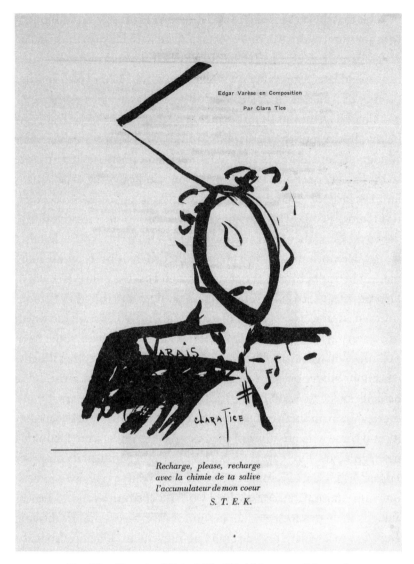

Clara Tice, 'Portrait of Varèse', *The Blind Man*, no. 2 (May 1917).

numerous extravagant costume and drag parties that were attended by the era's artistic and literary luminaries. Guests attending the Blind Man's Ball were asked to dress up for the occasion or risk being banished to seats in the boxes: the 'axioms du bal' read, 'The dance will not end till the dawn. The Blind Man must see the sun. Romantic rags are requested . . . guests not in costume must sit in bought-and-paid-for boxes.'[34] Not to be outdone by their guests, the *Blind Man* contributors assembled eclectic outfits: Clara Tice dressed as a radiator, Mina Loy as a cross between one of her own lampshade creations and a Pierrot, and Beatrice Wood arrived in a Russian folk costume. It was, Wood recalls in her autobiography *I Shock Myself* (1985), a 'riotous affair' that was attended by 'the whole art world'.[35]

Mina Loy's contribution to the *Blind Man* magazine – 'O Marcel – – – otherwise I Also Have Been to Louise's' – offers both a response to *Fountain* and an artistic experiment in its own right. A collage-like prose poem, it pieces together snippets of conversation buzzing through the room at the Blind Man's Ball. It is interesting to note that Loy refers to Walter and Louise Arensberg's salon as 'Louise's'; this title also encodes a nod to Louise Norton, one of the conspirators behind *Fountain*. In among the fragmented, half-finished discussions that Loy includes, we glimpse various members of the Arensberg circle: Duchamp is in conversation with Loy throughout, but we can also pick out Clara Tice, Charles Demuth and Carl Van Vechten. Although *Fountain* is not directly referenced, the piece contains an allusion to the scandal that surrounded it, specifically Arensberg's and Duchamp's resignations from the board of the Society of Independent Artists. The suggestive language that Loy includes throughout the poem recalls *Fountain*'s playful irreverence and *Rogue* magazine's urbane wit. Sexual double entendres (on the subject of tongue sandwiches), gossipy asides and continual requests for cigarettes and alcohol tease the reader, hinting at the licentious behaviour and risqué scenes taking place without revealing too much. Like *Fountain*, 'O Marcel' begs the question: is this a joke or is it art? Could it, in fact, be both? The cry of 'Censorship!' that appears towards the poem's end alludes to *Fountain*'s rejection, reminding us that irreverence is an integral feature of boundary-pushing art.

Loy ends 'O Marcel' with the words 'Compiled by Mina Loy', and, in the process, declares herself an impersonal recorder rather than the author of the piece. With this signature, she aligns her text with *Fountain*. Like the upturned urinal, 'O Marcel' is a readymade: Loy has taken (as opposed to created) spoken words and placed them in a new context. Just as *Fountain* questions the role of the artist via the exhibition of factory-made, mass-produced objects as art, Loy mechanized the role of the writer. In her editorial for the *Blind Man*, Wood makes the case for this new mode of artistry: 'Whether Mr. Mutt with his own hands made the fountain or not has no importance. He CHOSE it. He took an ordinary article of life, placed it so that its useful significance disappeared under the new title and point of view – created a new thought for that object.'[36] Alongside work by Wood, Tice and Norton, Loy's contribution to the *Blind Man* captures the dynamic salon spirit and serves as a reminder that the *Fountain* was just one part of the New York avant-garde's experiment in breaking down the boundaries between art and life.

5

BEATRICE WOOD:
Mama of Dada

April 19, 1917 to see Roché. See Arthur Cravan drunk at his
lecture at Independents. With Mrs Arensberg to Steiglitz's.
Mother tells me I am losing my reputation.[1]

The colourful entry that Beatrice Wood scribbled into her diary on
19 April 1917 was typical of a hugely momentous year. Even in a
life as lively and lengthy as Wood's – she remained active and irrepressible up to the grand old age of 105 – 1917 was particularly eventful:
it was a year that began with the then 24-year-old actress feeling 'so very
much more sophisticated than two years ago' thanks to her entanglement with Marcel Duchamp, Henri-Pierre Roché and the Arensberg
circle; it ended with a dramatic move to Canada following heartbreak
and a crisis of confidence. Wood kept a diary for more than eighty
years and its pages offer a fascinating glimpse into the day-to-day life
of a woman who would carve out a reputation as the self-proclaimed
'Mama of Dada'. Her entries cover social events, efforts to earn a living
and personal upheavals: from making batik scarves for dancer Isadora
Duncan and dining with the Arensbergs, to shifts at the Sunwise Turn
bookshop and endless fraught confrontations with her mother.

Knowing, and wishing to solidify, the importance of her role in
New York Dada, Wood transcribed and annotated her diaries in 1998;
she clearly understood the importance of her role in New York Dada
and wished to ensure that her memories were accessible to an increasing number of scholars interested in the movement. A note in the preface
alerts readers to the fact that 'unfortunately where Roché and Marcel

Duchamp were concerned, I often disguised or left out meetings for fear that my mother (in looking at my diary) might see what I was up to.' The disappointed, almost apologetic tone offers an insight into the way Wood felt constantly torn between the old-fashioned expectations of her overbearing mother and her desire to live the life of a carefree, sexually liberated modern woman. It also speaks to the ways in which much of Wood's life can be viewed as a carefully considered performance – whether for her parents, her circle of artist friends or a public audience whose interest in Wood grew as her great longevity allowed her to claim cultural authority over New York Dada in the second half of the twentieth century.

Before becoming a fully fledged member of the Arensberg salon in 1916, Wood struggled to find an outlet for her creative free spirit. She had been an unruly child, desperate to escape the restrictive upbringing and moralizing of her old-fashioned parents. Her childhood home was far from happy: Wood recalls being sent to a boarding school in Manhattan (where her family lived) because her parents 'fought terribly and did not want [her] to witness their battles'. It seems that her mother channelled her own misery and dissatisfaction into an obsession with making her daughter into the perfect eligible young lady. Wood, however, had other ideas. From a young age, she rebelled against the 'dominating, aristocratic' woman whose ideas were positively Victorian: She 'devoted herself to protecting me from life . . . determined I should remain a virgin, perhaps forever, she dressed me in lace, taught me to curtsy and to remain silent unless spoken to.'[2]

Wood's description of her mother's attitude directly evokes Mina Loy's poem 'Virgins Plus Curtains Minus Dots', in which Loy describes young women dressed in lace and imprisoned at home until a marriage suitor can 'purchase' them. There was an eleven-year age gap between Wood and Loy (and a considerable difference in social class), but, nevertheless, their childhood experiences of growing up with domineering, old-fashioned mothers were similar. Like Loy, Wood was caught between the pull of outdated but still persistent ideals of morality and femininity, and the promise of a more liberated modern life. Both women were determined in their mission to fashion for themselves lives and identities that were radically different to those of their mothers.

Art offered an early escape that led both women to study in Europe, where they would experiment with new ways of being women in an era that promised freedom to live, to love and to pursue careers outside of the home. However, in different ways, Wood and Loy suffered life-long guilt and could never quite shake off the voice of Victorian-style puritanism shaming them for their choices.

Despite the many restrictions that Mrs Wood placed on her daughter, she encouraged her to cultivate an appreciation of art and culture in the belief that this would enhance Wood's chances of finding a wealthy husband. Wood grew up speaking fluent French and was educated in a series of exclusive girls' schools in New York and Paris; summer holidays were spent touring European museums and galleries under the watchful eyes of a governess. Unwittingly, however, Wood's mother provided her with the tools she would need to enact a full-scale rebellion. As a young teenager, art and literature became Wood's sanctuary. With her head full of Oscar Wilde, Guy de Maupassant, Colette and Flaubert, she began to nurture romantic notions of living the bohemian life of an artist, writing poetry in a Parisian garret. In school, she neglected all subjects except art and literature, and gained a reputation as a bad influence on the other girls, to the horror of her mother.

Wood's parents allowed her to take drawing classes at the Académie Julien in Paris in 1910 and then to travel to Giverny, with a chaperone, to paint. Wood, however, soon tired of the 'elderly spinster' (aged thirty!) accompanying her. She gave her chaperone the slip and took a room in a house full of art students and models. Perhaps coloured by nostalgia or simply imbued with the naivety of a privileged young woman, Wood remembered her dingy attic room as a 'paradise' where she happily created innumerable terrible paintings. Needless to say, Wood's paradise was short-lived. Receiving word of Wood's escape from the chaperone, her elegantly dressed mother rushed over to Giverny, clambered up the stairs to the garret and dragged her daughter out. Wood was promptly shipped back to New York to attend a finishing school.

One year later, Wood made her return to Paris, but this time with the ambition of becoming an actress. She had gained her parents' approval to study at the Comédie-Française; in her memoirs, Wood claims that her mother believed a career as an actress was more suitable

Jessie Tarbox Beals, *Beatrice Wood*, c. 1922, gelatin silver print.

and respectable than that of an artist, so she begrudgingly agreed to the trip. In the spirit of compromise with her wayward daughter, Mrs Wood lined up a range of Paris-based tutors to take her under their wing (including Frances Robinson-Duff, a well-connected American voice coach and actress); she also arranged for accommodation with a seemingly respectable aristocratic family, the Nieuports. It soon became clear that Mrs Wood had underestimated her daughter's ability to seek out action and excitement; Wood's spirit of rebellion prevailed once more. In Robinson-Duff and her fashionable host Madame de Nieuport, Wood found mentor–mother figures who encouraged her to embrace her burgeoning womanhood and sexuality. Ditching the childish frills and lace her mother insisted upon, she learnt how to dress like a high-society Parisian, how to flirt and how it felt for 'a man to hold you close'. The latter was a point insisted upon by Robinson-Duff, who told Wood that in order to move gracefully and act well, she must first understand what it is like to be in love. This most certainly was not what her mother had in mind.

Alongside lessons in love, Wood found time to soak up all the vibrant, innovative avant-garde culture that Paris had to offer. She attended the opening night of Stravinsky's shocking *The Rite of Spring*, where Najinsky's dancers contorted to the strange sounds of Stravinsky's modern score. Infamously, some furious audience members started a riot, but Wood was delighted (by coincidence, Marcel Duchamp was also in the audience that night, but his path would not cross with Wood's until years later). During Wood's second stay in Paris, a whole new world opened up – a world where sexuality, creativity and free expression merged, and one in which women could play a role. To her frustration, Wood's French paradise was, once again, all too brief. This time, forces much more powerful than her mother intervened: as France plunged into the chaos of the First World War, she was forced to return to New York. Back home in America, Wood was emboldened to seek out new opportunities for the creative and sexual liberation she longed for.

Becoming Modern at the Sunwise Turn

In her autobiographical writing, Wood relished playing up to the myth that she was a wide-eyed ingénue until Duchamp, Henri-Pierre Roché and the Arensberg circle initiated her sexual and artistic awakening. She casts herself as a naive young woman, unaware of modern art and utterly inexperienced in passion and romance. Yet there is much to suggest that Wood was, in fact, a cultivated and cultured young woman by the time she began frequenting the Arensberg salon; in other words, Wood's myth-making made for a compelling backstory, but it did not quite match the realities of her early adulthood. Her early education and the time she spent in Paris meant that Wood had a good grounding in art and literature. However, Wood's first real initiation into modern art and new ways of thinking occurred in New York, a few years before her fateful meeting with Duchamp. It came about thanks to writer, artist and bookshop-owner Mary Mowbray-Clarke, a woman who gets little credit in Wood's autobiography, but who was a significant mentor and friend.

Mowbray-Clarke offered the restless young Wood direction and a sense of purpose. The fact that Wood plays down this relationship in later life is indicative of the degree to which, through her autobiography and late-life 'performance', she consciously created the narrative of a 'good girl gone bad', led astray by older men Duchamp and Roché. In reality, Wood's friendship with the multitalented and well-connected Mowbray-Clarke brought her into contact with progressive artists and politics long before she became part of the Arensberg circle. A letter that Wood sent to Mowbray-Clarke during her journey to Paris in October 1912 stands as a true testament to the latter's influence on her young friend: in it, Wood relays a conversation with two attractive male passengers who informed her that 'they were delighted [she] was going to Paris, as there all the "feminist" ideas would be taken out of me'; clearly amused, Wood adds how she wished 'they could have seen and talked to you'.[3]

Wood first met Mowbray-Clarke while studying at the Finch School, a liberal arts college in Manhattan that had been established by the prominent suffragette and educator Jessica Garretson Finch in 1900. An undated photograph shows Wood among a group of fashionable young women students, kitted out in paint-splattered smocks; the girls stand behind their art teachers, Mary and her husband, sculptor John Mowbray-Clarke (the couple also first met at the school). In 1908, the Mowbray-Clarkes bought a farm in Rockland County, a rural area 25 kilometres (15 mi.) north of Manhattan. They transformed the Brocken, as the farm became known, into a popular artist colony over the next decade, where their circle of artists, writers, activists, anarchists and intellectuals visited to escape the city and discuss the latest developments in art, culture and politics. Writer Harold Loeb later recalled that the Brocken group were 'in revolt against our commercial age'.[4] Like many of their friends and associates, the Mowbray-Clarkes were driven by a desire to revolutionize the arts in America. Away from the Brocken, both John and Mary were influential and well-known figures in New York's arts scene: Mary's commitments were limited in the years immediately following the birth of their only son in 1908, but John, as a founder member of the AAPS, played a part in organizing the Armory Show.

After becoming friendly with her tutors at the Finch School, Wood began receiving regular invitations to the Brocken. The excitement of being among brilliant, talented artists and writers must have thrilled the adventurous young Wood, but it is clear from correspondence that she also threw herself into the domestic daily life of the Brocken. In an undated letter received during one of her stays there, Wood's mother expresses her surprise to hear that her daughter had been doing chores – 'I can't think of you doing washing. God help the clothes.' She also

Students at Finch School, New York, *c.* 1912.

Beatrice Wood at the Brocken, *c.* 1912–14.

sends 'love and gratitude to the Clarkes', perhaps giving them too much credit for what she perceived to be a domesticating influence.[5] In contrast to the fractious relationship with her mother, Wood found a mentor and confidante in Mowbray-Clarke. The Brocken became a surrogate home, providing the stable sense of family that was lacking in her volatile upbringing.

A fond and intimate exchange of letters between Wood and Mowbray-Clarke through the 1910s attests to the closeness of their bond. In July 1912, Wood wrote to Mowbray-Clarke from Massachusetts declaring she was 'homesick' for the Brocken, and they kept in regular contact throughout Wood's trip to Paris later that year.[6] As the letter that Wood sent from the ship en route to Paris suggests, Mowbray-Clarke clearly introduced her to progressive feminist ideas and helped open Wood's eyes to new possibilities beyond the dull life of marriage and homemaking that her mother encouraged. Her stays at the Brocken brought her into contact with the latest radical theories and movements driving modern art. Although she was not in the United States during the time the Armory Show took place, Wood was privy to the planning of it and no doubt was kept informed about the scandal by Mowbray-Clarke.

Through Mowbray-Clarke, Wood also gained her first opportunity to play an active role in New York's new modern cultural landscape. In 1916, Mowbray-Clarke and her friend Madge Jenison (a writer from Chicago) recognized a need for a modern bookshop in New York. They envisioned a 'different kind' of bookshop than that which already existed in America, a store that would 'pick up all that is related to modern life'.[7] They wanted to stage poetry performances, show and sell art, and create a relaxed space, where patrons would be free to browse and lounge, with no pressure to buy a book. After they secured a rundown building on East 31st Street (close to 291 gallery), the Sunwise Turn was born. Mowbray-Clarke and Jenison's bold ambitions for their shop are evident in the surviving marketing material: letterheads and advertisements include a description of the Sunwise Turn as 'the Modern bookshop', an epithet that situates it within the progressive, post-Armory Show modernizing mission sweeping New York City. For the bookshop's logo, the pair chose a sketch of the shop's quirky exterior (a red-brick, cottage-style building), symbolizing the extent to which the shop itself was almost as important as the business of selling books.

The decoration of the interior was also carefully chosen to reflect the Sunwise Turn's modern ethos and its function as a relaxed, semi-domestic space. The bill for interior decoration reveals that Mowbray-Clarke and Jenison spared little expense in choosing vibrant, Fauvist textiles and stylish pieces of furniture: they spent at least $512 on brightly coloured soft furnishings and modernist tapestries.[8] Clara Davidge assisted with some of the interior-design work and lent her own furniture. Mowbray-Clark's lecture 'The Small Bookshop', given at the New York Public Library in 1922, touches on how integral the design and decoration of the building was to the Sunwise Turn's aims, over and above traditional standards of good business sense:

Even our mullioned windows and our great tiled wall sign are a protest against the mediocrity of the eternal plate-glass. Every hide-bound advertiser would tell us that we cannot sell books as well from small windows as from large ones, but we think we do a few things to people besides sell them books, and architecture with personality is not often enough a consideration in America in spite of our sky scrapers.[9]

Indeed, the Sunwise Turn did many things besides selling books. Similar to one of the art shops in Greenwich Village, it functioned as an exhibition space and sold prints, art objects and homewares. Its catalogues and stock lists from its eleven years in business give an insight into the eclectic range of items and artwork that was shown there, including furniture and other designs made by Roger Fry and Vanessa Bell's London-based Omega Workshop, textile art by Marguerite Zorach and Martha Kantor, scarves and accessories by Nancy Shostac, and lampshades by Warren Earle Cox.

When plans for the Sunwise Turn first began to gather momentum, Mowbray-Clarke invited Wood to be part of her exciting new venture. Wood invested $100 (other shareholders included modern-art patron and Museum of Modern Art founder Lillie Bliss and influential modernist publisher Alfred Harcourt), and, by April 1916, she spent much of her time assisting in the store. In her diary, Wood records regular shifts at the shop alongside dinners and other meetings with Mowbray-Clarke. She was also involved in arranging Sunwise Turn's programme

Mary Mowbray-Clarke at the Sunwise Turn bookshop, *c.* 1916.

of public talks and performances; Wood herself gave a memorably woeful reading of Amy Lowell's poem 'Patterns' (1915), while Lowell watched on, less than impressed.[10] Mowbray-Clarke even arranged for a small exhibition of Wood's drawings at the Sunwise Turn in March 1917, which was a generous show of support for a young, unknown artist. Wood also introduced Mowbray-Clarke to Duchamp, who arranged for her to purchase several copies of a book of lithographs by Marius de Zayas.

Mowbray-Clarke's respectful correspondence with Duchamp belies the scepticism she expressed as Wood grew closer to Duchamp and the Arensbergs. Wood's diary entries for May 1917 suggest that an argument broke out over her key role in editing and publishing the second issue of the *Blind Man*, which celebrated *Fountain*: on 9 May, she notes that 'Mrs Clarke disapproves of Blind Man Magazine. Sick over situation.' A few days later, she refers to Jenison's 'fury' at the *Blind Man* episode. Clearly, Mowbray-Clarke and Jenison were scandalized not only by what they had heard about *Fountain* itself, but by the playful arguments made in its defence that were published in the *Blind Man* magazine. The Sunwise Turn crowd was progressive and relatively radical, but it upheld certain standards for art and literature; it was serious in its intention to bring about a revolution in American arts – values that felt, from their perspective, at odds with New York Dada's risqué irreverence. This incident serves to emphasize why, even in the liberated atmosphere of the Society of Independent Artists, *Fountain* was censored. Wood's distress, as recorded in her diary, implies that Mowbray-Clarke felt Wood was keeping bad company. In addition to aesthetic differences, Mowbray-Clarke likely shared Wood's father's concerns about the potential consequences of putting her name to the *Blind Man* and risking the wrath of the Comstock obscenity law.

Both Mary and John Mowbray-Clarkes' parental concern for Wood is clear in the diary entries that she recorded during her visits to the Brocken, particularly during the tumultuous months of 1917. In August, as Wood fell into depression and despair following the end of her relationship with Henri-Pierre Roché, she notes that they advise her to 'marry or act, not drift'. They approved of her idea to join a theatre company in Montreal, Canada, feeling that Wood (by then 23 years old) needed to get away from her mother and create a life for herself. Mowbray-Clarke's support during this crisis is just one example of the significant impact she had on Wood during the 1910s. Long after their days at the Finch school, Wood continued to learn from and be guided by Mowbray-Clarke; as a mother–mentor figure, she offered both personal and practical support that helped Wood develop creatively and emotionally, away from the oppressive authority of her mother.

By playing down Mowbray-Clarke's influence, Wood continues the critical neglect that has led to her impact on the New York arts and literature scene (and that of the Brocken as a creative site) being overlooked. A young Peggy Guggenheim also worked as a shop assistant at the Sunwise Turn in 1920. Like Wood's, her experiences there under the guidance of Mowbray-Clarke (and among 'many celebrities and writers and painters' who frequented the shop) had a profound impact on the direction her life took. Guggenheim looked to Mowbray-Clarke as a role model of sorts, describing her, years later, as a 'goddess . . . so serious and so good and so wonderful about her work, idealistic, absolutely devoted to what she thought she was doing'.[11] Both Wood and Guggenheim would be significantly shaped by their time at the Sunwise Turn and, with their respective lifelong interests in education (Wood) and supporting the arts (Guggenheim), they carried the influence of Mowbray-Clarke with them throughout their lives.

Through examining Wood's close friendship with Mowbray-Clarke, a slightly different picture emerges of her life prior to meeting Duchamp, Roché and the Arensbergs in 1916. It reveals Wood's rich and thrilling initiation into New York's art world, which gave her access to spaces where intellectual debates around issues such as feminism, socialism and the transformation of modern culture flourished. At the Brocken and the Sunwise Turn, Wood began cultivating ideas about the self and society through art. This experience (in addition to the fact that she spoke fluent French) meant that she was well equipped to hold her own among the Arensberg circle of artists, writers and intellectuals.

Beatrice and the *Blind Man*

By mid-1916, although Wood was not quite the naive innocent she
presents in her autobiography, her life was lacking direction. She continued to pursue acting, with little success, and lived in her parents'
home under the watchful eye of her mother. A chance invitation was
to re-energize Wood and change the course of her life. Knowing that
she spoke French, her friend Alissa Frank invited Wood to join her on
a visit to a young Frenchman who was laid up in hospital and wanted
visitors to chat with. The patient in question was avant-garde composer
Edgard Varèse. Wood found Varèse interesting, but they didn't hit it
off. She was much more interested in another of his visitors, a sombre
and enigmatic Frenchman who, she soon found out, was the artist
behind one of the Armory Show's most notorious exhibits – Marcel
Duchamp. Duchamp was equally charmed by Wood and he quickly
introduced her to his friend Henri-Pierre Roché. Duchamp and Roché
became Wood's entrance to a dizzying world where art, sex, parties and
pleasure collided; it was more thrilling and outrageous than anything
she had previously encountered at the Sunwise Turn or the Brocken.
The timing of their meeting could not have been more serendipitous.

Duchamp had recently taken up residence in the apartment above
the Arensbergs', attracting an array of friends and associates who had
also left the turmoil engulfing Europe for the bright lights of New York.
With Duchamp as the star attraction, the Arensbergs' salon became one
of the city's go-to spots for cultured types seeking all-night parties, flirting, dancing and intense games of chess. The eclectic artworks on the
walls set the tone and amplified the salon guests' irreverent, avant-garde
attitude. Wood's recollections of her first visits to the Arensberg salon
offer a flavour of what a shocking, overwhelming and truly amazing
experience it was to step through the doors of 33 West 67th Street in
the 1910s. With her head spinning 'in disbelief', Wood recalls entering:

> A sitting room full of oriental rugs, carefully chosen early
> American furniture . . . but there on the walls – not only in the
> sitting room but in the hall, the bedroom, bath, and kitchen
> – hung the most hideous collection of paintings I had ever

Unknown photographer, Marcel Duchamp with Francis Picabia and Beatrice Wood, Coney Island, 1917.

seen. Walking into this incredible home I caught my breath, suppressed a giggle, and sat down in a state of shock. One by one I confronted each disconcerting image as it shrieked out at me . . . Nearby on a pedestal was a Brancusi brass that shot up in the air out of nowhere and made me uncomfortable. Scattered throughout the room were works by Picabia, Gleizes, Braque, and Sheeler, African carvings and pieces from a mixture of periods.[12]

Like the baffled visitors to the Armory Show a few years earlier, Wood felt uncomfortable and amused by this startling, provocative display of avant-garde art. Despite her professed ignorance, she had encountered modern art during her time with the Mowbray-Clarkes. However, encountering so many radical, highly experimental works of art in an ordinary apartment was a different experience. In an echo of Louise Arensberg's first impression of the Armory Show's most avant-garde works, Wood suggests that she initially felt an active dislike, even revulsion, at the shattered forms and disjointed figures scattered across the walls, as if the artwork was launching an attack on her senses.

Despite the salon's dizzying effect, Wood was seduced – not only by Duchamp and Roché (at long last, the passionate affairs that the romantic young Wood dreamed of beckoned), but by the vitality, the daring creativity and the possibilities that flourished in the Arensberg salon. On her second visit, Wood returned with an open mind and found that the artwork began to speak to her in a more powerful way than any of her lessons at art school. Matisse's *Mademoiselle Yvonne Landsberg*, the painting she initially declared 'the most awful' of the lot, was the first one to make sense. Wood remembers gazing at the portrait's 'angular lines' , with Joseph Stella and Charles Sheeler discussing colour theory in the background, until it revealed its 'wondrous beauty' to her: 'Matisse had spoken and at last I listened.' This moment contrasted sharply with the years she had spent being dragged through European art galleries by governesses. At the Arensbergs', Wood could truly feel the work of art in front of her, experiencing it as part of the vibrant sensations, conversations and cultural happenings that surrounded her during visits to the salon. She had also come to learn that understanding – in a traditional, rational sense – was simply not relevant to modern art; when she informed Duchamp that his ready-mades were 'beyond' her comprehension, he replied 'cela n'a pas d'importance.'[13]

Between flirtation and high jinks, Duchamp and Roché encouraged Wood to experiment with making art and using it as a vehicle for creative self-expression. Duchamp allowed Wood to work in his studio, where his critiques of her sketches helped hone her creative eye in ways that would prove crucial to her artistic development. Even in Wood's career as a ceramicist decades later, she was guided by the aesthetic principles she learnt working alongside Duchamp. In December 1916, just two months after Wood first met Roché and Duchamp, one of her sketches was published in *Rogue* magazine. Her work, *Mariage d'une amie*, was in illustrious company: it appeared in the same issue as Mina Loy's play *Cittàbapini* and Gertrude Stein's *Mrs. Th——y*, both formally experimental works that had been sent from Europe (Loy was then based in Florence, and Stein in Paris). In Wood's version of the story, she suggests that this drawing came about as the result of a challenge Duchamp set her. During a conversation about modern art, Wood declared that 'anyone can do such scrawls' and Duchamp replied 'try'.[14] Wood's description of the sketch she presented to him is typically self-deprecating (a 'tortured abstraction'), yet the fact that she was happy for it to be submitted to *Rogue* suggests some belief in its merits. We also know that when Wood declared *anyone* can create modern art, she was not speaking as an amateur: Wood had previously studied art in elite schools, learned from progressive artists like the Mowbray-Clarkes, and mixed with creative, intellectual groups who were bringing modernism to America.

As a critique of love and marriage created by a modern young woman, the sketch was a perfect fit for *Rogue*. On first impression, *Mariage d'une amie* looks like an abstract tangle of black and white lines. However, Wood's chosen title offers a clue to its meaning. Around the time that Wood completed this sketch, her close friend Elizabeth Reynolds had recently married Norman Hapgood, a divorcee 26 years her senior. With this particularly contentious marriage of a friend on her mind, Wood felt moved to comment on the effects of marriage, specifically the effects felt by a young woman married to a much older man. In the foreground of the sketch, phallic, snake-like forms emerge as two separate forms: a curvaceous feminine figure being squeezed by a thick, black jagged pole. Around the entwined figures, roughly sketched squares suggest stark and prison-like buildings, enhancing the overall sense of claustrophobia. This stifling entanglement is clearly a symbol of the loss of freedom that marriage heralded for women. The fact that Wood called this work 'Marriage of a Friend' (with the feminine form of the noun) highlights her personal sense of loss, alluding to the fact that marriage stifled the carefree nature of their friendship as young, single women.

Wood continued to develop loose-line, cartoonish sketches that expressed wry critiques of women's lives and relationships, a style and subject-matter that she would return to throughout her life. In 1917, she playfully captured scenes from the social lives of the Arensberg circle, immortalizing the night that Wood, Duchamp, Mina Loy and Charles Demuth piled into bed together after the Blind Man's Ball in

— Beatrice Wood

Mariage D'une Amie

Rogue, III/2
(November 1915).

187

Lit de Marcel (1917). She also created playful visual records of chess games between Duchamp and Picabia (*Soirée*, 1917), and recorded her experiences of working alongside Duchamp (*7.45 p.m. Beatrice Waiting for Marcel*, 1917–18). Wood's style – combining a deceptively childlike simplicity with sensuous eroticism, humorously cutting to the heart of human desires and jealousies – was perfectly suited to the creative scene that sprang up around the Arensberg circle, later known as New York Dada. Duchamp and the Arensbergs clearly felt that she captured the spirit of the moment as they asked her to design the poster for the Blind Man's Ball. Her sketch of a stickman thumbing its nose while doing a silly walk became a Dada icon. Its childlike simplicity was amusing and effective. Without trying too hard, Wood perfectly characterized New York Dada's irreverent, clownish spirit and anti-art ethos.

Wood's wild year with the Arensberg circle also coincided with the planning for the Society of Independent Artists' inaugural exhibition at the Grand Central Palace (10 April to 6 May 1917). Wood joined with other members of the Arensberg circle to assist in organizing the exhibition and edited the accompanying magazine, the *Blind Man*. The first issue featured statements and comments by Wood, Roché and Mina Loy on the role of art and the artist in modern society. It set out a challenge for New York to 'take responsibility' for art and do better than a 'provincial town'.[15] The second issue (May 1917) was much more explosive. By this time, the *Fountain* scandal had erupted, leading to arguments, splits and fraught debate within the Arensberg circle and beyond (Wood's aforementioned quarrel with Mowbray-Clarke and Jenison underscores what a hot topic this was within the New York art world). Wood, Roché and Duchamp decided that the *Blind Man* would defend the artwork, with essays and opinion pieces that functioned as tongue-in-cheek ripostes to those who had rejected *Fountain* from an exhibition that was supposed to have no rules and no judges. Wood wrote the editorial, defending the fictional Richard Mutt from charges of obscenity and plagiarism, and closed with the reminder that 'the only works of art America has given are her plumbing and her bridges.'[16] She also contributed the satirical 'letter from a mother', which urged that the beauty, purity and nobility of art be preserved against 'people without refinement, cubists, futurists'.[17]

Wood happily agreed to have her name and address registered as the publisher (fearing risk of deportation, Duchamp and Roché did not want their names officially associated with it). However, this meant that all final copies were sent to Wood's family home, where her father intercepted the mysteriously large packages that had arrived for his daughter. Shocked and disgusted by the material he found, he urged Wood not to circulate the magazines – not simply for the sake of her reputation, but also because of the likelihood she would be prosecuted under the Comstock obscenity law, which forbade the distribution of so-called obscene publications through the post. This was doubtless a blow to Wood's relationship with her parents, which was already incredibly strained at this time (even Roché's novel *Victor* makes constant references to Wood's arguments with her mother and her mother's threats to cut her off financially). But Wood claimed that she was not troubled by her father's warning. With characteristic bravado, she later reflected that prison would simply have been 'another new and exciting experience'.[18] It was only the thought of the repercussions high-profile figures who had donated to the *Blind Man* or written for it (including Gertrude Vanderbilt Whitney and Frank Crowninshield) might face that caused her to change tack. As a compromise, the editors decided that the *Blind Man*'s second issue would only be distributed by hand.

To the disappointment of her parents, Wood still managed to cause something of a scandal. In addition to editing the *Blind Man* magazine, she decided to exhibit artwork in the Independents exhibition. One of the two works she submitted, *Un peut (peu) d'eau dans du savon* ('A Little Water in Some Soap', 1917), turned out to be the exhibition's most shocking work – *Fountain*, of course, was not included, so it only gained notoriety retrospectively.[19] In a review for the 21 April 1917 issue of *American Art News*, a journalist singled out *Un peut d'eau* as 'the keynote of the childish whim, the unbridled extravagance, the undisciplined impudence and immature ignorance and even derangement that have been allowed full and free fling in the first jury-free exhibition of the Society of Independent Artists'.[20]

In *Un peut d'eau*, Wood used the childlike, Dada style she had developed over the past year to disrupt the classical tradition of the female nude. Showing the headless torso of a female nude in a bathtub with a (real) bar of soap strategically resting on her groin, Wood created a prosaic riff on Botticelli's *Birth of Venus* (1485–6). The title is often presumed by critics to be an error, with the two nouns mixed up (as if Wood intended the more common-sense phrase 'a little soap in some water' rather than 'a little water in some soap'), yet the fact that Wood was a fluent French speaker suggests this was intentional. Wood's phrasing places emphasis on the 'little water' rather than the soap, drawing explicit (in both senses of the word) attention to the wetness of the woman's genitals. Through a visual reference to the *Birth of Venus* and the myth of the goddess that sprang fully formed from sea foam, Wood's modern nude conveys a sense of intimacy and sexuality that is not dependent on a man: reclining in orgasmic bliss, Venus' act of self-creation is here transformed into sensual self-pleasure.

Un peut d'eau wasn't a straightforward celebration of female sexuality. The fact that the woman depicted in the drawing is headless neutralizes her agency; in this way, Wood disparages the tired trope of the objectified nude. By attaching a (real) bar of soap to the work, Wood embedded a particularly modern critique of the ways that women and women's bodies were objectified not only in art, but in America's increasingly rampant advertising and consumer culture. *Un peut d'eau* links sex and sensuality to mass-produced beauty and hygiene products, as well as to the ideals of purity and femininity that were used to market them. For those viewing *Un peut d'eau* in 1917, the image would likely have called to mind a notoriously risqué 1910s advertisement for Woodbury's Facial Soap.

The Woodbury Soap Company was one of the first companies to deploy sexualized advertising copy when they launched their slogan 'A Skin You Love to Touch' in 1911; the phrase was the brainchild of Helen Lansdowne Resor, one of America's pioneering women advertising executives and an active supporter of the suffrage movement.[21] Woodbury's appeal to sensuality and sexuality was in stark contrast to other brands, which used sentimental images of babies or middle-class women to evoke a sense of purity and moral uprightness. In Woodbury's advertisements, their slogan was accompanied by a provocative image of a well-dressed couple engaged in an intimate embrace, each with cheeks flushed by passion. The male figure holds the woman close, seemingly intoxicated by her skin; the woman's robe has slipped provocatively from her shoulder, and, in one of the earliest versions of the advertisement, she stares boldly at the viewer. Soap no longer represents cleanliness and virtue, but instead becomes seductive, a means to a sexual encounter.

Wood's allusion to Woodbury's advertisement is typical of her playful, sexually forthright approach and the contradictory impulses that define her work – part feminist, part stereotypically feminine and deferential to men. The link between Woodbury's 'A Skin You Love to Touch' slogan and *Un peut d'eau*'s soap tempts the viewer to touch the nude intimately, setting up an uncomfortable association that confronts its viewers – particularly its male viewers – with their own contradictory desires and expectations. *Un peut d'eau* repudiates the way that women's bodies are policed and their pleasure is limited: female sexuality is exploited and objectified in art and advertising, but simultaneously branded taboo and obscene by society. From experience, Wood knew only too well the conflicting pressures to be sexual and virginal, a modern woman and a good girl, which society placed on women (particularly those who, like Wood, were the first of a new generation struggling for greater freedom and self-expression). The press and public's shocked reaction to *Un peut d'eau* only confirms Wood's message – so too does the fact that some men left their business cards tucked into its frame.

Wood returned to suggestive images of touch and tactility in her later work. In 1992 she published *Touching Certain Things*, an ostensibly frothy memoir of Wood's close relationship with Helen Wood (unrelated) and their trip to Europe. The book is illustrated with a series of sketches of the same name, which Wood made between 1932 and 1933. There is a clear erotic undertone in her depiction of the two women together, with Wood's sensuous, expressive line drawings capturing Helen's beauty and vitality. 'How Lucky Men Are. I Fingered the Exquisite Silk with my Forefinger', for example, shows Wood lounging in bed with Helen, whose nightgown has gaped open to bare her breasts. Both of Helen's arms are under the covers, and she has closed eyes in an expression of bliss. Wood gazes at Helen while her hand hovers over the fallen strap of Helen's nightgown, as if she might have just pulled it down, or else she is reaching to touch her bare skin; Wood's other arm is mostly hidden under the covers, but the outline suggests that it too is stretched in Helen's direction. The sketch's tongue-in-cheek title asserts heteronormative standards (women's sexuality belongs to men), while also indicating that Wood herself takes pleasure in women's bodies and envies male entitlement to them. This is typical of the double game that Wood played throughout her life, switching between knowingness and naivety, a serious sensuality and absurdist humour.

Beato Post-Dada

Duchamp was the first of the Arensberg circle to beguile her, but, in typical Duchamp style, he was always slightly out of reach and impossible to fathom. He continued to exert a strong influence on Wood and their friendship would, at times, become something more over the course of that eventful year; however, Duchamp could not offer Wood the passion that she had longed for since her furtive readings of *Madame Bovary* as a schoolgirl. Instead, Duchamp's friend and compatriot Henri-Pierre Roché became Wood's first serious lover. By the time the two met, Roché was in his late thirties and a cultivated man of the world, working variously as a journalist, diplomat, art collector and advisor. Unlike Duchamp, Roché was gregarious and a skilled networker who, in Gertrude Stein's words, was 'a general introducer. He knew everybody, he really knew them and he could introduce anybody to anybody' (indeed, Roché was responsible for the fateful meeting between Stein and Picasso).[22] Wood felt instantly at ease with him, describing their relationship, years later in her autobiography, as 'like an old married couple'. Despite being besotted with Roché, Wood was open about her attraction to Duchamp. Roché, who was notorious for his aversion to monogamy, found this amusing. Her lust for the emotionally detached Duchamp played out like a game between the three of them, with the two older men delighting in their guileless young protégée.

In later life, Wood recalled her relationship with Roché as a revelation. She described the ways that he not only inspired her artistically, but also 'released [her] from prudish views about sex, and made it a loving and creative experience'.[23] As with many episodes of Wood's life, it is impossible not to suspect that she edited this version of events to suit her narrative. While Wood credits Roché for liberating her from 'prudish views', in reality she struggled to accept his polyamorous attitude towards relationships. What Wood did not know was that Roché was also carrying out affairs with two of her close friends (Louise Arensberg and the journalist Alissa Frank), alongside liaisons with Louise Norton and Isadora Duncan.[24] When Wood discovered Roché's betrayal, she was devastated. The idea of sharing him with other women was intolerable. Her anguish was only enhanced by the feeling that she was 'neither modern nor reasonable' for her inability to accept this kind of open relationship. Again, Wood's experience reveals the many pitfalls that lay in wait for young women seeking to live modern, liberated lives on their own terms.

Wood's diary entries from this period are typically brief yet revealing: she still continues to spend time with Roché but frequently notes feeling 'very sad', 'sick' and weepy about the state of affairs between them. What started off as a jest in which Wood was a willing participant perhaps ended up feeling more like a joke at her expense, as Roché focused his attentions on Louise Arensberg and Duchamp was his usual enigmatic self. The lack of direction she felt before meeting Roché, Duchamp and the Arensbergs seems to return, indicated by references to her low moods and the Mowbray-Clarkes' pep talks ('marry or act, [don't] drift').[25] On 9 August 1917, Wood records a seemingly snap decision to go work in a theatre in Montreal, Canada, likely spurred on by her depressed state of mind. Unsurprisingly, Wood's mother was appalled at her daughter's latest impulsive and unconventional life choice. For once, however, she was right: the move that took Wood far from the friendships and creative partnerships she had made during the wild year she spent as part of the Arensberg salon was disastrous. Overcome by loneliness in a strange city and frustrated by her mother's controlling behaviour, Wood became involved with a shady Belgian theatre worker called Paul Ransom. Ransom suggested that they marry because it would help Wood shake off her mother's grip on her life, then arrange a swift annulment later; Wood – this time genuinely naive and gullible – accepted. She regretted her decision almost immediately.

After a joyless marriage ceremony, they couple returned to New York, where it became clear that Ransom had married Wood for money. He was a reckless and abusive husband, whose gambling habit soon plunged the couple into poverty – a huge shock for a pampered young woman brought up with all the comforts of wealth and privilege. Ransom exploited Wood's open nature and played on the difficult relationship with her mother, knowing that she would not confide in her parents. Wood's life had changed dramatically since her whirlwind year at the heart of the Arensberg salon. She moved to a cheap flat in Greenwich Village, taking odd jobs and selling her precious art books to make ends meet, though there were still times when the couple could not afford to eat. During visits to her parents' house, Wood recalled looking on with concealed horror as they threw perfectly good food away after lavish dinners. There were further humiliations to come. After initially asking Wood to arrange a $500 loan from the Arensbergs, Ransom went behind her back to borrow thousands more. He pledged Wood's anticipated inheritance from her grandmother as collateral. The Arensbergs' lawyers ended up contacting Wood's parents to arrange repayment, alerting them to the precarious, miserable situation their daughter had ended up in.

Around the same time, Wood discovered a second, even more shocking betrayal. Ransom had left behind a wife when he moved from his native Belgium to Canada – he was a bigamist. For once, Wood had reason to be grateful for her mother's interfering nature. Despite Ransom pleading innocence, Mrs Wood travelled to Europe to track down his wife and family (including a son). Once his bigamy was confirmed, Wood's parents organized the annulment of their marriage, ending four miserable years. Free from Ransom, Wood began a journey of self-realization and creative expression. She discovered Theosophy, a modern spiritual religion that drew on the teachings of Hinduism and Buddhism. She also left New York in search of new creative vistas. Like the Arensbergs, she was drawn to the West Coast and, in 1948, she made Ojai, California, her permanent home.

In Ojai, Wood finally found an outlet for her creative talent in pottery. Typically, Wood hid her ambition and skill behind a pose of amateurism and flippancy. She suggested that she began pottery classes simply to make a teapot that would match a set of plates she had bought on a trip to the Netherlands; she recounts her clumsy attempts as an enthusiastic but untalented student struggling to learn the craft.

In reality, Wood pursued this new career with single-minded determination. She studied with innovative ceramicists Glen Lukens and husband-and-wife team Gertrud and Otto Natzler, selling some of her beloved art books to fund tuition. The ceramic works she created during her long career as a potter merge Dada's playful irreverent spirit with what Jenni Sorkin describes as a 'camp, queer aesthetic'.[26] The vases and vessels she created were glazed with a metallic lustre that Wood enjoyed experimenting with. Shimmering with rich gold and copper tones, her ceramics look like enchanted relics from another world. Some are adorned with circular patterns or figures in relief, like the pre-Columbian artefacts in the Arensbergs' collection. Wood's friend Anaïs Nin described the pottery as possessing a dramatic presence, with the 'rhythm and the lustre of both jewels and human eyes'.[27]

Alongside opulent chalices and pots, Wood crafted kitsch figurines that reimagined her earlier Dada work in ceramics and riffed on similar themes. Figures of women with titles like 'Career Woman' and 'Not Married' continue Wood's wry commentary on the politics of sex and gender. Her 'naughty' little human figurines highlight the absurdities of relationships and life, in a typically humorous style. Wood's *joie de vivre* shines through these pieces, which always find humour in the absurd without tipping into nihilism. They are deliberately, comically naive, very different in style to the more elegant, decadent modernist language of her pottery. Acknowledging the fact that some people found her figurines ugly, Wood references the impact of Dada on these purposefully kitsch creations: 'a lot of people think they're horrible. Maybe they are . . . But I purposely keep these figures unschooled. I've been told that my pottery is elegant . . . But these figures are something entirely different. And I think that's the impact of Marcel in a certain direction that I don't want to keep them schooled.'[28]

In 1980, Wood also made a replica of *Un peut (peu) d'eau dans du savon* (the original was lost) in glazed earthenware (complete with heart-shaped soap); much like the writing of her autobiography, this was a statement that staked Wood's claim in the historical Dada avant-garde movement. Just as Duchamp authorized replicas of his readymades throughout the post-war years, Wood similarly sought to highlight her own contributions to New York Dada, which was now part of art

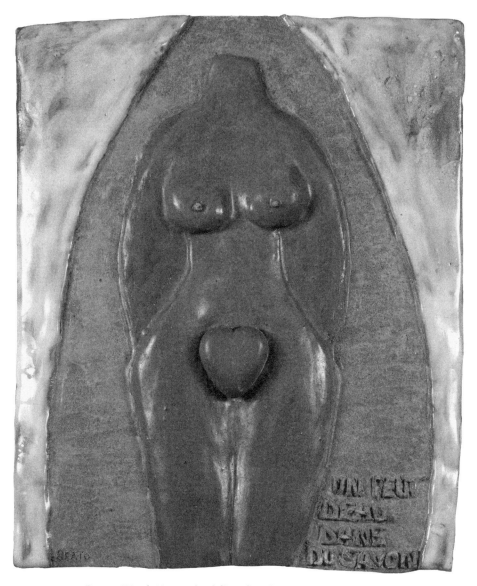

Beatrice Wood, *Un peut (peu) d'eau dans du savon*, 1917–77, ceramic.

history. Wood's commitment not only to keep working but to live an active, public life up until her death highlights the courage and determination that had always guided her. In the male-dominated art world, Wood ensured that she would be remembered – even if that meant playing up to stereotypes or carefully linking her personal mythology with that of modern art's recognized male geniuses.

Shocking!

Wood left behind an archive packed full of interviews, diaries and autobiographical texts when she died in 1998. In all this material, she appears completely candid and happy to discuss the intimate details of her life. However, the narratives she constructs are shot through with contradictions and inconsistencies. A degree of confusion is to be expected over the course of a life as long as Wood's, but some of these anomalies suggest something more deliberate. In fact, Wood seems to play on the fact that autobiography is, necessarily, a collage of subjective memories, desires, confessions and impressions; the facts of a person's life are filtered through memory, emerging in a different form. Like the process of making and firing pottery, writing a memoir is an art that combines skill, personal touch and chance. Wood played up to the performative, constructed aspects of autobiography, crafting a narrative that positioned her as a truly Dada character. This reflected a role she played in her life, particularly with her avant-garde friends. Recalling visits to the Arensbergs at their Hollywood home in the 1930s and '40s, Wood describes how she adopted and exaggerated a clown-like persona:

> They wanted to hear about every new man I met and insisted that I bring each one to meet them. I embellished my tales and enlarged the flirtations; I so appreciated the wealth of culture they brought into my life, I wanted to bring spice and enter-tainment into theirs. I think my daily absurdities were a relief to them after listening to some of their more highbrow visitors.[29]

In describing the Arensbergs' rather staid and serious life on the West Coast (compared to the all-night parties of their New York salon days), Wood reveals more about the way she performs a version of herself. There are clear parallels between the way she 'acts up' for the Arensbergs and the way she amuses and teases the reader of her auto-biographical works with the 'absurdities' of her life. Absurdity, indeed, was a concept that Wood returned to repeatedly in her work and as a frame for her life. In an interview in the 1980s, she notes how it was 'one of the absurdities of life that of all that group [from the Arensberg salon] I am probably the only one left alive'.[30] Clearly Wood found it amusing and appropriately Dada that she, the whimsical ingénue who was taught to parrot French swear words at the Arensbergs' soirées, was left to claim the title 'Mama of Dada'. More seriously, however, Wood also used this absurdity to deflect from distressing incidents, particularly her disappointing and, at times, abusive relationships. The persona that she constructed allowed her distance from some of the damaging episodes of her life.

As we reassess Wood's role in New York's 1910s avant-garde movement, it is vital to take into account the self-consciously crafted nature of her autobiography and not confuse Wood with the tragicomic persona she created. *I Shock Myself* is part of Wood's lifelong interest in exploring notions of sexuality, sensuality, creativity and the comical absurdity of the human condition. From the rebellions of her school days to the sexually voracious, glamorous image she cultivated in old age, Wood was driven by a desire to challenge taboos and push boundaries – particularly those imposed on women. Wood presents her involvement with the 1910s New York avant-garde scene as that of an art groupie, a dazzled young woman in thrall to two cultured older men. Yet the work she created and the interests she pursued during this time tell a distinctly different story. When she first encountered Duchamp and the Arensberg circle, she was an educated young woman already experienced in mixing with an older, intellectual crowd. The fact that she was prepared to show work to Duchamp, who was, during those post-Armory Show years, one of the 'most celebrated' and most infamous artists in New York, also reveals the self-confidence, determination and spirited nature that would drive her to later success as a ceramic artist and art world celebrity.

Perhaps the biggest lesson Wood learnt at the Arensbergs' salon was the power of shock, specifically shock as cultural strategy and currency. Wood gained the confidence to be provocative in this environment, but she also added her own already-formed attitude of rebellion and an astute understanding of sexual politics. She embodied the restless energy that was driving a generation of young women to find new, modern ways of living. Her active roles in the events of 1917, both as creator of the Society of Independent Artists exhibition's most scandalous (displayed) work and as an editor of the *Blind Man*, place her at the centre of the movement that became known as New York Dada. The delight she took in creating provocative work upends assumptions about the masculinity of New York Dada and its aesthetics of shock and sexuality. In later years, her irrepressible wit and creativity ripped up the rule book for older women: in her determination to stake her claim in the art world, to be sexual and, simply, to be seen, Wood reshaped the role of women in modern art.

Unknown photographer, *Djuna Barnes and Mina Loy*, 1927.

6

MINA LOY:
The Art of Modern Living

When Mina Loy stepped off ss *Duca d'Aosta* in New York City in October 1916, it did not take long for her to arrive at the door of the Arensberg salon. She had left her home and her two children in Florence the previous month, determined not only to build her career as an artist and writer but to taste life in the capital of American art and culture. She had already travelled widely in Europe, moving between key centres of modernity in London (where she grew up), Paris, Berlin and Munich, mixing with circles of artists and intellectuals at the vanguard of new trends in art, literature and philosophy. New York was the next step in Loy's aim to make a success of her art and poetry; after years of unhappy marriage and childrearing, this was also an opportunity to fully realize a life unconstrained by the traditional morality and gender roles that had shackled her mother's generation. By the time she reached New York, Loy was 35 years old and already an accomplished painter, designer and writer of poems, essays and plays. Yet despite her talent, she had made only a limited impact on the art world due to the demands of domesticity and bouts of depression. She had made friends and allies while living in Italy, from both Florence's circle of American expatriates and the bombastic Italian Futurist movement, but her life there lacked creative stimulation, opportunity and community. The departure of many of her American friends at the outbreak of the First World War turned Loy's attention to the United States. Europe seemed stuck in the past, but New York beckoned like a shining beacon of modernity across the Atlantic.

On a personal level, Loy had much to escape from, particularly her loathed husband, the minor British artist and photographer Stephen Haweis. Loy married Haweis out of necessity in 1903 after discovering she was pregnant. At first, marriage also seemed like a way to escape her mother's control, but (much like Beatrice Wood) she soon found she had only traded one frustrating, constrictive and disappointing relationship for another. Their married life was filled with misery and misfortune, beginning with the death of their infant daughter Oda in 1905. During the years that they spent living in Paris and then Florence, Haweis was serially unfaithful, jealous and unsupportive of Loy's own artistic career and a neglectful father to their children.[1] In Loy's unpublished autobiographical writing, she paints him as an affected, decadent aesthete, bound to the cultural legacy of late Victorian London and his beloved mother, Mary (an art critic and writer who died before Haweis met Loy). Stephen and Loy's Florentine home was cluttered with relics and curios from his mother's estate, such as an Etruscan vase filled with the ashes of her pet dog and a print of Aubrey Beardsley's *Mademoiselle de Maupin* (1897). As their relationship deteriorated, Stephen came to represent a backwards-facing, lifeless, repressive form of Victorian culture that Loy despised. Both couples had extramarital affairs, but Stephen's relationship with a model in 1912 proved to be the final straw. He took off on a trip to Australia and America in 1913, refusing Loy's requests for divorce – in part because he continued to receive money from Loy's small allowance. Left alone with the children and craving creative stimulation, Loy felt the need to reinvent herself, to build a new, modern life free from old-fashioned morals and traditions.

In Florence, Loy became involved with a network of influential Americans who were shaping and spreading the latest trends in politics and art. She was a regular at Mabel Dodge's eclectic parties at the Villa Curonia, and the two women developed a lively correspondence through which they exchanged thoughts on feminism, art and philosophy. Dodge became a close confidante and mentor for Loy through these years of rapid upheaval. Despite differences in wealth and upbringing, Dodge modelled a mode of modern living that was not bound by old-fashioned values and moral codes. In particular, Dodge's interest in feminism (rooted in radical Greenwich Village) impressed and inspired Loy, as did her bold attitude towards life. In Dodge, Loy found a woman who was fearless in the pursuit of her own sexual desires, having had a number of affairs with men and women. Her friendship with Dodge was a lifeline that provided both a fresh understanding of sexuality and the confidence she needed to imagine a life outside the bonds of marriage. At this time, Loy began a determined effort to write radically experimental poetry that critiqued women's place in society. She also began to put feminist politics into practice in her own life, making a break from her husband.

At the vibrant Villa Curonia, Loy came into contact with a dazzling crowd who, like her, were seeking new forms of expression, new ways of living and fashioning themselves. Through Dodge, Loy was introduced to Gertrude Stein. At this point, Stein had attracted a degree of critical interest following the 1909 publication of her novel *Three Lives* a few years earlier (it was published at her own expense), but she continued to struggle to find publishers that would take on her more experimental new works. Despite differences in their personalities and creative styles, Loy found something of a kindred spirit in Stein. In her *Autobiography of Alice B. Toklas*, Stein remembers Loy as one of 'the very earliest to be interested' in her work, after Stein let Loy read a draft of *Making of Americans*.[2] Stein notes that Stephen Haweis was also enthusiastic, but he betrayed his old-fashioned cultural aesthetic by insisting that she should add commas to make her writing easier to read. Loy was much more in tune with Stein's style: in Stein's words, she 'was able to understand without the commas. She has always been able to understand.' Soon, Loy would put her intuitive understanding of modern poetry's fractured rhythms into practice, with her own intriguingly enigmatic verses.

Stein and Loy shared a key ally in their respective quests for gaining recognition in America in the figure of Carl Van Vechten. The gregarious Van Vechten was an art critic, photographer and man about town who made it his business to be an authority on the latest innovations in art and culture. Like his friend and mentor Mabel Dodge, Van Vechten was skilled in associating – and promoting – himself with exciting new talents. Loy met Van Vechten at the Villa Curonia and the pair struck up a lively correspondence after he returned home to the United States. Through 'Carlo', as Loy affectionately referred to him in their many letters, she gained a link to New York's experimental arts scene. The books, magazines and gossip he sent gave her an insight into the cultural trends and ideas flourishing there, feeding her imagination and encouraging her sense that New York offered everything she was looking for. While Van Vechten helped Loy stay abreast of cultural life in the United States, Loy helped Van Vechten build a reputation among his New York circle for being abreast of innovative European avant-garde work. Eager to show off his 'discoveries', he began liaising with editors of little magazines, successfully arranging for the Nortons to take Stein's and Loy's work for *Rogue* magazine.

Van Vechten's updates from New York were a vital source of hope and encouragement for Loy while she languished in Florence. He became a trusted confidant as she gained belief in her abilities as a writer and began to explore daring issues surrounding women and sexuality in her poetry. Their lively and fond correspondence provides a fascinating insight into Loy's aims and inspirations in the years before her momentous move to New York: in one letter, she describes exciting encounters with work by Picasso and Wyndham Lewis, and a performance by Nijinsky.[3] Her frustrations at the financial and practical barriers that obstructed her plans (particularly balancing her creative life with her domestic responsibility) are also clear. In September 1914, she sent Van Vechten a number of fashion illustrations with the hope that he could sell them to designers and make her enough money to provide for her family and pay for her passage to New York.

In New York, Loy envisioned a new life where she would be free to write, make art and, crucially, make money. She also hoped to obtain a divorce from Haweis there, which was an easier process in the United States than in Italy. Unlike many of the artists, writers, intellectuals and impresarios that built the early twentieth century's modern-art movements, Loy did not have huge inherited wealth to fund her artistic career. She came from a lower-middle-class background and grew up in Kilburn, then a relatively shabby part of London. Her father, a Jewish tailor, had emigrated from Hungary to London to seek his fortune. He had made something of an unlikely match with Loy's mother, a puritanical English matriarch who harangued and severely policed Loy throughout her youth.

Loy's autobiographical poem 'Anglo-Mongrels and the Rose' (the section was published in a 1923 issue of the *Little Review*) reveals aspects of her childhood.[4] She characterizes her mother as a neurotic, domineering woman, obsessed with upholding the strictures of patriarchal Victorian society. In the poem, Loy also provides a glimpse into the family's unfashionable London home, with kitsch oleographs hanging on the wall and imposing heavy furniture filling every corner. Her mother is shown to dominate this oppressive space, swathed in typically Victorian petticoats, long dresses and tight corsets. In such a stifling environment, the young Loy learns to feel ashamed of her body and constricted by the conventions of Victorian patriarchy. Loy would spend much of the 1910s escaping the internalized shame that was the legacy of this late Victorian childhood. Like Beatrice Wood, Loy's efforts to fashion herself into a liberated New Woman were dogged by the nagging voice of a domineering, old-fashioned mother, always at the back of her mind.

Futurist Superwoman

As Loy became part of New York's avant-garde scene (first from a distance, then as an active member of the Arensberg circle), her credentials as an (almost) Futurist added an extra layer to the intrigue and mystery that surrounded her. In the press, 'Futurism' had become a catch-all term for any art that was modern, experimental and shocking. Like 'Cubism', it entered the public imagination after the Armory Show, evoking ideas of wild artists in bizarre clothes creating nonsensical artworks. In fact, there were few examples of actual Futurist art at the Armory Show because most members of the group refused to exhibit their work there. This meant that, for the American avant-garde, real Futurism remained a largely strange and fascinating movement that they had little direct contact with. By combining Futurism with feminist sexual politics in her experimental free verse, Loy offered an utterly unique perspective on a new aspect of modern avant-garde culture.

For Loy, Futurism occupied a complex place in her development as an artist and as a modern woman. The mental and sexual liberation she sought after breaking from Haweis was both enabled and complicated by her encounter with Futurism. Her enthusiasm for Futurism's radical energy was bound up with the intimate relationships she engaged in with its two rival leaders, Filippo Tommaso Marinetti and Giovanni Papini. The movement itself was ultra-masculine and male-dominated: the Futurists revered the machine, speed and technology as agents of a man-made modernity, one that would triumph over the natural world and decadent, old-fashioned values (both of which were identified as feminine). When she first became acquainted with Marinetti, Futurism was a revelation for Loy. Her poem 'Aphorisms on Futurism' expresses her enthusiasm for the boundless sense of regeneration, possibility and vitality that the movement offered. Futurism's dynamic forms shape the very words on the page, with Loy using bold block typography and expressive punctuation to grab the attention of her reader. Perhaps in some ways this was also a personal manifesto, a mantra to remind Loy of what she could achieve if she shook off her malaise and her links to those who were stuck creating conservative, stale art – such as her husband. 'Aphorisms on Futurism' also marked a particular personal success: it was Loy's first published piece of writing, appearing in the January 1914 issue of Alfred Stieglitz's prestigious *Camera Work* journal.

As much as the movement's commitment to new forms attracted Loy, she soon began to question its gender politics. Her ill-fated affairs with Marinetti and Papini contributed to Loy's sense of disenchantment with the limited possibilities Futurism offered her. Both men viewed Loy as an exceptional woman, distinguished by her intelligence, wit and artistic capabilities (and, no doubt, her beauty). Their opinion of the female sex in general was much lower. Women did not feature in the great nationalist regeneration of Italy that Futurism envisioned, other than to reproduce. The Futurist 'superman' would preside over a total break with outdated institutions and stultifying ways of living, but women were too maternal, too earthy, too animalistic to play active roles in this dynamic future. Marinetti wrote several misogynistic, fascist tracts that set out his point of view, such as 'Against Feminine Luxury' (1920), a eugenicist call for masculine Italian men and fertile women to procreate and ward off 'feminine luxury' and 'prostitution'.[5] The Futurists believed that mechanized warfare was necessary to violently and decisively sweep away the past and usher in a new, electric future. Their love of war and ambitions for Italy's violent cultural supremacy foreshadowed the rise of fascism, nationalism and eugenics policies through the 1920s and '30s. Unsurprisingly, Marinetti later became a fervent supporter of Benito Mussolini's 'revolutionary nationalism' and took Futurism into a second, explicitly fascist stage in the decades following the First World War.

For Loy, whose experiences at Mabel Dodge's salon had led her to think critically about gender politics and the societal roles – and rules – that imprisoned women, this was not a compelling vision. In February 1914, she confessed her doubts about the movement in a letter to Dodge, declaring that she was 'in the throes of conversion to Futurism – but I shall never convince myself – There is no hope in any system that "combat le mal avec le mal" ["fights evil with evil"] . . . and that is really Marinetti's philosophy.'[6] Later that year, after her affairs with Marinetti and Papini had ended in frustration and disappointment, she would channel the energy and linguistic innovations she had learned from the Futurists into a spirited riposte. Her 'Feminist Manifesto' (unpublished in Loy's lifetime) is a radical call to arms that challenges patriarchal views of women and urges women to take control of their own futures by rejecting dependence on men.

From a contemporary perspective, parts of the manifesto are strikingly modern but some elements are troubling. Lines referencing 'race-responsibility' key into racist eugenicist ideas that circulated in Futurist theory. The jarring moments that disrupt Loy's 'Feminist Manifesto' serve as reminders that many early feminist texts and avant-garde movements were couched in systems of white supremacy and racist belief systems. Perhaps Loy's own faith in the Futurists' enthusiasm for eugenics was shaky, or perhaps she suffered a general loss of confidence at the boldness of her own manifesto statements; either way, Loy wrote another letter to Dodge dismissing her manifesto as a 'tirade' that contained unoriginal ideas. She never sent this work to *Camera Work*, *Rogue* or any other New York magazines, and it remained unpublished until after her death.

After *Camera Work* published Loy's 'Aphorisms on Futurism' in January 1914, Van Vechten was successful in placing her Futurist-inspired works in several other New York-based little magazines. As the Armory Show had highlighted, New York's modern-art scene was not yet close to competing with European capitals of modernism, which still held unrivalled authority. Loy's presence was therefore sought after by magazines eager to prove their cultural legitimacy and authenticity. *Rogue*, in particular, saw in Loy a kindred spirit who embodied its progressive, irreverent ethos: her wit, irreverent attitude and radical voice, mixed with her ability to speak about sexuality, childbirth and modern love, spoke to the magazine's ideals. Her poetry conjured up striking visions of modernity – department stores, night clubs, bustling city streets – and explored what life was like for women in the modern world, in a similar style to *Rogue*. With a total of eight appearances (including two plays and a sketch), she was its most regular contributor and one of the few contributors based outside of the United States. Loy scholar Suzanne Churchill notes the fact that *Rogue* included 'the date and place of composition – [for example] "February 28; 1915, Firenze",' underneath her poems, which 'highlights Loy's position as a representative and translator of the European avant-garde'.[7] In other words, Loy provided a degree of authenticity that was essential while New York's fledgling arts scene was still in the shadow of European modernism. Loy's own feelings about *Rogue* were mixed. She wrote of her dislike of the magazine's name to Van Vechten, and suggested that, in her opinion, the 'drawings are poor'. However, the ever-fashionable Loy found a kindred spirit in Dame Rogue (alias of Louise Norton), and enthused about her 'Philosophic Fashions' articles in the letters to Van Vechten: the 'fashion articles [are] devine [*sic*]'.[8]

Rogue's editors, Allen and Louise Norton, found the magazine's characteristic sharp wit echoed in Loy's satirical works, which often lampooned the self-importance of her avant-garde peers. *Collision* and *Cittabàpini*, two plays that appear in the August 1915 issue of *Rogue*, take aim at one of Loy's favourite targets, the Futurist Superman. In each, a male Futurist character attempts to dominate and control his environment (variously the natural world and a mechanized city) but is instead reduced to an insignificant dot – he is swallowed up by the city and burnt by the sun. These pieces positioned Loy as an arbiter of European avant-garde art, particularly Futurism, which her intrigued American audience had heard about but never encountered. Loy's association with *Rogue* was important in raising her profile among the New York avant-garde, but it was her appearance in another Arensberg-backed modernist magazine that really put her on the radar: *Others*, a little magazine dedicated to free-verse poetry that was more serious and literary than *Rogue*.

In the pages of *Others*, Loy joined a coterie of experimental modern poets who were pushing the boundaries of poetry, including Ezra Pound, Marianne Moore and William Carlos Williams; with a high proportion of women contributors, *Others* quickly established a reputation for defying convention and challenging traditional views on gender, sexuality and society. Churchill suggests that the journal swiftly acquired 'a public image as a "queer" space that defied both poetic and sexual propriety'; in other words, *Others* was a literary version of Greenwich Village, its pages encompassing versions of the queer radical politics and experimentation that flourished in the Village.[9] A large part of the public perception of *Others* rested on Loy's 'Love Songs', a short poem sequence that would form part of the larger piece 'Songs to Joannes'. Kreymborg's bold editorial decision to include this poem in the magazine's first issue immediately signalled the uncompromisingly avant-garde intent of *Others*.

Loy's 'Love Songs' is a shockingly irreverent satire on the traditional fairy-tale love story. In this poem, Loy utterly breaks from tradition by alluding to the fleshy, messy reality of sexual relationships. By the standards of early twentieth-century society, Loy's frank, unromantic approach to sex was outrageous. Even the poet Amy Lowell, a proponent of modern free verse, was disgusted: she branded 'Love Songs' obscene and declared that she would refuse to appear in the same journal as Loy. Kreymborg, however, was delighted by the publicity. In April 1917, he dedicated a whole issue of *Others* to the full sequence of 'Love Songs', which was, by then, retitled 'Songs to Joannes' in a thinly veiled nod to the man who inspired the poem: Giovanni Papini.

In its expanded version, 'Songs to Joannes' tells the distinctly unromantic, uncourtly version of Loy's love affair with Papini, through a kaleidoscope of fragmentary scenes. Undaunted by the reaction to 'Love Songs', Loy added more provocative, unsentimental visions of sexuality and love. There are allusions to a possible abortion or miscarriage (that Loy may have experienced during her relationships with Papini or Marinetti), as well as to other taboo topics such as the female orgasm and bodily fluids. The lover Joannes's ego impedes any real, productive connection between the couple, but Loy's poem conjures up an enchanted, queer space where binaries between male and female, nature and technology and the human and natural world can be broken down – if stereotypes of masculinity and femininity are first overcome. With its powerful, groundbreaking exploration of intimacy from a female perspective and its unsentimental attitude to sex, 'Songs to Joannes' expresses many of the ideas that were swirling around the Arensberg salon and Greenwich Village in the 1910s.

Reflecting on the backlash against the first appearance of 'Love Songs' in the January 1915 issue of *Others*, Kreymborg remarked that Loy's 'detractors . . . derided her elimination of punctuation marks and the audacious spacing of her lines'.[10] Yet, if we read on, it becomes clear that the main problem was not the experimental free-verse style of the poem: 'had a man written these poems,' Kreymborg suggests, 'the town might have viewed them with comparative comfort. But a woman wrote them, a woman who dressed like a lady and painted charming lampshades.' In his opinion, the question that perplexed the disgusted public was simple: 'if Loy could dress like a lady, why couldn't she write like one?' The reaction to 'Love Songs' demonstrates just how much resistance women artists and writers faced in their efforts to freely express their desires and the contradictory, complex realities of their inner lives, even within artistic circles. Through her radical feminist poetry, defiance of traditional gender roles and striking personal style, Loy blazed a trail for the modern woman and set the tone for New York's playfully subversive avant-garde scene.

'Her clothes suggest the smartest shops,
but her poems would have puzzled Grandma'

By the time Loy headed for New York, her name carried serious weight in avant-garde circles and intrigue surrounded her. As soon as she arrived, Loy contacted her friend and fellow artist Frances Simpson Stevens, whom she had met through Mabel Dodge in Florence. Very little of Stevens's work survives today (and much of her life is a mystery), but in the 1910s she was a noted avant-garde painter who brought Futurist styles to New York; the Arensbergs purchased her painting *Dynamic Velocity of Interborough Rapid Transit Power Station* in 1915 and it remained a part of the collection that was transferred to the Philadelphia Museum of Art in 1950. Stevens introduced Loy into the Arensberg salon, where she was welcomed as a perfect addition to their eccentric, intellectual, cosmopolitan circle. Indeed, as a woman with first-hand knowledge of the latest innovations in European avant-garde art, who spoke four languages and dressed in self-designed, strikingly modern dresses and hats, she quickly became one of the salon's star members.

The attention of the New York press was also piqued by her arrival. In February 1917, a reporter for the *New York Evening Sun* set out to find the ultimate modern woman, a woman who summed up the new sexually liberated, artistic, fashionable atmosphere that was sweeping the city. With a little direction, the reporter's search ended with Loy, even though she had only been in the city for four months. They ran an article about Loy that declared her 'clothes suggest the smartest shops but her poems would have puzzled grandma'; her other modern attributes were listed as the ability to write free-verse poetry, design lampshades and magazine covers and to 'tell [you] why futurism is and where it came from and who'.[11] In little time, Loy joined Clara Tice as one of the New York media's favourite fashionably shocking women artists.

Members of New York's avant-garde were equally drawn to Loy's wit, style and mystic intellectualism. Her experiences of moving through Europe's artistic circles gave her a certain prestige – and cultural currency – that members of the Arensberg salon and Greenwich Village artists were impressed by. Poet and editor Alfred Kreymborg evokes a sense of the intrigue that Loy's arrival provoked:

During the war, a curious woman, exotic and beautiful, came to New York from foreign shores: the English Jewess, Mina Loy. Visiting the shrines of modern art and literature in Paris and Florence, and being accepted as a coeval in the maddest circles, Miss Loy, who is an artist as well as a poet, imbibed the precepts of Apollinaire and Marinnetti [*sic*] and became a Futurist with all the earnestness and irony of a woman possessed and obsessed with the sum of human experience and disillusion.[12]

Djuna Barnes, who would become a close friend of Loy's over the next few decades, also singled Loy out as a particularly notable new addition to the New York avant-garde scene. At that time, Barnes was working as a journalist, writing regular satirical features about life in Greenwich Village for the *New York Evening Sun*. In 'Becoming Intimate with the Bohemians', Barnes invites her reader into an opulently decorated and self-consciously artistic apartment, where 'a copy of *Rogue* on a low table open at Mina Loy's poems' serves as a marker of the occupant's progressive taste, along with Japanese prints, a box of cigarettes, candles and tapestries.[13] Barnes suggests that Loy had become a name to drop among the cultural elite, a way of showing off one's good taste and progressive attitude. The fact that Barnes chose to reference Loy's name – rather than other *Rogue* contributors, such as Clara Tice, Gertrude Stein or Wallace Stevens – shows just how notorious she was in New York at this time.

After arriving in the city, Loy threw herself into its social whirlwind of parties, costume balls and plays. She contributed to the *Blind Man* and was one of the ringleaders on the evening of the Blind Man's Ball, leading the group, including Beatrice Wood and Marcel Duchamp, to extend the festivities at the Arensbergs' apartment (and then to crash out on Duchamp's bed together). Loy even acted in *Lima Beans*, a short play written by Kreymborg and produced by the Provincetown Players. She was much admired during this time. William Carlos Williams recalled poet Marianne Moore staring in awed envy, 'with her mouth open', at Loy's leopard-skin coat.[14] Moore confirms her fascination with Loy's striking fashionable style in a 1921 letter to fellow avant-garde poet H.D., describing a meeting with Loy in which she wore 'gold slippers, a green taffeta dress, a black Florentine mosaic brooch, long gold earrings and some beautiful English rings. We discussed [theatre practitioner and lover of Isadora Duncan] Gordon Craig, whom she knew, George Moore, and the hollowness of fashionable life.'[15] Moore created an ambiguous portrait of Loy's beauty, style and cerebral wit in 'Those Various Scalpels' (1917), a poem that archly suggests that Loy's appearance and her poetry share the same cold, sharp surface.

The year Loy spent in New York between 1916 and 1917 seemed like a golden time for her. When the publisher James Laughlin asked her for a biography to accompany a reprint of some of her poetry in 1950, her brief response included the line 'Only jolly time I ever spent/ Was as the gu[crossed out] frequent guest of Mr and Mrs Walter[crossed out] arensberg ———'.[16] Her break with the Arensberg circle came in the hulking form of Dada poet, boxer and provocateur Arthur Cravan. Cravan landed in New York in 1916, via France and Spain. After the outbreak of war in Europe, he left Paris to dodge the military draft and, on his travels, left a trail of chaos in his wake. By the time he arrived in New York, he was infamous for outrageously insulting most of the European artists who exhibited at the 1914 Société des Artistes Indépendants show in Paris, being defeated in a bizarre boxing match against Jack Johnson in Barcelona and sparking a rumour that his uncle Oscar Wilde was still alive. His anarchic behaviour continued in the United States, much to the fascination, disgust and, perhaps, begrudging admiration of the Arensberg circle. Penniless and without a fixed address of his own, Cravan spent most of his time in New York lounging at the Arensbergs in a stupor, chatting up women who might give him a bed for the night or sleeping rough.

During their initial meetings, Loy was distinctly underwhelmed by Cravan. Yet gradually she found herself irresistibly attracted to the man she would name 'Colossus' in the mythologized story of her life. It is hard to understand what exactly Loy saw in this boisterous and brutish contrarian, though perhaps his admiration for her intellect offered a sense of security after the demoralizing years she had spent with Stephen Haweis. Many members of the Arensberg circle expressed their surprise and confusion at this unlikely pair, even from a distance of several decades. In a 1977 interview with Loy's biographer, Juliette Gleizes remained puzzled over 'why a woman as refined as Mina Loy [married] a brute like Cravan'; similarly, Louise Norton suggested, years later, that the Arensberg circle was 'disappointed' by Loy's marriage to Cravan, and, when asked about Loy and Cravan in a 1957 interview, Duchamp recalled, 'I didn't like [Cravan] very much, nor him me.'[17] Nevertheless, Cravan had a magnetic effect on Loy, an effect that changed the course of her life.

The United States' entry into the war in April 1917 put an end to Loy and Cravan's time together in New York. The country erupted in a patriotic fervour and scrutiny was cast on anyone suspected of draft dodging. This sparked an exodus of many of New York's avant-garde artists and writers, some returning to Europe, others heading to different states or going to South America; all were keen to escape the atmosphere of fear, jingoism and censorship that had settled over spaces where radical, socialist and pacifist values flourished, like Greenwich Village. Groups of inspectors also targeted areas popular with the city's artist communities, keen to root out draft dodgers. This was bad news for Cravan, who was forced to resume his haphazard travels, heading first for Canada and then changing course to Mexico. Once settled there, he began bombarding Loy with declarations of undying love and pleas for her to join him as soon as possible. His letters suggest that their time in New York had not been quite as idyllic as Loy would later recall: in one, he begs, 'why weren't you more trusting? ... If you had said just once "I love you" you would have seen how tender I can be', assures Loy he will take care of her, and threatens suicide.[18] Cravan's desperate, emotionally manipulative tone suggests that Loy had reservations about starting a new life with this unpredictable character. However, perhaps seeking some hope in troubled and uncertain times, Loy allayed her fears. In January 1918, she left New York behind and set out on the long journey to Mexico City to reunite with him.

What happened next became the stuff of legend. Loy married Cravan in Mexico, but there was little honeymoon enchantment. Still in the grip of a decade-long revolution, Mexico was politically volatile and poverty-stricken. Lacking work, money and food, Loy and Cravan neared starvation but were unable to leave the country due to an issue with Cravan's papers. To make matters worse, Loy soon found that she was pregnant. The couple decided to take separate routes out of the country, with Loy taking a passenger ship to Buenos Aires and Cravan (still without the correct passport document) sailing to Chile. After setting off in a small, battered boat Cravan vanished without trace.

Transatlantic Househunting

Years of turmoil followed Cravan's disappearance, during which a grief-stricken Loy returned to visit her family in England and give birth to her baby. We can only speculate as to how the prim, Victorian Julia greeted her wayward daughter – now divorced, penniless and pregnant with the child of a poet–boxer who had mysteriously vanished. Unsurprisingly Loy didn't stay long after the birth of her baby, a daughter she named Jemima Fabienne Cravan Lloyd, in tribute to Cravan. Soon, she returned to Florence to reunite with her two older children after three years abroad. Again, there are no records of Loy's return, but it must have been bewildering for both parties: Loy greeting a daughter and a son who bore little resemblance to the children she left three years earlier, and Joella and Giles struggling to recognize this half-stranger who was engulfed in grief for a man they had never met, with a new baby sibling in tow.[19] In Florence, Loy's behaviour became increasingly erratic – tormented by a conviction that Cravan could still be alive, perhaps in prison, she decided to embark on yet another journey, back to New York.

Post-war New York at the turn of a new decade was changed from the wild and carefree days Loy had experienced there in the mid-1910s. The United States itself was emboldened by its victory, but the years following the end of the First World War were marked by racism, xenophobia and civil unrest: the Red Summer of 1919 saw a surge in white supremacist terrorism directed at African American communities across the United States, as well as hostility towards German and Italian Americans, and a fear of socialism and communism fuelled by the Russian Revolution. Prohibition (which began in January 1920) also signalled a turn to conservatism and increased efforts to police the lives of working-class African American and immigrant communities. The artistic circles that Loy mixed in were largely privileged enough to avoid the effects of this shift. Even so, the ideals of openness, cosmopolitanism and radical freethinking that flourished in the Arensberg salon could no longer be taken for granted.

Although Loy had faced an emotionally draining few years, her work continued to have an impact on the New York avant-garde, and her name still carried currency in its experimental magazines. In 1917, publishers Jane Heap and Margaret Anderson moved their progressive modernist magazine the *Little Review* to New York. It became a supportive venue for Loy's work and printed enthusiastic praise for her work by poet Ezra Pound. Heap and Anderson published several of Loy's poems, including sections of the semi-autobiographical 'Anglo-Mongrels and the Rose', and 'Lion's Jaws'. The latter was printed alongside a dramatic portrait of Loy by Man Ray in which she meets the viewer's gaze with a steely side-eye glare. She looks stylish and self-possessed, signalling that she was still a chic, confident modern woman whose 'clothes suggest the smartest shops but poems would puzzle grandma'. *Lunar Baedecker*, her first published collection, was released by the Paris-based Contact Publishing Company in 1923.

In the early 1920s, Loy continued to develop a persona in the American press that traversed the boundaries between high art and feminized design, and modernism and the commercial. In 1921 she appeared in several newspapers in an article entitled 'Would You Be "Different"? Madame Loy Shows How'.[20] Assuming the reader's familiarity with Loy, the article informs them that 'Madame Mina Loy is keeping busy these days creating for several houses here frocks and hats that should satisfy the most ambitious of those who seek to be different.' In 1925, Loy also wrote an article for American fashion magazine *Charm* that aimed to demystify modern poetry from the perspective of a modern(ist) woman. Loy's essay is fascinating in the way it uses modernist poetry to navigate larger issues of commerce and culture. Deploying simple yet effective images, Loy suggests that the 'new rhythm' in poetry is in sync with everyday modern life by drawing parallels between free verse, jazz and sport (she might also have added Clara Tice's joyful sketches).

The reality of Loy's life in the 1920s was a little different. She urgently needed to resolve the question of providing for her children (who were

Mina Loy

still living with their governess in Florence) but lacked the means to do so. Bringing them to New York seemed impossible; she hatched a scheme to move to Paris and start a restaurant but lacked the capital to start up such an enterprise. In the letters she wrote in attempts to raise funds (first to Arthur Cravan's mother, Nellie Grandjean, and then to her old friend Mabel Dodge), her desperation is clear. Both women ignored her. In spite of the uncertainty, it was clear that Loy had to return to her children – along with Joella's pleas for her to return came news that Stephen Haweis had taken their son Giles away and threatened to sell the Florence house. As well as these pressing family concerns, visions of a new life in Paris among its newly swelled expatriate artistic community proved tempting. Despite the grief and complex personal problems that she was grappling with, Loy was not ready to give up pursuing her creative vision. Soon, she set off on yet another transatlantic journey; this time, she would not return to New York until Europe was on the brink of a second devastating world war.

After brief periods in Florence and Berlin, Loy made it to Paris. Once again, she was part of dazzling circle of avant-garde artists and writers. A 1923 photograph captures her in a typically chic fur coat and a smart hat, smiling among a jovial group of prominent cultural figures: Man Ray, Tristan Tzara and Jean Cocteau crouch beside her, flanked by Jane Heap and Margaret Anderson, Kiki de Montparnasse, Ezra Pound and several others. Sylvia Beach describes Loy and her two daughters as the 'three raving beauties' of 'the Crowd' that hung about Shakespeare and Company. Beach's comments reference Loy's multitalented creativity, but also acknowledge the difficulties she faced in balancing earning money with devoting time to her art: 'when you went to Mina's apartment you threaded your way past lamp shades that were everywhere: she made them to support her children. She made all her own clothes . . . she wrote poetry whenever she had the time.'[21]

In Paris, Loy finally found a financial backer for her business idea (now a lampshade shop rather than a restaurant) in the form of the glamorous heiress and arts patron Peggy Guggenheim. The shop, however, proved to be a mixed blessing: on the one hand, Loy's enchanting lampshades drew attention from arts and design magazines and had a degree of commercial success; on the other, the work distracted her from writing and painting, and she was also in competition with the big department stores, which began selling cheaper copies of her work. Guggenheim also proved to be a mercurial patron, prone to shifting her interests (and investment) elsewhere. After the shop folded in 1930, Loy spent a few years liaising with artists in Paris on behalf of Levy, who by then had married Joella and set up a New York gallery to show-case Surrealism in the United States. Her efforts were crucial in setting up links between Levy's gallery and European Surrealist artists, includ-ing Salvador Dalí and Giorgio de Chirico. Her time among the Surrealists also resulted in one of Loy's most intriguing written works, the novel *Insel*, which was unpublished in her lifetime, despite Loy's efforts to interest James Laughlin's New Direction Press in releasing it (but Laughlin did publish a collection of her poems under the title *Lunar Baedeker and Time-Tables* in 1958). By 1938, the threat of war forced Loy to join the masses of people fleeing Europe for the United States.

Refusées

The woman who arrived in New York in 1938 was more jaded and dispirited than the one who had stepped off the boat from Italy more than twenty years earlier. Aged 56, Loy was self-conscious about her appearance, impoverished and less confident in her creative vision. Her daughters were grown up, and often despaired over (what they per-ceived as) Loy's sometimes maudlin, stubborn and difficult attitude. To their alarm, Loy largely shunned the old crowd of artists and writers whom she had once known. Instead, by 1955 she had moved into a boarding house on the down-at-heel Lower East Side. She became the grand dame of an eclectic, almost bohemian household in a house that was part *Alice in Wonderland*, part 'jungle', where one found anything from 'frantic cats' to fish heads on the floor, 'bums on the stairs' and an eclectic, ever-changing cast of residents.[22] This description is provided in a letter to Loy's daughter Fabienne from her friend Irene Klempner, whose own mother 'Klemp' lived with Mina. Irene describes how the pair would 'hold court like the red queen and the white queen' in the kitchen, where 'artistic ideas and examples [were] the stuffy air you breathe[d]'.[23] Despite, or perhaps because of, the chaos, Loy felt so at home in this eccentric set-up that she chose to move with the household when they relocated to a larger property.

To the greater horror of her daughters, Loy made friends with the local homeless population, mostly men who had lost their jobs and struggled with alcoholism. Loy empathized and identified with this downtrodden Bowery community, feeling herself to be similarly adrift on the margins of society. These relationships fuelled a startling new burst of creativity, marking Loy's second New York art phase. She wrote a sequence of poems, named 'Compensations of Poverty', in response to her experiences of life around the Bowery. Alongside poetry, she embarked on a series of assemblage artworks that acted as companion pieces to the 'Compensations of Poverty' series. Her assemblages were made using the detritus of New York's streets. In their recollections of Loy, her boarding house 'family' recall seeing her return from regular walks around the neighbourhood carrying bundles of rags and other rubbish that she picked up on the city streets. There, she would set about turning her piles of junk into works of art, constructing street scenes featuring the drunk and dejected bums who littered the Bowery. Burke describes how Loy's housemates would loiter outside in the hope she would ask them in because, they felt, 'things were happening' in there.[24] Loy would shrug off her creative experiments as something she did to pass the time.

Loy's housemates were correct. The assemblage pieces that she created in her cluttered room were serious artworks that used ephemeral materials and litter to comment on the city's cycle of consumption, waste and poverty. The dedication and effort she poured into creating them suggest that this was a project she cared about; they were carefully crafted, in dialogue with a series of poems that both complement and expand upon the assemblages. When Loy's daughters finally lost patience and removed their mother to Aspen (where they both had settled) in 1953, her friends in New York preserved the pieces and contacted various galleries and dealers in an attempt to get them shown.[25] Loy's old admirer Duchamp shared her enthusiasm for this late body of work. It was characteristic of Duchamp to support women artist friends, whose work was largely forgotten in the post-war years. In 1958, he collaborated with gallery director David Mann to salvage the assemblages that had been left behind in Loy's apartment and put them on display.

The result was a solo show – 'Refusées' – held the following year at New York's Bodley Gallery, where a young Andy Warhol had one of his earliest shows. The title (French for 'rejected', presumably chosen by Duchamp, echoing the nineteenth-century French Salon des Refusés), makes a link between the refuse that the work is made from and a protest: the physicality of the pieces, and the people they depict, resists society's scorn. Loy's work confronts the viewer with objects and bodies that have been discarded, returning them to our gaze. Being an almost-homograph of refugee, 'Refusées' also hints at the mass displacement that occurred as a result of the Second World War, which of course included Loy herself and many other members of Paris's art community. The exhibition brought together some of this old crowd, including some former Greenwich Villagers. Djuna Barnes, by then a self-proclaimed recluse, ventured out to join Berenice Abbott, who photographed some of the assemblages. Barnes's and Loy's former patron Peggy Guggenheim also attended and bought an assemblage work entitled *Househunting*, which would later be passed on to Loy's biographer Carolyn Burke (one of the rare assemblage pieces to survive).

Critics were largely disinterested or bemused by the show, but it led to the last moment of artistic recognition that Loy would live to see: the artist, collector, patron and entrepreneur William Copley purchased *Communal Cot* while at the exhibition and, later in the year, Loy was awarded the Copley Foundation Award for Outstanding Achievement in Art. As a Copley Foundation board member, Duchamp, no doubt, had a hand in this. Yet this was more than a favour from an old friend; Duchamp recognized the worth of Loy's assemblages and the significance they held both for her aesthetic project and for the wider avant-garde movement. There are, indeed, intriguing crossovers between her technique and that of young post-war Neo-Dada artists like Robert Rauschenberg and Claes Oldenburg, who also drew inspiration and the physical material of their art from the litter-strewn streets of the Lower East Side. Loy continued to make assemblages in Aspen, but her work was never again exhibited in her lifetime. The Bodley Gallery show was a poignant send-off, in the city where the cosmopolitan Loy found all-too-fleeting moments of success and happiness.

Loy was confined to the footnotes of modernism as it developed through the mid-century, but her biographer Carolyn Burke and her editor and executor Roger Conover led a timely revival of interest in her work in the late 1980s and '90s. In his introduction to *The Lost Lunar Baedeker*, Conover describes an episode in 1920s Paris when rumours that 'Mina Loy' was a 'hoax of critics' or a myth persona circulated among its artistic circles: she was too provocative, too much the quintessential modern artistic woman to be true. To dispel this chatter, Loy made a dramatic entrance to the salon of Natalie Barney, where she declared, 'I assure you I am indeed a live being. But it is necessary to stay very unknown . . . to maintain my incognito the hazard I chose was – poet.'[26]

In reality, Loy's life was a difficult balancing act between different personas and roles – some that were chosen, and some that were forced on her by circumstance. Her restless intellect expressed itself through a range of creative mediums and her determination to monetize her artistic talent to support her family pulled her in several directions. Loy's reputation as the 'ultimate modern woman' was an illusion that she managed to briefly hold together in the late 1910s, but it slowly crumbled throughout the following decades under the demands of domestic duties and financial need. Loy moved to New York in 1916 seeking a new, modern life, but she ended up running into the same old problems that disrupted (and continue to disrupt) many women artists and writers: namely, the impossibilities of successfully making art, earning a living and raising children. In 1918, the same year that Loy struggled to balance her career, her affair with Cravan, and the needs of the children she'd left behind in Florence, Crystal Eastman wrote that

> women who are creative, or who have administrative gifts, or business ability, and who are ambitious to achieve and fulfil themselves . . . must [if they have children] make up their minds to be a sort of superman [and have] . . . a more determined ambition than men of equal gifts.[27]

In this way, Loy succeeded at being more of a superhuman than her Futurist lovers Marinetti or Papini dreamt of, but it still wasn't quite enough.

Despite these difficulties, Loy's work conceptualized a mode of modernism that was, by turns, sensuous and prickly, cerebral and mystical, urbane and otherworldly. Loy's free-verse poetry broke the rules of form and taste, channelling a voice that was vital and formative for the 1910s New York avant-garde; it was the language of the modern woman, who cast off old sentiments and formal niceties along with her corset. With her dress designs, paintings and lampshades and written manifestos, she extended her vision into everyday life: each facet of her creative practice represented her belief that art could bring about a democratic renewal of the world and that the artist is a prophet, gifted (and burdened) with the power to guide society via their creative visions. In her later life, Loy embodied the image of the modernist 'prophet crying in the wilderness' that she imagined in a 1929 essay on Gertrude Stein, but in recent decades, Loy has slowly re-emerged, in another act of reinvention. The complexities and conflicts of her creative vision and her restless search for a visionary, revolutionary form that could reimagine ways of being in the world still have much to offer today.[28]

7

STETTHEIMER SALON:
Chateau Stettheimer and the Cellophane Sisters

[Florine] and her two sisters, Miss Carrie and Miss
Ettie, presided over a salon that had considerable
to do with shaping the intellectual and artistic impulses
of the period . . . at the dinners and receptions which
followed in quick succession in their house. . . hardy
ideas were put into words which echoed sooner
or later in other parts of the city.[1]

If the Arensbergs' salon was the riotous home of New York's irreverent Dada scene, the Stettheimer salon was an opulent dream world. Presided over by three creative, wealthy and eccentric sisters – Carrie, Florine and Ettie – it was more exclusive than the Arensbergs' but played just as pivotal a role in the city's avant-garde culture during the 1910s and '20s. The salon began to take shape in 1914, when the sisters and their mother, Rosetta, returned from decades spent travelling around Europe. They took up residence in a townhouse at 102 West 76th Street in the exclusive Upper West Side and set about decorating the home in their favoured decadent rococo style. In 1926, they moved to a duplex apartment in the suitably grand and eccentric Alwyn Court. Opened in 1909, Alwyn Court aimed to attract wealthy families looking for the opulence of a grand house with less upkeep. With its ornate terracotta facade decorated with crowned salamanders and ornamental pilasters, the building stood out like a French Renaissance mirage in the middle of Manhattan. It was, in other words, the perfect fit for the equally eccentric and idiosyncratic Stettheimers and was immediately christened 'Chateau Stettheimer' by their good friend Carl Van Vechten.

Stepping through Alwyn Court's gothic entrance and up to the apartment was like stepping out of the city and into a dazzling world of fantasy. The Stettheimer aesthetic was characterized by camp feminine excess: shimmering cellophane curtains, lace doilies, beaded crystal lampshades and elaborate *trompe l'oeil* furniture were everywhere, and floral arrangements covered every room. It was an eccentric and unique space that transported guests into the Stettheimers' private fantasy. Adorning the walls in elaborate gilt frames, Florine's paintings amplified the effect, merging fantasy and illusion. Florine also kept a studio

Arnold Genthe, *Florine Stettheimer's Studio*, 1936.

in the Beaux-Arts Building in Midtown Manhattan, where she would spend nights away from the family to focus on work, and sometimes host parties to unveil new paintings. This bijou apartment was as opulent as the main Stettheimer residence, with shimmering cellophane curtains, a bedroom swathed in lace, and a luxurious red velvet carpet: Henry McBride, a close friend of the sisters, noted that its decoration was 'very closely related, in appearance, to the work that was done in it'.[2] Florine transferred some of her designs from the canvas onto furniture and wall panels, turning the Stettheimer apartment and her studio into immersive works of art.

The combination of cellophane and lace provides a perfect visual metaphor for the Stettheimers. The delicacy and old-fashioned femininity of lace signalled the eccentricity of their exclusive matriarchal sphere. By contrast, cellophane was a modern, glamorous material. The historian Judith Brown describes how it was used in *Vogue* shoots and even made an appearance in the lyrics of Cole Porter's 'You're the Top' (featuring a whimsical list of modern pleasures, the song lyrics read remarkably like one of Florine's poems); it 'offered the modern imagination new ways of seeing the mundane world' and it 'offered modernists a material with all the plasticity and possibility of language'.[3] Brown quotes a reviewer of *Four Saints in Three Acts* who praised the visual language of Stettheimer's cellophane backdrop, which, combined with the other elements of the libretto, signified 'intelligibility without meaning', like James Joyce's *Ulysses*, T. S. Eliot's *The Waste Land*, Surrealism or Dada art. Their impact in a domestic dwelling was heightened: the lace drapes and cellophane curtains combine to transform the Stettheimer apartment and Florine's studio into spaces of subversive femininity.

Modernist Sisters among the European Avant-Garde

The trio of sisters and their mother became a tight-knit group after their father abandoned the family and emigrated to Australia. Their two elder siblings, Stella and Walter, each married and made separate lives for themselves. Carrie, Florine and Ettie continued living together as an entwined, matriarchal household until their mother's death in 1935. We cannot be sure exactly why each sister decided to remain single and live in this atypical family unit; some critics suggest that Rosetta was demanding and forbade her younger children from deserting her, as their father had done. There are clear signals, particularly in Florine's and Ettie's work, that the traditional path of marriage and motherhood held little appeal. Florine succinctly expressed the predicament in which many women who left their family home for a new married life found themselves, in one of her wry short poems: 'Sweet little Miss Mouse/ Wanted her own house/ So she married Mr Mole/ And only got a hole.'[4] In Ettie's semi-autobiographical novel *Love Days* (published in 1923), her protagonist Susanna feels that 'whenever her potential motherhood, marriage, death were touched on in conversation . . . [it was] as though some one else were being referred to, and the chief emotion produced in her was one of estrangement from the speaker who so unpleasantly identified her with that other person.'[5] Florine and Ettie each allude to a sense of personal freedom that was incompatible with marriage. The fact that Ettie associated marriage and motherhood with death shows just what an extreme end to all possibilities she found those states to be.

The sisters were close, but there was often friction in their relationships; in a 1933 letter to Alfred Stieglitz, Ettie complained, 'we differ so often & so much on important & general matters that I'm sure they resent this grouping of ourselves as much as I do.'[6] Barbara Bloemink, Florine's biographer, refers to frequent quarrels and fallings out, particularly between the more independent-natured Florine and the highly strung Ettie. Florine's longing for greater freedom from family duties and uninterrupted time to devote to her art caused consternation among the rest of the group. Her decision to live separately from Carrie and Ettie following Rosetta's death in 1935 came as a shock; for Florine, it was a chance to finally focus on her art, away from all distraction. Ettie's decision to destroy large parts of Florine's diary after her death got rid of many details about her intimate relationships, quarrels and opinions, leaving us with only a limited insight into her inner life. Nevertheless, Florine's paintings and poetry offer evocative insights into the sisters' lives, their parties and Florine's own perspective on her beloved city as a modern woman and a modern artist.

The Stettheimers' matriarchal sisterhood gave them a supportive family environment outside of the traditional heteronormative family set-up with a husband/father at its head. The disappearance of the Stettheimer patriarch granted Rosetta and her daughters autonomy over their lives, which was, of course, enhanced by their vast family wealth. Modern feminist thinking further emboldened them: from a young age, Florine and Ettie were supporters of the suffrage movement (Florine's biographer Barbara Bloemink suggests that they likely attended the First International Feminist Congress in Paris in 1896) and identified with emerging arguments for women's independence and enfranchisement. Like many young women of the time (particularly those with the means to support themselves independently), the Stettheimers turned to the arts for fresh opportunities to create new identities and networks away from the traditional paths of marriage and motherhood. Their personal and economic independence granted them the freedom to devote themselves to a range of passions, pursuits and people: to their community of friends and creative collaborators, and to making a life that revolved around art, literature, style and creativity. Their home in Manhattan became a lively salon, where domesticity became a creative act for the purpose of entertaining friends and bringing about creative expression.

Before settling down in the city, the sisters and their mother had several long excursions in Europe. From the 1890s to 1914, they moved between capitals of modernity, such as Paris, Munich and Vienna, immersing themselves in a thrilling cultural education that shaped the rest of their lives. Ettie, the most cerebral of the sisters, studied at the University of Freiburg, gaining a doctorate in philosophy for her work on William James in 1907. Florine took art classes and toured galleries, eager to experience all forms of art – from Renaissance masterpieces to decorative rococo art and modern experimental Cubist works – and submit them to her critical eye. At the 1912 Salon d'Automne, Florine encountered Raymond Duchamp-Villon's sensational architectural installation *La maison cubiste*. It featured a Cubist-inspired facade of a house, which visitors stepped through into a bedroom and a decorative 'Salon Bourgeois' to see a selection of Cubist paintings. The interior, designed by André Mare, was an early example of Art Deco, with stylized floral patterns and bright colours adorning the soft furnishings, wallpaper and furniture. *La maison cubiste* suggested new possibilities for the forms of modern art to be applied to decorative designs and household objects and presented a holistic approach to art that encompassed everyday life. Traces of *La maison*'s influence can be felt through the opulent decoration of the Stettheimer salon, as well as Carrie's later Dollhouse artwork.

The immersive experience that *La maison* created would undoubtedly have appealed to the Stettheimers' love of theatre. When in Europe, the sisters sought out the most exciting, innovative performances of dance and drama. Many reflected new, progressive ideas that were reshaping notions of sexuality and gender roles, such as Oscar Wilde's *Salome* and Henrik Ibsen's *Hedda Gabler*. However, nothing captured the sisters' imaginations quite like performances by the Ballets Russes. In a diary entry written in June 1912, Florine raved about an early performance of the controversial *L'Après-midi d'un faune* in Paris, noting her particular admiration for Léon Bakst's costume designs. The faun became a recurring symbol of gender fluidity and sexuality in her own later paintings, a figure she clearly identified with on a deep level. The power of costume to mediate aspects of a performance would also inform Florine's designs for Gertrude Stein and Virgil Thompson's *Four Saints in Three Acts* in the 1930s. For Carrie, who harboured an unrealized desire to design stage sets, the Ballets Russes influenced her elaborate personal style, through the daring Bakst-inspired Paul Poiret couture costumes that she wore at parties.

Florine summed up the joys and freedoms the sisters enjoyed on their European sojourns in one of her characteristically lively poems: she celebrated 'living in the Latin Quarter/ and flanéing in the Bois', wearing gowns designed by Callot Soeurs, being 'thrilled by the Russian Ballet/ and cakes made by Rebattet' and eating Marquise chocolate and French petit pois.[7] The poem sets up a camp collision of high and low culture, decadent sensuality and playful *joie de vivre* – a familiar tone that runs through much of her writing and artwork. When the Stettheimers returned to New York full-time following the outbreak of the First World War, they carried this spirit with them. The household that they created and curated together symbolized a creative experiment in living a life devoted to art and culture. From the mid- to late 1910s, Florine developed her style as a painter, experimenting with methods and forms she had encountered in Europe while moving towards her own singular style. As Florine honed her identity as an artist, the Stettheimer sisters collectively transformed themselves into the city's most unique patrons and creators of the avant-garde. All three were makers of creative worlds, both individually (Ettie in her novels, Carrie through her Dollhouse and Florine in her paintings) and collaboratively as the designers and hosts of their unique domestic space and social gatherings. Before long, the sisters had firmly embedded themselves and their salon in the cultural map of the city and were at the centre of a diverse network of writers, artists and public figures.

Just like at the Arensberg salon, Marcel Duchamp played the role of co-conspirator and guest of honour (Bloemink suggests that the sisters likely met him at the Arensbergs'). Clearly intrigued and also keen to support his art, the sisters employed Duchamp as a French tutor, despite the fact that they were all proficient in the language. Duchamp soon proved to be a perfect addition to their circle, frequently joining their salon soirées as well as trips to their summer house André Brook in Tarrytown, a village near the eastern bank of the Hudson River. There was a particular sense of recognition and understanding between Duchamp and the Stettheimers. The camp, subversive irreverence of Florine's paintings and Carrie's Dollhouse project chimed with some of the interests he was exploring in his own art. With Ettie, Duchamp shared a love of philosophy, language and wordplay. Their rapport took on an intimate, sometimes flirtatious tone. When Duchamp visited André Brook in August 1917 while Ettie was absent, he was moved to write to her: 'naturally the house was empty without you'.[8] In a letter sent in July 1922 (the month that they both celebrated their birthdays), Ettie sent Duchamp a 'Pensée-cadeau' (thought-gift) in the form of an enigmatic short poem:

> Je voudrais être faire sur mesure
> Pour toi, pour toi –
> Mais je suis ready-made par la nature
> Pour quoi, pour quoi?
> Comme je ne le sais pas j'ai fait des rectifications
> Pour moi – [9]

The poem seems to allude to an awkward incident that occurred at their last parting (in a prior letter, Duchamp describes hiding tears in his eyes because he knows Ettie doesn't like 'men who cry'). Ettie puns on Duchamp's experiments with art objects, describing herself as being readymade by nature, which means that she cannot be made to measure for Duchamp – or any man. It restates her independence as a self-contained being, with the final 'for me' suggesting that Ettie is giving herself to herself, rather than giving herself to a man.

Ettie's exchange with Duchamp is one of many examples of how the sisters maintained their integrity and independent natures not only in the face of wider society's pressures but among their talented and dynamic friendship group. Even in supposedly progressive, artistic circles, many women ended up playing second fiddle to men who made them into muses or helpmeets. The Stettheimers would not be relegated to secondary roles. Florine's poetry suggests that she shared Ettie's aversion to marriage. Some surprisingly sensual pieces hint at flirtations, but she often reveals feelings of disappointment: a poem titled 'To a Gentleman Friend' begins 'you fooled me you little floating worm'.[10] Ultimately, the Stettheimers were their own muses, and their guests were supporting actors in their dynamic lived art practice.

The Salon

Art critic Henry McBride was enchanted by Florine's painting *Birthday Party* (also known as *La fête à Duchamp*) when it was shown at the Second Annual Exhibition of the Society of Independent Artists in 1918.

> One of the most joyous of the paintings [at the Society of Independent Artists' Second Annual Exhibition] is the 'Birthday Party' by Mrs. [*sic*] Florine Stettheimer . . . All the people at the party are extremely well known in the most advanced Greenwich Village circles . . . I blushed at not having heard of them. Not to know the fair artist of the picture is to argue oneself unknown . . . [Stettheimer] has painted herself into the party and she has some rather good things to say for herself

... The more I think of it the more miffed I am that I wasn't asked to that party.[11]

Shortly after viewing it, he rectified his ignorance of the Stettheimers and their circle, ensuring that he secured an invitation to future parties. As McBride suggests, the Stettheimers' parties brought together an eclectic who's who of New York's cultural scene. In her eulogy for Florine, Georgia O'Keeffe quoted Van Vechten's declaration that 'in prohibition days the three Stettheimer sisters were the only people he knew who could have a large dinner party without liquor and be successful with it'.[12] The Stettheimer magic more than made up for a lack of alcohol.

Florine's paintings offer us a glimpse at the dazzling, luxurious events that the sisters hosted. Her vivid palette and sensuous, decadent scenes perfectly evoke the atmosphere of the salon. *La fête à Duchamp* – the work that captured McBride's imagination – is a typical lively group scene, in which Florine captures the fizzing atmosphere, furtive conversations, pleasures and performances that made up the Stettheimers' social scene. Like several of her other paintings, it deploys Florine's durational narrative technique, whereby moments from different points in time are woven together in one scene. Along with her use of rich colours and flattened perspective, the mini-sequences of different guests' journeys through the scene draw the viewer into the Stettheimers' world; Florine conveys something of the dynamism and buzz of Stettheimer parties, breathing life into the static space of the canvas.

La fête à Duchamp commemorates the party that the sisters threw in honour of Duchamp's thirtieth birthday at their summer home in Tarrytown. The painting captures events spanning Duchamp's moment of arrival on a bright sunny afternoon up until the end of the night, under the glow of lanterns. In the top left corner, Duchamp and Francis Picabia pull up outside the house in Picabia's hot-red sports car; at the bottom of the canvas, they are shown entering the garden, and then gradually progressing through the scene (Picabia joins Henri-Pierre Roché on the grass, while Duchamp – identifiable only by a peek of his shoe and trouser leg – sits with Fania Marinoff under a canopy). The top third of the painting depicts a transition to a candlelit night scene, with the guests gathered around tables for intimate conversations. The tone is celebratory but, as in other similar group scenes, Florine added a few visual jokes at the expense of certain male guests: Florine can be seen turning away from a hectoring, gesticulating Albert Gleizes, as if relieved to spot Duchamp. Towards the bottom right of the painting, Ettie concentrates on a book while two Leo Steins surround her. By painting him twice, she emphasizes the way he was relentlessly demanding Ettie's attention. Florine also cruelly mocks Stein's use of a hearing aid, showing him clutching it to his ear as he attempts to break Ettie's focus. Remarks made by Duchamp in a letter sent from Buenos Aires reinforce the sense that the sisters had little time for pompous or pretentious men: seeking news of their gatherings, he asked: 'Have you had a lot of "diners" this winter? New Faces? . . . Do you see Roché from time to time? Or has he fallen from favour with you? For you are very demanding. And I consider myself fortunate to have managed not to displease you and that you have not tired of me.'[13]

Unlike the Arensbergs, who hosted an eclectic revolving cast of characters and felt duty-bound to share their art collection with a wider circle, the Stettheimers limited their parties to a more intimate, trusted group of friends and acquaintances. The sisters supported certain artist friends financially, but their salon was not a means to gain influence, to flatter prominent artists or to otherwise ingratiate themselves with prominent progressive figures. This attitude has typically been understood as a feature of the sisters' rarefied, introspective world; indeed, an element of the Stettheimers' snobbery was at work here. Ettie and Florine could be highly strung, critical and impatient. In this way, the Stettheimer salon serves as a reminder that such spaces could offer a home for art and experimentation outside of traditional institutions, but they could also be part of a culture of gatekeeping and exclusion. However, there were other reasons for the Stettheimers' strict invitation-only policy. The salon's exclusivity afforded both the sisters and their guests' privacy in which they were free to express themselves away from the prying eyes of censorship and other darker forces that were prevalent in society.

As a secular Jewish family of German descent, the Stettheimers were disturbed by growing anti-immigrant and anti-Jewish rhetoric both within the United States and in Germany. Wartime nationalism during the First World War had fuelled support for the Klu Klux Klan and other white supremacist movements that sought (successfully) to reduce immigration into the United States in order to 'preserve the ideal of U.S. homogeneity'.[14] The lynching of Leo Frank, an American Jewish man falsely charged with rape and murder in 1915, was a flashpoint in the swelling climate of antisemitism. This was by no means limited to the fringes of society or certain states. High-profile figures gave legitimacy to dangerous antisemitic rhetoric. Henry Ford, one of the most famous Americans of the 1910s and '20s, regularly provided a platform for hate speech and conspiracy theories in the newspaper he owned, the *Dearborn Independent*. Ford's antisemitic rhetoric was, in historian Hasia Diner's words, 'no different than what Hitler [was] saying in his beer hall meetings in Munich at the same time'; Ford's immense popularity ensured that these comments were reported widely in the media.[15] Diner suggests that this hostile environment forced Jewish Americans to 'question how really they [were] being accepted as Americans' and make 'pronouncements about how American they were'. Jewish immigrants who were politically active were also targeted for deportation by denaturalization policies, Emma Goldman being the first and most famous case.[16]

Florine was far from a political painter, but issues surrounding antisemitism and immigration surface in some of her allegorical paintings in subtle ways. *New York/Liberty* (1918) presents a celebratory vision of New York, seen from the perspective of someone arriving on a ship bound for Ellis Island. Mixing references to the United States' past and present history, Florine symbolizes New York's heritage with a small Dutch sailor and an Indigenous American man standing together, holding a badge commemorating the time and place. It is a hopeful yet naive patriotic vision, which highlights her enthusiasm for mixing fantasy and reality to create her own vision of the world. More sinister themes nevertheless crept in. In *Beauty Contest: To the Memory of P. T. Barnum* (1924), a carnivalesque scene of an elaborate beauty pageant (something that Florine recorded contempt for in her diary), an array of mostly blonde, blue-eyed women parade in front of male judges. Centre right, one woman waits to hand a bouquet to the winner, her bridal outfit covered in small red swastikas. Alluding to Florine's belief that beauty contests were a 'B. L. O. T.' on 'American civilization', the swastika woman associates mindless pomp and pageantry, the valorization of certain beauty standards, and women's status as objects on the marriage market with the growing popularity of fascism. Bloemink suggests that 'in 1920s America, with its various segregated Jewish communities, it would have been unthinkable for a Jewish woman, no matter how beautiful, to win a beauty contest.'[17] Indeed, Bess Myerson, the first and only Jewish Miss America, faced antisemitic public protests, cancelled sponsorships and bans from certain country clubs when she won the contest in 1945.[18] Florine's *Beauty Contest*, painted two decades previously, is darkly prescient.

Florine also touched on incidents of antisemitism that were closer to home. *Lake Placid* (1919) is a typical opulent scene of the Stettheimer's social milieu – in this instance, an afternoon swimming and sailing on Lake Placid. In the typical style of fashionable wealthy women, the sisters are shown to be sporty and active, and one of their friends (Hazel Seligman) is even water-skiing. Like Clara Tice's sketches for *Vanity Fair*, Florine's painting celebrates the outdoor pursuits and public freedoms enjoyed by modern women. But what is ostensibly a joyful depiction of an afternoon's swimming takes on a deeper meaning when one considers the name that Florine chose for this painting. Lake Placid was a popular resort for rich American families but it was mired in antisemitic discrimination: Jewish people were banned from many of the area's clubs, hotels and restaurants by white supremacist members of high society, who claimed they were ill bred and lacking in refinement. In defiance, some wealthy Jewish families purchased land in the area and developed their own camps. The Stettheimers' cousin Edwin Seligman was among them and, in 1919, they vacationed at his summer residence, Camp Calumet. *Lake Placid* shows some of their companions, including Seligman and his daughter Hazel, sculptor Elie Nadelman, gallerists Marie Sterner and Rabbi Stephen Wise and Peruvian diplomat the Marquis of Buenavista. As a Catholic, the marquis was part of another group widely banned from resorts and clubs around the lake. *Lake Placid* reads as a pointed riposte to the antisemitism and discrimination that overshadowed this holiday idyll.

Even among their friends in the art world, the Stettheimers were confronted with expressions of antisemitism and disturbingly relaxed attitudes towards Nazism.[19] Artist and patron Katherine Dreier, a close friend of Duchamp's and a co-founder of Société Anonyme (of which Florine was a member), remained an apologist for Hitler's Germany late into the 1930s. Dreier visited Germany regularly up until 1937 and knew, through friends such as Wassily Kandinsky (who left Germany in 1933 after the Bauhaus closed under pressure from the Nazis), of the increasing authoritarianism and persecution. Yet she defended the regime, only appearing slightly concerned when modern art was threatened, for example during the Nazis' 1937 'Entartete Kunst' exhibition. In her correspondence, Dreier frequently expressed what art historians Robert Herbert, Eleanor Apter and Elise Kenney describe as a '"lady-like" anti-semitism' that, with hindsight 'permitted more violent forms to thrive when encouraged by political forces'.[20]

Dreier's views were echoed by a one-time member of the Stettheimer inner circle, artist Marsden Hartley. A lifelong Germanophile, Hartley wrote approvingly of Hitler's regime during a visit to Germany in the mid-1930s in letters to the artist Adelaide Kunst, adding that his praise was limited to issues 'outside of the Jewish question which of course is tragic'.[21] To another friend, he declared that 'if the Nazis must have the Jews out of politics, out of art, out of banking, that is their business.'[22] The Stettheimers would not countenance any apologies for the Nazis' antisemitic oppression. In *Marsden Hartley: Race, Religion, and Nation* (2006), Donna M. Cassidy describes how Ettie 'criticized Hartley's German work because of its entanglement – and what she perceived as Hartley's sympathy – with this racist regime'.[23] Hartley felt that he was the injured party. In a letter to friend and fellow modernist Paul Strand, he informed Strand that he was no longer in touch with the sisters due to Ettie's 'cruel and unforgivable' treatment of him. Hartley's explanation glosses over his expressed sympathy with Hitler and the methods of Nazism, making only a vague reference to Ettie's anger at the fact that he 'happened to [have been] in Bavaria and the racial question – etc'.[24] Hartley had been a close friend of the sisters and they had supported him financially but, in the 1930s, he was no longer welcome at the Stettheimers' soirées.

The exclusive nature of the Stettheimer salon also meant that guests were free to experiment with gender and express queer sexual identities, something that was risky and potentially dangerous in wider society. Florine and Duchamp delighted in subverting the boundaries between genders, and the salon was a welcoming, safe space for a number of gay and bisexual artists, writers and critics, including Van Vechten, McBride, Hartley, Charles Demuth and Cecil Beaton. Although queer culture flourished in parts of New York through the 1910s and '20s, there were continued crackdowns, raids and attacks on the rights of anyone caught running venues that welcomed gay, lesbian, bisexual and transgender clientele. Popular gay bathhouses were frequently targeted by undercover police and agents acting on behalf of the notorious New York Society for the Suppression of Vice. Proprietors could be severely penalized and, if they were immigrants, deported: this fate befell Polish Jewish feminist Eve Adams, who was jailed and then sent to Poland after being arrested by the Vice Squad following a raid on her tea room Eve's Hangout (also known as Eve Adams' Tearoom) in Greenwich Village.[25] Despite the Village's radical, bohemian reputation, it was vulnerable to the enforcement of homophobic, xenophobic laws. By contrast, the Stettheimers' world of fantasy and luxury offered an escape – for the privileged few who were invited – from society's rules and expectations.

In their apartment and Florine's studio in the Beaux Arts Building, the Stettheimers transformed their small corner of New York. Combining a gallery for Florine's work, a living space and a party venue, these sites pushed at the boundaries between what would usually be considered domestic, private space and the public world. Their salon soirées were almost like surreal art installations, where fantasy and play made even the city outside seem a little unreal. This atmosphere chimed perfectly with the irreverent, mocking spirit of New York Dada. It was also a space in which the sisters themselves could create a radically alternative way of living that centred creativity, beauty and a community of like-minded people. Wealth and privilege enabled their independence. Nevertheless, it was bold for a group of women to reject the norms that governed most people's lives during those early decades of the twentieth century, to turn away from marriage and motherhood and instead embrace the arts, sisterhood (however conflicted) and the company of an eccentric cast of outrageous avant-garde artists and writers. While domesticity still curtailed their creative opportunities to some degree, their boundary-breaking work and creative salon reimagined the world through art – together they created a vision that was both feminine and radically avant-garde, decorative and modernist, European and American.

Carrie Stettheimer's Salon in Miniature

In 1923, Florine completed a trio of portraits depicting herself and her sisters Carrie and Ettie. The images are typical of her later style: rich with opulent, decorative detail, and paint thickly applied in jewel tones. Each sister is depicted as sylphlike, androgynous and ageless, despite the fact that they were then aged between 48 and 54. Florine defies the stereotype of the middle-aged spinster to celebrate her sisters' creativity and their rich inner lives. She uses colours, symbols and clothing to highlight the sisters' differing personalities and interests. In her own self-portrait, Florine sits on a red blanket, flame-like under a cool yellow sun and floating in an expanse of bright white. Her androgynous body is dressed in a sheer cellophane dress paired with nude high heels and she gazes out, beyond the viewer, with heavily made-up eyes. In contrast to the dazzling white backdrop behind Florine, the portrait of Ettie presents her in a dark, moonlit scene. She floats in the night sky on a ruby-red chaise longue, wearing a dark dress and a pensive look. Florine often depicted Ettie in a lounging position, hinting at her sister's elegantly louche lifestyle. Yet she is also careful to acknowledge Ettie's intellectual pursuits: a book rests beside Ettie with her name written on the cover, symbolizing her activities as a writer and scholar. Florine paints her with a wide-eyed, intense stare, alluding to Ettie's curious, pensive nature.

Of the three images, the portrait of Carrie is the most fascinating. Much less is known about Carrie: her role as manager of the Stettheimer household was demanding, leaving her less time for creative pursuits and leisure than her sisters. After her death, she left no diaries and very little correspondence, making it near impossible to get a

Arnold Genthe, *Carrie Stettheimer*, 1932.

sense of her personality and interior life. Clues remain, however, in the letters and recollections of their friends. Like her sisters, Carrie enjoyed art and culture, and she found time (around her domestic duties) to pursue interests independent of her mother, Ettie and Florine. She made frequent trips to Paris to shop for the latest fashions in haute couture and catch up with artist friends in Europe. Her shopping trips were legendary among the Stettheimers' social circle; in a 1927 letter to Florine, Henry McBride jokingly described Carrie pounding the rue de la Paix (Paris's centre of couture, home to designers such as Elsa Schiaparelli and Jeanne Paquin) and returning home to 'put Bendel Brothers in the place they belong'.[26] Like her sisters, Carrie used costume and couture to take control of her image and make herself modern. As a hostess and *salonière*, Carrie placed great emphasis on her appearance, taking the many opportunities presented by the Stettheimer's soirees to dress up in the latest couture outfits that she picked up in Paris. Carrie's taste in fashion was extravagant and modern, and she used clothes to signal her creativity and her appreciation of new styles.

Florine's portrayal of her older sister in the 1923 portrait offers a rare, intimate insight into Carrie, one which emphasizes her creativity and daring sense of style. One of the most obvious differences between the painting of Carrie and those of Ettie and Florine is their poses: whereas Ettie and Florine lounge in a state of repose, Carrie is upright and active. She is also grounded in a semi-interior space, not floating in the cosmos like her sisters. Nevertheless, there remains a high level of performance and fantasy in this portrait. Carrie takes centre stage, quite literally: theatrical gold- and silver-trimmed curtains frame her and separate her from the family group gathered in the background. The large rug Carrie stands on gives the appearance of a stage, and the pose she adopts (one foot pointed forwards, left arm presenting the doll's house beside her) is that of a performer. Her outfit adds to the sense of drama. Demonstrating her love of modern haute couture, she is dressed in an elaborate shimmering outfit, complete with harem pants and a matching hat; her clothes evoke Paul Poiret (one of Carrie's favourite designers) and the costume designs of the Ballets Russes' Léon Bakst. Her outfit is similar to a dazzling costume that Florine describes her wearing the previous year, featuring 'white satin slippers, white turban and [a] new metal dress'.[27] The material of her dress was likely lamé, an expensive woven metal fabric often used in Bakst's costumes and, as such, a fashionable choice for 1920s evening wear.

The care that Carrie took over self-fashioning reflected Florine's distinct mode of portraiture, which she developed in her later paintings. Just as Florine depicted herself and her sisters as ageless, gender-fluid, sexual (but not sexualized) beings, so too did Carrie present herself in a way that defied the expectations of a middle-aged, unmarried woman. In 1922, when Florine described her stunning white satin and lamé outfit, Carrie was 53 years old. In an era obsessed with the modern (young) woman, the Stettheimer sisters would have been considered old spinsters. Carrie's choice of outfits demonstrates a defiant disregard of the ageist, sexist norms of her day. The turbans and jupes-culottes that she favoured in the early 1920s align Carrie with a daring look that was coded feminine, sensuous and erotic.[28] In Paris, the fashion for jupes-culottes posed what Nancy Troy describes as a 'sartorial [challenge] to traditional gender roles, racial and national identities'; the trousers provoked a shocked response from critics in the press, much of it steeped in 'racism and anti-Semitism [and] anti-feminism' and fearful of women's efforts to 'claim from men parity of costume, as well as all other equalities'.[29] Poiret defended his designs from charges of indecency by claiming that they were outfits intended for the private domestic interior, not the public world; but both Carrie and Florine wore these trousers in semi-public forums (at parties and in portraits), each making bold statements about their own image.

Despite the glamorous attire Carrie wears in her portrait, she is busy working. In her right hand, she holds a tiny chair ready to be set in place in the imposing dollhouse beside her. This large dollhouse is Carrie's life's work: an unusual art project that saw her recreate and reimagine aspects of the Stettheimers' home and lifestyle in miniature. She began the work in 1916 and continued for two decades, abandoning it only in the wake of the disruption caused by their mother's death in 1935. The fact that the dollhouse is so prominently situated in the painting symbolizes the central role it played in Carrie's life. Florine suggests that it is almost an extension of Carrie, as if the painting is as much a portrait of the dollhouse as it is of its creator. In this way, Florine gives weight to Carrie's decades-long project, signifying respect for her sister's creativity. A small sign on the side of the dollhouse reads 'Carrie Stettheimer. Designer. Decorator. Collector', highlighting her expertise and authority. These three titles show the combined knowledge and artistic flair that fed into the creation of the dollhouse and transformed it into a work of art.

Florine Stettheimer, *My Sister, Carrie W. Stettheimer*, 1923, oil on canvas.

In the portrait, Carrie's concentration on her dollhouse has taken her away from the other Stettheimers, who can be seen chatting over cups of coffee in the top right of the painting (Ettie is shown in her characteristic languorous pose, relaxing with a cigarette). By portraying Carrie alone with her work, Florine shows that she managed to carve out time to focus on the dollhouse and prioritized it in her life. Carrie did indeed leave the family home to work on her dollhouse, hiring a room at the nearby Dorset Hotel in which to work. Art, it seems, gave Carrie independence and interests away from her family and domestic duties; but of course, the Stettheimer home and salon were the source of her inspiration. There is a certain playfulness in the way that Florine has depicted the family in the background as just about doll-size, as if Carrie might pick them up and place them inside the dollhouse. It is an amusing touch that draws deeper parallels between Carrie's and Florine's world-making, particularly the way that each sister transforms and transcends the everyday whirlwind of parties and social occasions that the Stettheimers were caught up in, turning it into the stuff of art (and, in the process, memorializing it). Like Florine in her paintings, Carrie lends the Stettheimers a magical, timeless quality through her art. In different mediums, each sister captures the ephemeral aspects of their lives – fashion, parties, friendships, interior design – and transforms it into a lasting work of art.

Ettie's view of Carrie's life and achievements was less celebratory than Florine's. Writing after Florine's and Carrie's deaths in 1944, Ettie expressed her feeling that Carrie had been prevented from fulfilling her creative potential due to the demands of running the household and the pursuit of her other passions, 'reading, learning and conversation'. During their mother's illness, Carrie did indeed shoulder the burden of care and had much less time for herself (however, all three sisters contributed, and Florine's output also lessened during these difficult years). Ettie laments the fact that Carrie's tiring domestic chores drew her from what was – in Ettie's mind – her true vocation: stage design. In Ettie's opinion, Carrie's Dollhouse was simply a 'facile and posthumous substitute' for the more worthy, prestigious work of stage design. Despite these feelings, Ettie completed parts of the Dollhouse left unfinished after Carrie's death and donated it to the

Museum of the City of New York in 1945 (where it remains to this day). It was unveiled to great fanfare in December 1945, including a fittingly glamorous party attended by old friends and art world luminaries, such as Georgia O'Keeffe. The museum's acceptance of the Dollhouse into its permanent collection bestowed on it institutional prestige and cultural currency. However, the fact that Ettie donated it to a museum rather than a gallery frames the work as a curious piece of history rather than an art object. Ettie may have felt that the work was a facile compromise, but both the Museum of New York and Florine (as signalled in her portrait of Carrie) acknowledge it as a significant cultural object. By giving it such prominence in the portrait, Florine appears to foresee its role in the Stettheimers' legacy.

The Dollhouse is a statement of Carrie's interest in mixing art, fantasy and the everyday. Carrie's efforts to bring art into the everyday were not only vital to transforming the Stettheimer home into a vibrant salon but represented a mode of avant-garde experimentation with ways of living and expressing one's self that was akin to Greenwich Village bohemianism. Through design and theatrical flourishes, she elevates femininity and domesticity to the realm of art. She even ensured that the Stettheimers' dinner parties were injected with a camp, otherworldly aesthetic. Guests were treated to beautifully prepared menus and unusual dishes: in June 1934, she served cocktails, lobster in mayonnaise aspic (jelly) and the whimsical-sounding 'feather soup' to a gathering that included Cecil Beaton and Virgil Thompson. Her menu for the birthday party that the Stettheimers threw Van Vechten in 1933 was carefully composed along a pink theme, with dishes including salmon, strawberry ice cream and pink champagne on a pink tablecloth with a pink floral table display.

Ettie's ambivalent opinion of the dollhouse's worth highlights the fact that this kind of work or creative practice was not valued during the first half of the twentieth century; from a modern-day perspective, as we come to new understandings of decorative art and other acts of making and performance that have been cast aside as feminine or domestic, Carrie's Dollhouse emerges as a unique intervention in the New York avant-garde of which the Stettheimer salon was at the centre.

Inside the Dollhouse

Featuring sixteen elaborately decorated rooms spread across two floors, Carrie's Dollhouse was an act of camp world-making that encapsulated and exaggerated the magic of the Stettheimer salon. It drew on elements of the real-life architecture and decorative schemes of the apartments that the Stettheimers occupied in New York. The exterior of the house was custom-made by a carpenter, to replicate the Stettheimers' vacation home in Tarrytown in upstate New York, André Brook (a location that also features in some of Florine's paintings). Some of the decor – cellophane curtains, opulent red-and-gold furniture – is familiar from photographs of the Stettheimers' apartment and Florine's paintings. However, the Dollhouse is not an exact replica of any one location or room; rather, Carrie mixed and matched elements of reality to create her own style, letting her imagination run free in the painstaking acts of decoration and design she dedicated herself to.

Carrie's work on the Dollhouse was labour-intensive and thorough, to ensure that every inch of the space and the objects in it were unique. She hand-sewed tiny rugs and wove miniature carpets; she created replicas of their friends' books for the library, including a tiny Van Vechten title. Even the mah-jong tiles in the library, monogrammed silk-covered hairbrush and the feather-trimmed lampshades were hand-made. Although some small aspects were unfinished at the time of Carrie's death, Ettie and museum conservators were able to finish the work using a trove of luxurious fabrics that Carrie kept aside for the Dollhouse. As in the actual Stettheimer home, the multiple decorative patterns, use of cellophane and chintz flourishes push Carrie's Dollhouse beyond a traditionally feminine decorative style and into the realms of a high camp aesthetic of excess. The Stettheimers' love of excessive decoration, feathers and frou-frou parodied stereotypes of the middle-aged, upper-class spinster. Juxtaposed with modern art, modern materials (such as lamé and cellophane) and their avant-garde guests, the Stettheimer aesthetic took on a subversive tone.

The nursery is a particularly intriguing room; it was a work of pure imagination and memory, as it never existed in the adult Stettheimers' apartment. The nursery features collaged wallpaper, with a design of scattered pastel shapes along the lower walls and a striking Noah's Ark scene on the frieze above. In typical Stettheimer style, this is a playful twist on the traditional image of the ark: the animals are joined by a group of people, each kitted out in stylish, modern attire. Two women wearing short dresses and cropped hairstyles could represent Stettheimer sisters; another woman dressed in an old-fashioned long dress and bonnet, holding a parasol, is reminiscent of their mother. The frieze scene is a playful, joking addition to the Stettheimer myth, inserting the family into a founding fable of the history of mankind. Two deliberately childish drawings hang below, each featuring a figure of a girl with a short blonde bob. The child likely represents Carrie, showing that the inclusion of a nursery does not signify an unfulfilled wish to have a child, but rather the importance of those early years on the Stettheimer sisters. By including collage decor, scrawled portraits and a miniature dollhouse, Carrie clearly locates creativity within childhood and, in the process, taps into popular contemporaneous philosophical ideas surrounding links between the child and the artist.

Among the tiny toys scattered around the nursery, the presence of a miniature dollhouse (sadly now lost) adds a witty layer of self-referentiality that emphasizes Carrie's sense of humour. Similar touches elsewhere in the Dollhouse demonstrate Carrie's playfulness and pleasure in the element of surprise, an attitude that aligns with the New York avant-garde's Dada high jinks. The entrance hall, for example, is decorated with wallpaper that gives a *trompe l'oeil* effect of a baroque French garden, complete with columns of decorative marble arches and statues. This visual trick causes the viewer to do a double take, while the absurdity is heightened by its miniature scale. Other decorative features emphasize the room's camp theatricality: blue drapes and a beaded crystal lampshade create drama and also nod to Florine's paintings and studio. In this space, the drapes draw attention to the interplay between fantasy and reality, truth and illusion – although, of course, all is ultimately fantasy in the miniaturized world of the Dollhouse. Two other incongruous additions add to the surreal effect of the hall: a glass chandelier hangs from the ceiling, illuminated with a tiny electric bulb and, at the back of the room, a working elevator is hidden by collaged foliage; critic John Richardson refers to the latter as a 'Dadaist elevator – a machine without a mechanism', and, unsurprisingly, it was an addition that fascinated Duchamp.[30]

One of the most remarkable rooms is the ballroom. A grand room at the centre of the Dollhouse, the ballroom was marked as the room in which the Dollhouse's collection of artworks would hang. Carrie asked several of the Stettheimers' artist friends to recreate their paintings and sculptures in miniature and amassed around thirty pieces. The tiny collection represented some of New York's most exciting modern artists, several of whom had exhibited at the Armory Show. Marguerite Zorach contributed three Fauvist paintings, and William Zorach made a miniature of his *Mother and Child* sculpture. Gaston Lachaise added the second of the Dollhouse's two tiny sculptures – the alabaster *Female Nude* – as well as three other painted nudes and a woman's head. The female nude is a dominant theme in the collection, which subverts the tradition of grand, wealthy homes displaying portraits that reflect their patriarchal family lineages (however, most of the artists are men). Queer masculinity is also encoded in some of the paintings, for example Claggett Wilson's *Basque Sailors*, reflecting the way that the Stettheimer salon was a welcoming and inclusive space for queer artists.

Carrie's miniature collection is a tribute to the Stettheimers' close friendships and represents an exchange of influences and inspiration. Florine painted Louis Bouché's portrait in 1923; positioning him surrounded by lace curtains, she parodied *Mama's Boy*, the painting he recreated for Carrie. He also created a striking, stylized sketch of the three sisters in 1918, capturing the stylish elegance and confident poise each woman possessed. These exchanges were an extension of the salon's social network and strengthened the Stettheimers' place in the New York avant-garde. But perhaps the most significant token of friendship in the Dollhouse – and the most significant miniature painting in its collection – is Duchamp's tiny *Nude Descending a Staircase, No. 2*. The painting's notoriety meant that it functioned as an unmistakeable symbol of provocative, modern, avant-garde art, disrupting the quaint, childish associations of the dollhouse. Duchamp presented the miniature to Carrie for her birthday, with a personal message written on the back: '*Nu Descendant un Escalier Pour la collection de la poupée de Carrie Stettheimer à l'occasion de sa fête en bon souvenir*' ('Nude Descending a Staircase For Carrie Stetthimer's collection of dolls on the occasion of her birthday in good memory') signed '*Marcel Duchamp 23 julliet 1918 N.Y.*' '*En bon souvenir*' likely refers to Duchamp's impending departure for Buenos Aires on 13 August; as a token of the group's happy memories, the miniature painting is, literally, a souvenir of their relationship.

Carrie's Dollhouse greatly intrigued Duchamp. In his letters to the sisters, he regularly asked for updates on specific aspects of it (including the elevator) and Carrie's overall progress. Duchamp spoke of the Dollhouse with reverence and respect: in 1918, he wrote to Carrie asking, 'have you continued on your doll's house? I didn't say finished, that would be an insult.'[31] His recognition of the work as an ongoing – and unending – project shows that he acknowledged it as a piece of art. Considering Duchamp's own interest in questioning art, pushing its boundaries and playing tricks on the art world, he no doubt appreciated the way that this unusual, playful object subverted the boundaries between art and craft. The Dollhouse was undoubtedly an influence on Duchamp's own miniature project, *Boîte-en-valise*, which he began in 1935.

Boîte-en-valise is a 'portable museum', or archive in a box, housing tiny replicas of all Duchamp's work, including *Fountain* and other readymades. Each work was created using labour-intensive, hands-on methods, deploying techniques such as *pochoir* (a skilled form of hand-coloured stencil illustration), lithography and (for the three-dimensional readymades) papier mâché. Ironically, more physical work went into the creation of some of these pieces than the originals; this added another layer to the work's subversive play, in which art, craft and the commodity collide. By citing his alter-ego Rrose Sélavy in the title (its full title, in French, is *De ou par Marcel Duchamp ou Rrose Sélavy (Boîte-en-valise)*), Duchamp makes another link to the Stettheimers: the Stettheimer-inspired character he conceived during his years frequenting their salon becomes the co-creator of this work. The concept of the souvenir also returns, with the tiny reproductions reminiscent of kitsch tourist mementos (such as a miniature Eiffel Tower) or the copies of religious relics collected by pilgrims. Like the Stettheimers' work, Duchamp's *Boîte-en-valise* functioned as a form of self-fashioning: the work is a self-curated retrospective created during a time when Duchamp was far less celebrated as a master of modern art than contemporaries such as Picasso and Matisse.

Where Carrie collapsed the Stettheimers' world into a doll's house, Duchamp fitted his entire artistic vision into a suitcase. Both miniature worlds (that is, Dollhouse and *Boîte-en-valise*) expand our ideas of what art is and can be. Miniatures are often described in terms of interiority, retreat and seclusion. Susan Stewart refers to the miniature as 'a world of arrested time ... once we attend to the miniature world, the outside world stops and is lost to us'; 'the miniature, linked to nostalgic version of childhood and history, presents a diminutive and therefore manip-ulatable version of experience, a version which is domesticated and protected from contamination'.[32] It would be easy to frame Carrie's Dollhouse in the terms of a traditional gendered criticism that portrays the Stettheimer sisters as introverted and sequestered in a rarefied, fem-inine world. Yet, it was so much more – not least a modern work of art that was communicative, or, in other words, engaged with the Stettheimers' avant-garde social network.

Carrie's Dollhouse does, to a degree, stop time, but the effect is not simply nostalgic or domestic. Instead, Carrie creates a world that is part fantasy, part reality, which strives to capture the ephemeral spirit of the salon. Much like Florine's paintings, it celebrates the physical space that the sisters' crafted around themselves and made a lasting work of their creative art of living. Furthermore, the Dollhouse was never a sealed-off, static object. As we have seen, Carrie invited collaboration and welcomed conversations about its style with Florine, Duchamp and other friends. The fact that it remained unfinished after around two decades of work shows that Carrie considered its creation a much bigger feat than a simple pastime. It was an ongoing, ever-evolving project. Duchamp recognized in its unfinished nature the artist's lifelong mis-sion towards realizing their creative ambition (which, by its very nature, can never be fully achieved).

The carefully thought-out creative decisions that Carrie made during the many years she spent working on the Dollhouse further highlight the depth and scope of her vision. In particular, the absence of dolls has an impact on the Dollhouse's meaning and how the viewer reads it as an art object. On receipt of Gaston Lachaise's miniature paintings and sculpture in 1931, Carrie wrote to him:

> My dolls and I thank you most sincerely for the lovely drawings that are to grace their art gallery. I think that the dolls – after they are born, which they are not, yet – ought to be the happiest and proudest dolls in the world as owners of the drawings and the beautiful statue. I am now hoping that they will never be born, so that I can keep them forever in custody and enjoy them myself.[33]

A journal entry written by Florentine a decade earlier (19 August 1921) notes that she had made sketches for the 'doll portraits for Carrie's dollhouse picture gallery'.[34] Clearly, plans for dolls had been in place for much of the time Carrie had spent working on the Dollhouse (and Florine had been a collaborator at certain points), yet she opted to – as she suggested to Lachaise – keep the house for herself. This decision signals a resistance to the straightforward interpretation of the Dollhouse as a toy. The space and decoration are the centre of attention, removed from any sense of cosy domesticity that the presence of tiny inhabitants might bestow. Uninhabited, the Dollhouse is a space onto which viewers can project their own fantasies. In keeping with Carrie and Florine's love of the theatre, the Dollhouse is a stage for the viewer's imagination. It can transport us back – to a vision of the Stettheimer salon in all its luxurious, camp splendour – but it can also play host to new dreams. The Dollhouse invites us to reflect on how we organize and decorate the space around us, as well as how we negotiate the ideological boundaries placed between art, craft and domestic practices; with its playful humour, it also challenges expectations and understandings of New York's Dada movement. Carrie's Dollhouse remains a largely overlooked art object, more often seen as a curiosity than a significant creative project. Yet despite this, it plays a role in the development of twentieth-century American art: an exploration of the Dollhouse takes us on a journey to Betye Saar's assemblages, via Joseph Cornell's enchanted boxes; it takes in Andy Warhol's 'transcendentally camp' style that toyed with high and low art forms (Warhol noted his love of Florine Stettheimer and

Carrie's 'fabulous dollhouse that I loved [visiting] at the Museum of the City of New York' in his 1980 memoir *Popism*).[35] Stepping into Carrie's excessive, stylized miniature world brings about a transformation that upends what we think we know about art, femininity and domesticity – in the Stettheimers' world, nothing is quite what it seems.

Florine Stettheimer, Painter of Modern Life

In the eulogy she delivered at Florine Stettheimer's funeral, Georgia O'Keeffe paid tribute to a woman who had collapsed the boundaries between art and life; an artist who managed to be both ageless and absolutely modern, who channelled the spirit of the metropolis in a feminine-coded visual language:

> Anything that I would say about Florine I would say about her painting. Florine was ageless – never anything but young . . . When we saw her she was always charming and fresh – dressed surprisingly so that she and her paintings were always the same sort of thing – bright and clear – she had all the charm of an old fashioned valentine but she also had the smartness and brightness, the newness of today . . . Florine put into visible form in her own way something that [all three sisters] were, a way of life that is going and cannot happen again, something that has been alive in our city . . . Florine was a city girl.[36]

Like O'Keeffe, Stettheimer was a visionary chronicler and creator of American modernism, working against the grain of the masculine modes that would come to define it. Whereas O'Keeffe came to be acknowledged as the 'mother of American Modernism', Stettheimer remains something of an eccentric great-aunt. Her paintings are quite unlike anything else being produced at the time, and her use of fanciful allegory, decorative patterns and a camp sensibility place her in a world apart from her contemporaries. In her lifetime, she shifted between insider and outsider status: as a wealthy, middle-aged woman, she defied expectations to marry and have a family, to keep a house and respectable company, to act her age. Even among privileged women who had attended art school and practised art, Stettheimer stood out for her determination to create work that was not derivative or in the shadow of the male gaze. She painted women enjoying other women's company, nude women enjoying their own bodies and people who disregarded the societal norms of gender and sexuality.

In defiance of a modernist cult of youth and society's obsession with the modern woman (inevitably defined by youth), Stettheimer developed her unique artistic style in her mid-forties. She continued to push the boundaries of that style into her seventies, developing work that was bigger and bolder and branching out into new forms. The 1934 performance of Virgil Thomson and Gertrude Stein's *Four Saints in Three Acts* marked a then 63-year-old Stettheimer's ambitious (and successful) shift to the design of theatre sets and costume, giving her the opportunity to realize her luminous visions in three dimensions. Costumes and backdrops were an obvious step for an artist who was forever playing at the boundaries between fantasy and reality. Her art reworks forms and tropes traditionally linked to feminine and domestic art to surprising effect; the self-consciously artificial, decorative surfaces of her paintings are multi-layered, deploying something that Linda Nochlin (in her groundbreaking essay on Stettheimer) refers to as 'an actively subversive component [that is] inherent to Camp sensibility'.[37] Like Beatrice Wood and Clara Tice, Stettheimer showed that pleasure and amusement could also be subversive, a technique with which to disarm the viewer and smuggle controversial ideas and images into the public consciousness.

The perceived femininity of Stettheimer's art and the cellophane-wrapped, lace-draped fantasy world that the sisters created in their luxurious living spaces convinced many critics that she was a decorative, whimsical, dilettantish artist. Her cautious attitude towards exhibiting only reinforced the idea that Stettheimer was insular and not part of New York's early twentieth-century modern-art movement. With her sisters, Stettheimer made space for modern art in New York while also, as an artist, making art that reflected and responded to modern life in the metropolis. She eschewed typically modernist cold abstraction and clean lines, instead filling her paintings with detailed eclectic scenes that convey the 'noise and colour' of modernity. Stettheimer's paintings

Arnold Genthe,
Florine Stettheimer, 1931.

pulse with the thrills and sensory overload of city life – she was, as
O'Keeffe declared in her eulogy, a 'city girl', and highly invested in the
political and cultural life of New York and the United States. In fact,
Stettheimer's work is anything but insular; her paintings are portals to
a world of pleasure, parties and parades, where people share communal
experiences, such as dancing, playing sports and shopping. Stettheimer's
women enjoy the freedom of the city: they are active and intellectual,
they wear androgynous styles and elaborate costumes – or cast off clothes
all together.

Even Stettheimer's choice of materials shows the influence of the
city and her will to channel something of its scale and surfaces into her
work. Stettheimer's paintings are large and imposing, something that
is easily lost when viewing reproductions of her work in books or on a
screen. With their shimmering surfaces, fine details and narrative scenes,
it is easy to assume (when seen on a screen or a page) that Stettheimer

created small, intricate works. Instead, her paintings are substantial in size and heavily textured pieces: she applied paint with a palette knife, building rich surfaces of vivid colour in thick impasto, evoking New York's whirl of colour, noise, light, jazz and textures. Highlighting the imposing size of her canvases, O'Keeffe noted that they were 'very large paintings for the time', decades before the large-scale canvases of Abstract Expressionism. When viewed at her salon unveilings (hung on the decorative walls of her studio), the effect must have been overwhelming and immersive. The paintings' size is one of several ways that Stettheimer places femininity and domesticity in tension with a masculine, monumental, urban mode more typically associated with modern art. Like her sister Carrie, Stettheimer envisioned new worlds, while also using art to reshape everyday life. Her paintings offer us a tantalizing peek into a privileged life that was lived in the whirlwind of modern New York, without failing to flag up its absurdities and sinister undertones: posturing male egotists, department store dramas and even the smiling face of antisemitism that lurks among the parade in *Beauty Contest: To the Memory of P. T. Barnum* (1924). The Stettheimer sisters preside over it all – patron saints or modern goddesses – creating a world free from the binds of age and gender.

Artist in a Man's World

Stettheimer's personal and professional life revolved around art and culture, but her relationship with the art world was complicated. She operated quite differently to many of her artist friends and associates, maintaining a high level of control over her art. She was reluctant to sell paintings and deliberately inflated their prices to ward off potential buyers. Similarly wary of exhibiting, Stettheimer participated in select group exhibitions and preferred to launch her latest work at private viewing parties held in her salon. O'Keeffe lamented the fact that Stettheimer did not make more effort to show her work, and Duchamp helped arrange opportunities to exhibit paintings when possible; he also sought permission from Stettheimer to place her poem about mosquitos in a Dada magazine, later writing to Man Ray urging him to 'squeeze it into one of [Tristan] Tzara's numbers'.[38] Despite her friends' encouragement and support, Stettheimer was uncompromising in her approach. Critics often cite the failure of her one and only solo show at New York's Knoedler Gallery in 1916 for her later reticence, but the reality is more complex. In the work she created after 1916, Stettheimer clearly developed a stronger artistic voice and gained confidence in her artistic vision, which was moving away from trends in modern art towards something much more unique and unusual; with a network of friends who could critique and review her work (and independent wealth), she didn't need to hold solo shows. Her caution in exhibiting also reflects the difficulties faced by modern women artists, particularly those who did not have older male artists (inevitably as lovers or husbands) to promote their work or support them in a protégée/ingénue role. Stettheimer's envy of O'Keeffe's success (expressed in letters to McBride) reveals the difficult situation that women artists found themselves in, whether or not they associated themselves with male artists and curators. O'Keeffe's relationship with Stieglitz brought compromise and emotional upheaval, but Stettheimer's independence cut her adrift from the much-needed support of influential men.

Stettheimer's friendships with artists and her career as an artist ran parallel with a distinct scepticism of the art world and some of the people operating within it. In particular, art's status as a commodity to be owned (in most cases by men) troubled her. Stettheimer's poetry gives an insight into her thoughts on the business of art: 'Art is spelled with a capital A/ And capital also backs it . . . the chief thing is to make it pay.'[39] In another poem, 'The Unloved Painting', she imagines one of her paintings reproaching her for selling it to a male collector. Typically, Stettheimer placed prohibitively high prices on her paintings, preferring instead to keep them and exhibit them in her salon and the Stettheimer home. Of course, there is a certain irony in the fact that her own capital allowed her to make this choice: unlike many of her peers, she did not need to make money from her work and so was free to create (and retain ownership of) paintings without giving a thought to the market.

Beyond being simply critical of business matters, Stettheimer questioned the dominance of male artists and masculine forms. She took pleasure in satirizing and poking fun at their pomposity in her poetry and, occasionally, in her paintings. The shocking provocations of modern art become, in Stettheimer's words, the tantrum of a little boy shouting 'look at my painting' (the public response is 'go play with a toy!').[40] Stettheimer's poems are tongue-in-cheek, yet they express an underlying exasperation with the male-dominated art world and a desire to do things her own way. In 'Must One Have Models', Stettheimer exclaims:

> Must one have models forever
> Nude ones
> Draped ones
> Costumed ones
> 'The Blue Hat'
> 'The Yellow Shawl'
> 'The Patent Leather Slippers'
> Possibly men painters really
> Need them – they created them[41]

Her reference to common tropes of portraiture (for example, Pierre Bonnard's *La châle jaune* (c. 1925), Henri Matisse's *Femme au chapeau* (1905), Pablo Picasso's *Woman with Blue Hat* (1901)), highlights how women models are equated with the item of clothing they pose in, and thus become part of the same economy of commodities. Her sly dig at men needing models works to both undermine the imaginative creativity of male artists and to criticize the fact that they were often exploiting their models for sexual relationships. Stettheimer never worked from posed models. Instead, she observed her family and friends during salon parties and other social events, later turning her impressions and observations into paintings.

In many of Stettheimer's portraits of male friends, there is often an underlying tone of satire, used to mock male egotism. The characteristic use of symbolism and allegory in her portraits demonstrates intimacy with her subject, but it can also be used to quietly undermine the subject's own efforts to construct a serious, imposing identity. In 1928, she surprised Stieglitz with a portrait that depicted him in the Room (or, the Intimate Gallery), a space that he opened in 1925 to showcase the top American artists working at that time (Stettheimer declined an invitation to exhibit her paintings there). Departing from her usual vivid palette, Stettheimer painted Stieglitz in monochrome to reference the central role photography played in his life. However, it also casts a gloomy tone over the painting, which evokes the depressed frame of mind Stieglitz was in around this time (something that O'Keeffe had described to Stettheimer in their letters). His serious expression and the hand that anxiously clutches his lapel adds to the overall sombre mood. Allusions to O'Keeffe haunt the image: her name is inscribed backwards on the wall behind Stieglitz, next to a very faint outline of her face in profile. The window scene on the left side recreates O'Keeffe's leaf-and-landscape paintings. Rich colours seep in at the edges of the canvas in the form of Charles Demuth and photographer Baron Adolphe de Meyer, whose hands and feet are just visible striding into view. Perhaps Stettheimer hints that Stieglitz drew colour from the artists he surrounded himself with. The painting also alludes to the difficult dynamic between Stieglitz and O'Keeffe, played out in his efforts to possess and define her through his photography (and her later resistance to this). For an artist who was as careful with her own self-image as Stettheimer, this was undoubtedly anathema.

Some of her male friends fared a little better. Duchamp was the subject of two portraits, both of which capture his enigmatic nature and reflect his own interest in manipulating identity through unconventional portraiture. A good deal of mutual respect existed between Stettheimer and Duchamp. They shared a scepticism of the art world: Stettheimer's criticisms of art's dependence on capital chimed with Duchamp's opinion that art was a 'game', in which a 'painting is declared good only if it is worth "so much" – [and] . . . accepted by the holy museums'.[42] Duchamp recognized something unique and dynamic in Stettheimer's paintings, and he regularly sought updates on her work when he was absent from New York. In one letter written from Buenos Aires in 1919, he wrote that he was 'keen to know what "groups" Florine has done since [he] left', adding that he felt 'group' was a more exciting and 'mobile' term than the boring, traditional 'composition'.[43] Considering that Duchamp himself had grown bored of painting shortly after *Nude Descending a Staircase*, this was high praise. After Stettheimer's

Florine Stettheimer, *Carl Van Vechten*, 1922, oil on canvas.

death in 1942, Duchamp was one of the directors of an exhibition of her work, a role he would repeat for other women artists who had been good friends, including Beatrice Wood and Mina Loy.

Stettheimer's two portraits of Duchamp demonstrate her understanding of his slippery, sometimes contradictory nature as an artist. In one, Stettheimer paints Duchamp as a disembodied head, with a ghostly, luminous pallor. The shape of his head and the rays of light framing his face suggest an electric light bulb. This alludes to Duchamp's prevailing interest in science and technology, particularly X-rays, radio-activity and the physics of electricity.[44] There is a striking similarity to Picabia's cover for the July 1917 issue of Dada magazine *391* (created by Picabia, the title was an obvious reference to *291*), which shows a grey light bulb with the words 'FLIRT' and 'DIVORCE' written inside it. The caption 'Américaine' underneath signals that this is a comment on the modern American woman: lewdly suggestive, it draws parallels between the modern woman and mass-produced objects, suggesting that the modern American woman is sexually threatening (flirt and divorce referring to promiscuity) but also cold and mechanical. By ref-erencing this image, Stettheimer turns the tables on Picabia's chauvinism: the American woman is switched for the male French artist. It encodes a subtle allusion to Duchamp's gender play, as well as his passion for America's technologized modernity. He was likely amused by the ways that Stettheimer's whimsical painting encapsulated his interests in America's Fordist culture, mass production and the American woman, while also casting him as a vaguely sinister saint.

In Stettheimer's second portrait, Duchamp shares the space of the canvas with his alter ego, Rrose Sélavy. The painting sits in a custom-made frame, adorned with metal letters of Duchamp's initials along all four sides – the repeated 'MD' signals Duchamp's obsession with iden-tity and his playfulness, with the sequence of letters collapsing the signifier of his selfhood into nonsense (that is, Duchamp's MD is lost in an unending circular repetition of 'MDMDMDM' and so on). In the painting, Duchamp lounges in a chair decorated with the French and American flags, to acknowledge his native and adopted countries. A horse's head floating above him represents the knight chess piece, sym-bolizing his love of the game, as well as the meeting of the surreal and the rational within Duchamp. Duchamp turns a long metal pole, oper-ating a mechanism that elevates the painting's second figure, Rrose Sélavy. The way that he mechanically sets her in motion draws parallels with his readymades (some of which were signed Rrose Sélavy). Rrose's fluid figure is dressed entirely in pink and her pale face is made up. Stettheimer displays Rrose as Duchamp's camp double: her painting gives a much greater insight into Rrose's role as an avatar than Man Ray's famous photographs. While the latter presents Rrose as a theatrical character that Duchamp dresses up as, Stettheimer's portrait suggests that Rrose is part of Duchamp.

In the context of Stettheimer's androgynous figures, Rrose clearly represents Duchamp's feminine spirit. It is likely no accident that Rrose bears a certain similarity to Stettheimer's depictions of herself. This highlights their kindred artist spirits; on a more light-hearted level, it also acknowledges the Stettheimer sisters' role in Duchamp's creation of Rrose. They inspired her image and Rrose also became part of the sisters' and Duchamp's private language of affectionate in-jokes. In correspondence Ettie sometimes took on the masculine alter ego Henry

Florine Stettheimer, *Marcel Duchamp and Rose Sélavy*, 1923, oil on canvas.

Waste (a pun on her name), and Duchamp would refer to Stettheimer as 'bachelor'. Indeed, Duchamp signed as Rrose in many letters to the sisters, much more frequently than to any other correspondents. The Stettheimers' creative sphere (encompassing the salon, parties and Florine's paintings) emerge as a defining influence on Rrose Sélavy's entrance into the world of New York Dada.

Nymphs and Nudes of New York City

Image and identity were central aspects of Stettheimer's art. By including portraits of herself, her sisters and mother, and her friends, Stettheimer created lasting visions of their lives together, paying tribute to their talents and idiosyncrasies. The many painted versions of herself she included in her work also allowed Stettheimer to control her public image and resist the idea that she was ever anyone's muse. As she rarely agreed to be photographed, these portraits define how we imagine her: she is immortalized as ever youthful (in defiance of middle and old age), androgynous and impish. In other words, she exists in the imagination as a creative, chic modern woman, cast in the otherworldly aura of her luminous paintings. Stettheimer's self-portraits also allow us a glimpse into how the artist saw herself. In group scenes, she usually places herself on the margins; ever the observer, Stettheimer paints herself painting her friends and sisters; sometimes, she is turned to meet the viewer's gaze, as if giving us a knowing nod and wink. Stettheimer's appearance at the edge of gatherings highlights her persistent feeling of being an outsider, largely due to her intelligence and forthright nature (characteristics considered unbecoming of an upper-class woman in the early twentieth century). In her poems, she wrote frequently of feeling in a world full of strangers and being forced to tone down her personality in company. Using the visual language of her paintings, she imagines dimming the light of her being until it is something 'soft, pink...modest, charming', lest a man extinguish it, or people are simply scared away; once the stranger leaves, she becomes herself once again.[45] This hints at the play between surface and depth that Stettheimer also sets up in her paintings, where femininity similarly masks witty observations and social commentary.

As an artist, Stettheimer's feelings of being on the outside freed her from convention. The fact that she was protective of her inner self and unwilling to change to suit a man, or fulfil the typical domestic role expected of women, meant that she was able to more or less devote her life to painting (although the expectations of her sisters and mother proved to be an unwelcome distraction). Her unique perspective plays with our expectations and assumptions. In Stettheimer's vision, rules and traditions do not apply, particularly when it comes to identity and appearance. The majority of her portraits and group scenes present her subjects as ageless, sylphlike figures that could slide from masculine to feminine, or vice versa, with one slight flourish of a paintbrush. Both age and gender are almost irrelevant, or, rather, they take on different dimensions in Stettheimer's painted world. Henry McBride noted that Stettheimer 'rejected age . . . and in the portraits turned us into the essence of what we were. The "too, too solid flesh" meant nothing to her. She weighed the spirit.'[46] As Stettheimer developed her mature style, she found the confidence to give full expression to this unconventional and, for its time, progressive understanding of the self.

Stettheimer's *A Model (Nude Self-Portrait)* of circa 1915 represents a bold step in the transition she made from the fairly unremarkable Post-Impressionist style of her early years to the camp aesthetic of her mature work. Stettheimer introduces the luminous white background, applied in thick impasto, that would become a recurring feature in her dream-like scenes. We can clearly see how the highly decorative Stettheimer apartment, with its cellophane drapes, Grecian pillars and rococo dazzle informed the creation of her painted world – and vice versa. Stettheimer paints herself in a more realistic manner than the sylphlike bodies that populate her later paintings, but her features are heavily stylized; the overall impression is more akin to an advertising illustration than a traditional painted portrait. As in many of Stettheimer's paintings, a frame within the frame (in this instance, a fringed curtain) adds an element of theatricality. Significantly, though, Stettheimer presents herself in front of the curtain, not behind it. This underscores the painting's reversal of the traditional dynamic of the female nude portrait. *A Model (Nude Self-Portrait)* positions the nude woman not as an object of consumption, but as an active subject. Alongside Jacqueline

Florine Stettheimer, *Studio Party (Soirée)*, *c*. 1917–19, oil on canvas.

Marval's *Odalisque au Guépard* (1900), which Stettheimer might have seen in Paris, it represents not only one of the earliest female nude self-portraits in the Western canon but one of the earliest examples of a woman artist defying the male gaze.

The unconventional power dynamic at play in *A Model (Nude Self-Portrait)* is re-emphasized through its later appearance as a painting within a painting, in *Studio Party (Soirée)* (1917–19). Stettheimer never showed her nude self-portrait at a public exhibition, but she did display it prominently in her salon. *Studio Party* is typical of Stettheimer's late 1910s and '20s style: a crowded group scene, luminous with a soft pink backdrop and rich jewel tones. The atmosphere is more tense than many of her usual scenes: the men brood and scrutinize; the women lounge, bored and languid. It hints at Stettheimer's anxiety over showing work and the discomfort she felt about male art critics, even friends like McBride. The reproduction of *A Model* is placed at the top right of *Studio Party*, occupying a much larger space than the real painting. It stares out at the viewer, facing the same direction as the salon guests (some of whom study a painting that the viewer cannot see), giving the uncanny effect that the figure in the portrait is part of the crowd. The two Florine Stettheimers in the painting (that is, the nude self-portrait and the depiction of the artist seated on a couch alongside her guests) mirror each other's pose, each resting their head on their right hand. This subtle cue underscores the link between the two. The fact that the self-portrait was given a central position in the salon suggests that, for Stettheimer, it was a key part of her mythology and the persona that she cultivated for her selected group of friends and peers. By maintaining ownership of *A Model* and regulating who was allowed to see it, Stettheimer subverted the patriarchal system of spectatorship and exchange that the female nude portrait traditionally was placed in.

Perhaps one of the most striking things about this daring self-portrait is Stettheimer's age at the time of painting (44): by society's standards, she was a middle-aged spinster, a far cry from the youthful ingénue typically selected to be an artist's model. In many ways this painting was a statement of Stettheimer's intent as she settled into a new life in New York, to continue taking up space and having an active, public life as an artist – a radical thing to express for an older woman in the early twentieth century. From 1915 onwards, Stettheimer continued to play with her own image, creating unconventional self-portraits and inserting herself at the edge of large group scenes. She was as meticulous in controlling her image as she was in controlling ownership of her paintings: by rarely allowing herself to be photographed, Stettheimer's self-portraits are the dominant source of images of her. Through these painted acts of self-fashioning, Stettheimer portrays herself as an ageless, often androgynous character. In *Family Portrait II* (1930), she cuts a smart, self-assured figure wearing a black trouser suit and her signature red high heels. Along with fashion, Stettheimer used portraiture as a way to construct her identity as a modern urban woman, inserting herself into the story of the city and its art world in the vibrant interwar period.

Even in her final works, such as the *Cathedrals of Art* (1941), Stettheimer portrayed herself as a fashionable young woman, despite the fact that she was around seventy years old at the time. Stettheimer imbued herself and her sisters with a subversive sexuality that, once again, defied expectations of women, particularly of their class and age (life expectancy for women in the United States would not pass sixty until 1921). In *Bathers* (*c*. 1920), Florine depicts her sisters as nymph-like visions, showering and relaxing on an idyllic outdoor terrace. The painting is an urbane play on the traditional scene of the goddess Diana bathing with her nymphs, disturbed by Actaeon. In Stettheimer's painting, the intruding Actaeon is left out and her modern goddesses are less fleshy: the two naked women are lithe and long, with skin glowing a pearlescent white. Ettie takes a seductive pose on the chaise longue,

Florine Stettheimer, *Bathers*, *c*. 1920, oil on canvas.

arms stretched above her head and one leg bent wide, exposing her vulva, which is simply outlined to mirror the slight curve of her breast. It is a remarkable image given the context of the time, Ettie's age and the fact that the painter was a woman. Seen from the side, with her arm folded against her chest, Carrie is androgynous. She peeks at the viewer through the streams of water cascading down from the shower. To her right, a jet of water hits her buttocks, its source is the golden mouth of a sculpted feline face – a detail that enhances the painting's strange, subversive sexuality.

In her paintings, Stettheimer creates a mode of queer temporality – a time of lasting play, pleasure and leisure, where age and gender are fluid. Through this approach, she not only turns the Stettheimers' unique fantasy world into something lasting, in a manner similar to Carrie's, but celebrates the sisters' defiance of the expectations and constraints traditionally placed on women's lives.

New York: An Amusing Thing, America Having Its Fling

When the First World War forced Rosetta and her daughters to end their jaunts around Europe and settle in Manhattan full-time, Stettheimer fell in love with a city that was undergoing rapid, thrilling changes. She rhapsodized over New York City in her writing: it was, she declared, a city that had 'at last grown young' and was now alive with jazz, dazzling lights and skyscrapers sprouting up on its ever-growing skyline. Its vibrant energy chimed with Stettheimer's love of life and fear of stagnation. Decades ahead of Andy Warhol and Pop Art, she revelled in New York's booming popular culture; Broadway's lights, the electrifying atmosphere of speakeasies and dance halls and the glamour of the department store all fed into her art. After her death, Stettheimer came to be considered an insular artist, whose decorative, feminine art was too domestic to be part of modernism's urban culture. Yet the experiences and spectacles offered by modern city life were a fundamental influence on her, and something that she explored in her paintings with increasing frequency as her confidence and unique style grew. Stettheimer's vision of New York reflects her privilege, in that it is free from the deprivation and segregation that afflicted the urban experience of poor people and those from African American or immigrant communities – and, of course, it was her privilege as a wealthy white woman that afforded her the freedom of the city and the distance to make it into a work of art.

In Paris, Stettheimer had written poetry celebrating her love of being a *flâneur* in the city's parks. Back in New York, she also became a keen observer of urban life. The role of *flâneur* suited Stettheimer's independent nature and her persistent feeling of being distant from and different to other people. Her paintings, however, give the sense of being in the middle of the action. Stettheimer's skill at both creating and subverting fantasy with her unique style of campy satire meant that she was ideally placed to capture life in jazz-age New York. She evokes the rhythms of bodies out seeking pleasure in the city streets, the vivid pops of colour and dazzling bright lights; her art and writing are alive with the poetry and jazz of the city. In a 1946 letter to Museum of Modern Art director Monroe Wheeler, in which he proposed the posthumous exhibition of Stettheimer's work, Duchamp declared her to be 'a New York painter . . . among the first artists who, twenty-five years ago, helped build up the "school" of New York'.[47] Unlike many of the other New York painters that would follow, Stettheimer presented and created a woman's city, alive with the joy and possibilities that the modern woman found there.

Spring Sale at Bendel's (1921) is a dazzling example of Stettheimer's skill in conveying women's pleasure in venturing out into the city. The painting depicts eager women shopping the sale at Bendel's, a luxury department store that stocked the latest in haute couture from Paris (and was the first American store to import clothing by Coco Chanel). Bendel's pioneered fashion and shopping as an experience: it was the first to offer a sale, to stage a fashion show and to provide women with an in-store makeover service. The store was also conveniently located just around the corner from Alwyn Court, ideal for the Stettheimer sisters to shop the latest arrivals from Parisian fashion houses. *Spring Sale at Bendel's* presents a wonderfully dynamic scene that looks, at first glance, more like a ballet or a drama than an image of women shopping. Mirrored screens and fringed curtains set a theatrical tone. In a typically crowded picture plane, women bend and stretch nimbly as they try on new dresses. In the centre of the painting, a shopper in green seems to fly through the air as she dives towards a pile of clothes; to our left, a woman performs a *plié* as she steps into a voluminous red skirt while, in front of her, another appears to be caught mid-cartwheel. The rich tones, areas of floral decorative patterns and overall sense of rhythm recall Matisse, but Stettheimer's crowded scene bursts with life. Her subjects are active participants in urban life (rather than passive posed models) and each is engrossed in a private act of dressing or examining fabric.

Spring Sale at Bendel's and another vibrant ensemble scene she painted the year before, *Asbury Park South* (1920), marked the start of Stettheimer's bolder ambition in capturing bustling moments of modern life. As in *Lake Placid*, *Asbury Park South* shows that Stettheimer was careful and deliberate in choosing settings that were significant for both positive and troubling aspects of life in 1920s and '30s America. It commemorates a beach trip that Stettheimer and her friends made to Asbury Park, one of the first officially segregated beaches on the East Coast. They were taken there by Van Vechten, who played a support- ive but problematic role as a patron and promoter of Harlem Renaissance figures and as a white voyeur in Black cultural circles (his photography of Black artists, writers and entertainers captured his subjects through a white gaze, deploying racist visual tropes that enforced harmful ste- reotypes).[48] Bloemink's thorough reading of the painting and its context shows that the beach was a flashpoint for anti-segregation protests and activism, as its Black community fought against white supremacists' efforts to ban them from the beach and its boardwalks. The wealthy real-estate developer who owned the land (James Bradley), enforced segregation in the 1880s, banishing Asbury Park's Black residents to its southern beach, away from the main attractions and close to where a sewer pipe discharged into the sea.

In contrast with the area's history of discrimination, Stettheimer's painting presents a joyful scene. She shows a crowd of exquisitely dressed African American beach-goers delighting in the haze of a sunny 4 July day. Similar to *Spring Sale at Bendel's*, each group is absorbed in their own pleasure: a trio of stylish girlfriends strut along the boardwalk to the right; on the sands, a man dangles a tiny American flag for the amusement of a baby and, in the background, bathers tumble and dive into the sea. Bloemink highlights the significance of Stettheimer's painting of Black figures in this work, which is far removed from the racist caricatures and stereotypes that were typical of most white depictions of African American people at this time. In *Asbury Park South*, each person is presented as an individual and Stettheimer observes 'the multiplicity of African-American skin tones'. Stettheimer's inclusion of Fourth of July celebrations seems to be a pointed comment that this is a quintessential American scene, that these people are equal and valued American citizens. However, she confines the flags and banners to the far left of the painting, allowing full focus to fall on the events playing out on the beach and boardwalk.

Right up until her death in 1944, Stettheimer continued to fashion herself as a painter of metropolitan life in America's (and, increasingly, the world's) most modern city. This culminated in some of her boldest works, the *Cathedrals* series, which were praised by contemporary art critic Paul Rosenfeld as 'Americana' and 'documentary caricatures' of the country's part-serious, part-childish spirit.[49] In Stettheimer's final unfinished *Cathedrals* painting – *Cathedrals of Art* – she turns her attention to the New York art world. As she astutely documents, it was very different to the environment that she had returned to in 1914, when the city was still reeling from the shock of the Armory Show and young American artists were struggling to make space to develop and promote their work. By the 1940s, a number of prominent (mostly male) curators, gallery owners and gallery trustees were vying for authority and power: the Metropolitan Museum of Art was attempting to modernize, partly by exploring potential mergers with the Whitney Museum of American Art and the Museum of Modern Art, with the ambitious Francis Henry Taylor at the helm. Within the institutions themselves, several fraught power struggles played out. Alfred H. Barr Jr (another ambitious young man) was demoted from his post as director of the Museum of Modern Art and left out of negotiations with the Met.

Within the riotous scene, Stettheimer satirizes this wrangling over the legacy and future of modern American art. Each of the key players is shown posturing and posing and the canvas is divided up to represent MOMA, the Met and the Whitney. The Met takes centre stage, physically encroaching on its two rivals. Representing one of only two women involved in the curation and direction of a New York gallery in the painting, Whitney curator Juliana Force cuts a sombre, isolated yet dignified figure at the top right. Behind her, a golden statue of Gertrude Vanderbilt Whitney signifies her legacy. Stettheimer here acknowledges Force's solo efforts to defend the Whitney's autonomy in the time after Gertrude Vanderbilt Whitney's death. Owners of smaller galleries, such as Julien Levy and Marie Sterner, were also staking a claim for their chosen artists and art groups; Stettheimer pokes fun at their more modest efforts by showing them clutching small symbols of artists they supported (Levy holds balloons, one with Dalí written on it, and Steiner holds a bust by Elie Nadelman), which are dwarfed by the more elaborate displays of the Met and MOMA.

Stettheimer's amused scepticism at the whims of the art world is embodied in this painting by 'Baby Art'. The baby appears several times in the image: he is photographed and worshipped as he emerges on the scene, before being led up the iconic steps of the Met by Taylor, wearing a little gold crown. He can also be seen at the top left corner, playing naked on a Piet Mondrian abstract canvas, while Barr watches impassively. Baby Art is a prescient comment about the way that novelty, celebrity and money came to dominate modern art. *Cathedrals of Art* shows the rapid trajectory of modern art, from the shock, scandal and mockery that greeted the 1913 Armory Show to cultural behemoth by the 1940s; it also anticipates the ascendency of Abstract Expressionism and Pop art as specifically American movements that dominated the post-war art market. The fact that *Cathedrals of Art* is a male-dominated scene also signals the shifts that had occurred since the 1910s heyday of bohemian Greenwich Village and the feted modern women who had, in Mabel Dodge's account, run the city. Although women had been (and would continue to be) vital to the development of modern art in America, their contributions and voices were increasingly marginalized in favour of male genius and male-dominated networks of critics, curators, collectors and artists.

After her great success as the set and costume designer for *Four Saints in Three Acts*, Stettheimer was in demand from curators of exhibitions in America and Europe. The year of the opera, Julien Levy wrote to Mina Loy in Paris informing her that 'the vogue here has changed radically (through Florine Stettheimer's designs for Gertrude Stein Opera) . . . the dealers are fighting with each other to give a Stettheimer show', in a letter encouraging her that her own feminine, otherworldly art might find a new audience.[50] Along with O'Keeffe, Stettheimer was one of two modern American woman artists whose work was regularly sought out for large shows in her lifetime. The rapid decline of her reputation in the decades that followed make it hard to imagine that Stettheimer had, at one point, been feted. As Stettheimer sensed, the art market would not be kind to modern women artists: women's art commanded a fraction of the price of their male peers' work, so it was neglected by dealers and collectors. Similarly, as the narrative of modern art was written by male critics and art historians, women were sidelined. When Stettheimer wrote that 'ignorance makes [art] sway' and 'the chief thing is to make it pay,' she predicted her own years in a critical wilderness.[51]

By reducing Stettheimer's aesthetic to domestic, decorative frippery, critics missed her subversive use of avant-garde strategies – as a means both to position herself as an artist at the forefront of the modern movement and to disrupt the avant-garde's masculine posturing. Situating Stettheimer's art in the context of modernist experimentation with time and space, McBride referred to her style as, among other things, 'cinematic' and 'Proustian'; the press release for the posthumous retrospective organized by Duchamp in 1946 described this approach as a 'fourth-dimensional simultaneity'.[52] The spaces of Stettheimer's paintings hold multiple ideas, identities and possibilities, creating a world unbound by the rules of our own. In Stettheimer's world, gender and age were fluid; feminine- and masculine-coded modes of art merge, destabilizing assumptions about what modern art looked like and what its acceptable forms and topics were.

The decorative, urbane and – in certain critics' view – frou-frou elements that Stettheimer incorporated masked alternative meanings, small acts of resistance that allowed her to subvert traditions in art, as well as contemporary claims on modern art that centred on men and so-called masculine, rational forms. In the same way, Stettheimer's group compositions operate on different levels: they show the pleasure of a privileged set of modern people, while recording intangible, ephemeral cultural moments of the New York interwar avant-garde. They also align Stettheimer with modern pioneers across a range of arts, including painting, writing, dance and performance, like visual manifestos of her aesthetic vision. By painting these networks, Stettheimer found her own way of recording modern-art groups (and positioning herself within them), independent of critics, collectors and gallery owners. Her paintings themselves become coded messages that collapse the distance between Stettheimer's moment and our own, inviting us to find new approaches to the story of early twentieth-century modern art in America.

CODA:

MAKE THE WORLD
YOUR SALON

It is a cold February night in New York and the year is 1997. From beyond the grave, the voice of Baroness Elsa von Freytag-Loringhoven bemoans her death 'by asphyxiation' in Paris seventy years ago and intones fragments of her poetry like incantations. The spirit of the baroness is channelled by the artist Carolee Schneemann, in attendance for a recreation of an Arensberg salon soirée curated by Steven Watson. Although other guests play the part of members of the salon, including Carolyn Burke as Mina Loy and Francis Naumann as Marcel Duchamp, no one inhabits their subject as fully, as intensely, as Schneemann.

Much of the innovative feminist performance art of the 1960s and '70s bears the traces of the baroness and the approaches to art-making that emerged from the Arensberg and Stettheimer salons and bohemian Greenwich Village. Artists such as Yoko Ono, Theresa Hak Kyung Cha and Hannah Wilke continued the feminist spirit of the early twentieth-century Village's restless women, but Schneemann was surely the most fitting reincarnation of the baroness. In infamous performance pieces such as *Meat Joy* (1964) and *Up to and Including Her Limits* (1973–6), Schneemann disrupts the boundaries between her body, art and the spaces of everyday life. Messily mixing elements of dance, painting, collage and assemblage, Schneemann's art foregrounds her own body as a site of avant-garde experimentation and generation. In the process, she challenged passive images of women in art; like the baroness, she harnessed the subversive power of a female body that is sexual (rather than sexualized) and fleshy, and one which overspills the limits placed on it by patriarchal society.

By choosing to embody the baroness for Watson's salon event, Schneemann established a link with her avant-garde foremother that transcended the near century dividing the baroness's death in 1927 and Schneemann's performance as her in 1997. This connection speaks of the many ways that the influence and ideas of New York's early twentieth-century radicals and rogues continue to echo through the decades, right up to our contemporary moment. They take on myriad new forms of expression and direction, but all spring from the spirit of boldness and subversion that was embodied by the women of 1910s and '20s New York. Their innovations in art, poetry, magazine-making and creative ways of living continue to unfold and inform the emergence of new feminist, queer avant-garde movements.

Recent acts of academic recovery are drawing some of these women out of the wilderness in which they languished for the latter half of the twentieth century. Yet despite critical neglect, their work has continued to influence later generations, and we can trace many subtle threads that connect contemporary and mid-century artists to the women of 1910s and '20s New York. Florine Stettheimer's legacy, for example, winds its way through her self-professed admirer Andy Warhol to the whimsical portraits of Vaginal Davis and the sensual absurdity of Ambera Wellmann's decorative, intimate paintings. In the context of what curator Apsara DiQuinzio calls 'gender alchemy' (a term borrowed from the work of sculptor Nicki Green), Stettheimer's depiction of gender fluidity takes on a new resonance.[1] Similarly, Marguerite Zorach (who, despite her fascinating career, currently lacks a critical biography) becomes more relevant as a contemporary interest in textile art offers new ways of framing and interpreting work previously dismissed as domestic. There is still much work to do in tracing lineages and excavating stories that were relegated to the margins of cultural history.

If the modern woman at the vanguard of 1910s and '20s New York cultural life teach us anything, however, it is the importance of networks and collective movements. The women who appear in this book were joined by countless other 'anonymous women' (in Mabel Dodge's words) who used art and creative practices to transform everyday life. They drew on friendships, political allegiances and professional and romantic relationships to achieve their visions and support wider aims to live lives free from the restrictions that had tied previous generations of women to the home, to husbands and children, to a small, dependent existence. They recognized a need for collaborative, unrestricted spaces where people could come together to imagine new ways of living and creating art, away from the limitations of an oppressive, patriarchal society. The salons, cafés and magazines that women such as the Stettheimers, Louise Norton, Louise Arensberg and Paula Holladay set up provided crucial spaces of counterculture, where ideas that were then taboo or radical could be discussed freely. Salons, in particular, modelled a dynamic part-public, part-private environment where hosts and their guests were free to exchange ideas, subvert gender roles and turn society's codes upside down.

Through their radical creative practice, artists and writers like Florine Stettheimer, Mina Loy, Clara Tice and Beatrice Wood sought to reimagine the world. They sought to prove that art and literature could – and should – be a democratic, essential and transformative part of society. For a moment, the cigarette-smoking, poetry-writing, smock-wearing, bob-haired modern woman ruled New York. She embodied modernism and seemed to herald a new era of freedom. Yet just as quickly as she dominated public consciousness, she faded from view – swept away by a conservative turn that followed economic depression and the horror of the Second World War. In the post-war years, the masculine Abstract Expressionist movement marked a new era of American male genius. The shift from cultural prominence to footnote in a history book is a stark example of how vulnerable women artists are to changes in taste and resurgences of conservatism, due to a lack of investment in their work and myriad socio-economic factors. From the perspective of our own era, it is a timely reminder that museums and collectors must invest in art by women and artists of colour in order to widen the narrative of art history (and art's future): exhibitions of artists from marginalized communities may be fashionable, but this does not necessarily translate into lasting change in terms of museum acquisitions and sales, or truly equal representation in the art world. The zeitgeist must not distract from the real work of questioning institutions and pushing them to be bolder and go further in their commitments to real progress.

While the stories of many early twentieth-century women artists and writers faded, their impact on art in America remained. Without their restless energy, experimental approaches and desire to harness the febrile, youthful spirit of the new century, American modernism would look very different. The transformation of New York City into a capital of modernity is largely unthinkable without their contributions to art, contributions that were woven into the very fabric of the city – from MOMA and the Whitney to Greenwich Village, traces of their influence linger. The modern woman of the 1910s and '20s made the city synonymous with boundary-pushing freedom and a subversive, tricksy mode of avant-garde creativity. In this, she sparked the dreams of later generations of radical freethinkers who would form their own collectives and mount fresh challenges to institutions and society. Mid-century spaces like Andy Warhol's Factory and Yoko Ono's Chambers Street loft, and groups such as the Heresies Collective, built on their legacy, taking efforts to collapse the boundaries between art and life in new directions. From the perspective of the early twenty-first century, certain aspects of the their era seem disconcertingly familiar. At a time of deepening inequality, global instability, threats to bodily autonomy and a resurgence in conservative values, it can feel futile to engage in creativity that is hopeful, joyful and provocatively future-facing. From their own turbulent moment in history, the radicals and rogues urge us to boldly reimagine what is possible, to take creative risks and follow Mina Loy's imperative call: 'make the world your salon.'

REFERENCES

INTRODUCTION

1 See Dawn Adès and Alastair Brotchie, 'Marcel Duchamp was Not a Thief', *Burlington Magazine*, CLXI/1401 (2019). See also 'Letters to the Editor: Did Duchamp Really Steal Elsa's Urinal?', *Art Newspaper*, www.theartnewspaper.com, 4 March 2020.
2 Jennifer Cooke, *Contemporary Feminist Life-Writing: The New Audacity* (Cambridge, 2020), p. 1.
3 Quoted ibid., p. 4.
4 Quoted in Judith Schwarz, *Radical Feminists of Heterodoxy: Greenwich Village, 1912–1940* (Lebanon, NH, 1982), p. 25.
5 Walt Whitman, *Leaves of Grass* (Garden City, NY, 1920), p. 108.
6 Saidiya Hartman, *Wayward Lives, Beautiful Experiments: Intimate Histories of Riotous Black Girls, Troublesome Women and Queer Radicals* (London, 2021), p. xv.
7 Ibid., p. xvii.

1 THE ARMORY SHOW: *Riot and Rebellion in New York*

1 Walt Kuhn, letter to Walter Pach (12 December 1912).
2 Donald Gallup, *Flowers of Friendship: Letters Written to Gertrude Stein* (New York, 1953), pp. 70–71.
3 *New York Evening Sun* (20 March 1913).
4 *New York Times* (16 March 1913).
5 Carl Van Vechten, *Peter Whiffle: His Life and Works* (New York, 1922), p. 123.
6 Christopher Long, *Paul T. Frankl and Modern Design* (New Haven, CT, and London, 2007), p. 82.
7 Walt Kuhn, *The Story of the Armory Show* (New York, 1938), pp. 24–5.
8 *New York Evening Telegram* (13 March 1913), p. 5.
9 Contemporary critics have demonstrated the importance of women to the Abstract Expressionist movement, but the dominant image projected at the time (and reified in the years following) was intensely masculine. For more on the women of Abstract Expressionism see Mary Gabriel, *Ninth Street Women: Lee Krasner, Elaine de Kooning, Grace Hartigan, Joan Mitchell, and Helen Frankenthaler: Five Painters and the Movement That Changed Modern Art* (New York, 2018).
10 *New York Evening Sun* (13 February 1917), quoted in Sandra Gilbert and Susan Gubar, *No Man's Land: The Place of the Woman Writer in the*

Twentieth Century, vol I: *The War of the Words* (New Haven, CT, 1988), p. vii.

11 Jennifer Pfeifer Shircliff notes that $5 in 1913 is the equivalent of $178 in 2014. See Jennifer Pfeifer Shircliff, 'Women of the 1913 Armory Show' (2014), *Electronic Theses and Dissertations*, https://doi.org/10.18297/etd/1322, accessed 1 February 2020.

12 Davidge's papers have not survived, nor have the records of her Madison Art Gallery, despite Davidge herself being active in social welfare in the 1900s and the art world of the 1910s.

13 Prior to opening the Madison Art Gallery, Davidge was a passionate social-reform campaigner, with a particular concern for improving conditions for working-class women. She lectured at the Pratt Institute on the topic, and wrote essays for magazines; for example, see Clara Davidge, 'What Society Offers Mary Grew', *The Cosmopolitan*, XV/1 (May–October 1893), pp. 223–7.

14 Kuhn, *The Story of the Armory Show*, p 4. Kuhn also suggests that Gertrude Vanderbilt Whitney provided some of the funds for the Madison Art Gallery.

15 E.S.H. [assumed to be Elizabeth Sage Hare], *Art Review*, 1 (January 1922), pp. 14–15. Hare was a painter and influential arts patron. Her niece Kay Sage became a noted Surrealist artist.

16 Ibid., p. 15.

17 Mabel Dodge, *Movers and Shakers* (New York, 1936), p. 39.

18 Dodge's biographer, Lois Palken Rudnick, notes that there was no suggestion Edwin mistreated Dodge or interfered in her life, beyond demanding fidelity after the scandal of her affairs in Florence. However, she had never been in love with him and clearly felt the pursuit of a more fulfilling sexual relationship to be integral to her life as a liberated, modern woman. See Lois Palken Rudnick, *Mabel Dodge Luhan: New Woman, New Worlds* (Albuquerque, NM, 1987), p. 9.

19 Dodge, *Movers*, p. 57.

20 Ibid., p. 69.

21 Gertrude Stein, 'Portrait of Mabel Dodge at the Villa Curonia', *Camera Work* (June 1913), pp. 3–5.

22 Dodge, *Movers*, p. 36.

23 Mabel Dodge, 'Speculations', *Camera Work* (June 1913), pp. 6–9.

24 Ibid., p. 9.

25 Mabel Dodge, 'Speculations, or Post-Impressionism in Prose', *Arts and Decoration* (March 1913), p. 172.

26 Dodge, *Movers*, p. 36.

27 Ibid., p. 35.

28 Dodge was an early proponent of psychoanalysis in America, undergoing analysis first with Smith Ely Jelliffe in 1916, then Brill. Patricia R. Everett has written extensively on Dodge's encounters with psychoanalysis: see *Corresponding Lives: Mabel Dodge Luhan, A. A. Brill, and the Psychoanalytic Adventure in America* (London and New York, 2016); and *The Dreams of Mabel Dodge: Diary of an Analysis with Smith Ely Jelliffe* (London and New York, 2021).

29 The pageant was, ultimately, a failure in that it failed to make money. It also led to arguments between the artists and activists, with the latter (falsely) accusing the former of stealing profits.

30 Quoted in Doris Alexander, *Eugene O'Neill's Last Place: Separating Art from Autobiography* (Athens, GA, and London, 2005), p. 32.

31 Dodge, *Movers*, p. 89.

32 Lincoln Steffens, *The Autobiography of Lincoln Steffens* (New York, 1958), vol. II, pp. 654–5.

33 Van Vechten, *Peter Whiffle*, p. 124.

34 'Many Inventions! 1914!', *New York Morning Telegraph*, Series IV: Scrapbooks. Mabel Dodge Luhan Papers. Yale Collection of American Literature, Beinecke Rare Book and Manuscript Library.

35 Mabel Dodge Luhan, *Intimate Memories: The Autobiography of Mabel Dodge Luhan*, ed. Lois Palken Rudnick (Albuquerque, NM, 1999), p. 37.

36 Dodge, *Movers*, p. 84.

37 First published in a 1920 edition of *The Dial* and written between 1915 and 1916.

38 Mina Loy, *The Pamperers*, in *The Stories and Essays of Mina Loy*, ed. Sara Crangle (London, 2011), pp. 162–82, p. 164.

39 *In Exaltation of Flowers* was donated to MOMA by Meyer's family, but, due to its vast size, it was quickly sold on to the Art Bridges Foundation. In 2017, the Dallas Museum of Art displayed the full mural and carried out new research into its rich symbolism. Renewed interest led to another contemporary exhibition, at the Chrysler Museum of Art, Virginia, in 2021.

40 Mrs Eugene Meyer interviewed by Emma Bugbee, *Barnard College Alumnae Monthly* (1934), pp. 10–11.

41 Agnes Ernst Meyer, *Out of These Roots: The Autobiography of an American Woman* (Boston, MA, 1953), p. 68.

42 Quoted in Marius de Zayas, *How, When, and Why Modern Art Came to New York* (Cambridge, MA, and London, 1998), pp. 196–7.

43 Agnes Ernst Meyer, 'How Versus Why', *291* (March 1915), p. 2.

44 Ibid.

45 References in the poem to 'snow covered roof tops' and the view of New York 'best from the back and from above' correspond with Stieglitz's *From the Back* series of photographs (1915/16), which were taken looking out from 291. In one, an advertisement for a *parfumerie,* with the face of a pierrot clown, is visible (the advertisement features the correct spelling of crème – with a grave accent, not, as Meyer suggests it should be, a circumflex!)

46 Agnes Ernst Meyer, 'Mental Reactions', *291* (April 1915), p. 3.

47 Ibid.

48 Willard Bohn, 'The Abstract Vision of de Zayas', *Art Bulletin* (September 1980), pp. 434–52.

49 Ibid.

50 Katharine Rhoades, 'I Walked into a Moment of Greatness', *291* (May 1915), p. 2.

51 In a further example of the bind faced by many women artists, Carles was entranced by Rhoades but was hostile towards women artists more

generally: O'Keeffe recalled that, when planning an exhibition with
Stieglitz, Carles declared, 'I don't want any goddamn women in the show!'
Quoted in Kirsten Swinth, *Painting Professionals: Women Artists and the
Development of Modern American Art, 1870–1930* (Chapel Hill, NC, and
London, 2001), p. 183.

52 Katharine Rhoades letter to Alfred Stieglitz (5 December 1914). Alfred
Stieglitz/Georgia O'Keeffe Archive, Yale Collection of American
Literature, Beinecke Rare Book and Manuscript Library.

53 See Herbert Seligmann, *Alfred Stieglitz Talking: Notes on Some of His
Conversations* (New Haven, CT, 1966). Rhoades did, however, continue
to be loosely affiliated with Steiglitz's circle, occasionally modelling for
photographs and keeping up a friendly correspondence with O'Keeffe.

54 Kathleen Pyne, *Modernism and the Feminine Voice: O'Keeffe and the
Women of the Stieglitz Circle* (Berkeley and Los Angeles, CA, 2007),
p. 263.

55 Stieglitz held an exhibition of drawings by Engelhard at 291 in 1916,
when she was ten years old.

56 William Innes Homer, *Alfred Stieglitz and Modern Art in America*
(Boston, MA, 1977), p. 194.

57 William Zorach, *Art Is My Life: The Autobiography of William Zorach*
(Cleveland, OH, 1967), p. 37.

58 Ibid., p. 23.

59 Ibid., p. 22.

60 Ibid., p. 43. In addition to the general hysteria that surrounded modern
art, William notes the antisemitism that was also bound up in anti-modern
sentiments: he recalls a Philadelphia critic announcing that 'East Side Jews
were running and ruining American art.'

61 Zorach, *Art Is My Life*, p. 41.

62 The Zorachs put Madison in touch with friends at the Theatre Guild of
New York, which led to her being cast in *Porgy and Bess* in 1927.

63 Quoted in Kate Kennedy, *Maine's Remarkable Women* (Portland, ME,
2016), p. 102.

64 Other Armory Show artists included Anne Goldthwaite, Margaret
Huntington and Ethel Myers.

65 Rebecca Hourwich, 'Art Has No Sex', *Equal Rights* (12 December 1925).

66 See 'Modern Tapestries in Colored Wools', *Vanity Fair* (October 1922),
p. 66.

67 Gertrude Vanderbilt Whitney Papers, 1851–1975, bulk 1888–1942, Box 10,
Folder 2: Journal, 1904–1911. Archives of American Art, Smithsonian
Institution.

68 Quoted in Wendy Goodman, *The World of Gloria Vanderbilt* (New York,
2010), p. 56. Whitney took part in an infamous legal battle for custody of
heiress Gloria (her brother Reginald's child) in 1934, which she won.

69 Gertrude Vanderbilt Whitney Papers, 1851–1975, bulk 1888–1942, Box 26,
Folder 1: Autobiographical Writings, 'My History', undated. Archives of
American Art, Smithsonian Institution.

70 Whitney records a kiss shared with Esther in her diary, but, in general,
Esther appears to be the more enthusiastic party. Esther composed a book

of love poems to mark Whitney's twentieth birthday, in which she declared 'I love you and I would give anything in this world if only you were Gertrude – anything but Vanderbilt.'

71 Greenwich House continues to play a vital part in the community, supporting all ages and people with substance abuse and other health issues. Pottery lessons began there in 1905, but Whitney's funds meant that a department for pottery could be established; this was joined by a music school in 1915.

72 The Whitneys moved into 871 Fifth Avenue in 1910 and Gertrude stayed there until 1942, just before her death. It was later demolished to make way for an apartment block.

73 Quoted in B. H. Friedman, *Gertrude Vanderbilt Whitney* (New York, 1978), p. 246.

74 Quoted ibid.

75 Avis Berman, *Rebels on Eighth Street: Juliana Force and the Whitney Museum of American Art* (New York, 1990), p. 7.

76 Oral history interview with Marie Appleton, 27 June 1977. Archives of American Art, Smithsonian Institution.

77 Helena Appleton Read, 'The Whitney Museum', *Vogue* (March 1930), p. 69.

2 GREENWICH VILLAGE: *Restless Women of the Smock Colony*

1 Quoted in Julia Van Haaften, *Berenice Abbott: A Life in Photography* (New York, 2018), p. 17.

2 Anna Alice Chapin, *Greenwich Village* (New York, 1925), p. 210.

3 Frank Shay, *The Greenwich Villager* (1921). Shay's bookshop was located on Christopher Street between 1920 and 1924 and was popular with the neighbourhood's bohemian artists and writers. The door of Shay's bookshop miraculously survived (covered with the autographs of the many movers and shakers who passed through it) and can now be viewed digitally as part of an online exhibition hosted by the Harry Ransom Center.

4 Max Eastman, 'Editorial', *The Masses* (December 1912).

5 Max Eastman, *Enjoyment of Living* (New York, 1948), p. 418. Eastman added that *The Masses'* 'relations with that entity [Greenwich Village] were not simple', gesturing towards the many competing and, in some cases, contrasting strains of thought that existed among the Village's bohemian community.

6 In fact, both *The Masses* and the *Little Review* faced legal action – the latter for publishing excerpts of James Joyce's *Ulysses* (in 1921) and the former for publishing 'treasonable material' that 'obstructed' recruitment to the U.S. military (in 1918).

7 Robert Schulman, *Romany Marie: The Queen of Greenwich Village* (Nashville, TN, 2006), p. 5.

8 Crystal Eastman, 'Birth Control in the Feminist Program', in *On Women and Revolution*, ed. Blanche Wiesen Cook (London and New York, 1978), pp. 46–8.

9 Saidiya Hartman, *Beautiful Lives, Wayward Experiments: Intimate Histories of Riotous Black Girls, Troublesome Women and Queer Radicals* (London, 2021).

10 Lillian Faderman, *Odd Girls and Twilight Lovers: A History of Lesbian Life in Twentieth-Century America* (New York, 2011), p. 87.

11 'Vast Suffrage Host Is on Parade To-Day', *New York Times* (4 May 1912), p. 22.

12 Clara Lemlich, 'The Inside of a Shirtwaist Factory', *Good Housekeeping*, LIV/3 (March 1912), pp. 367–9.

13 Winnifred Harper Cooley, *Harper's Weekly* (1913).

14 June Sochen, *The New Woman: Feminism in Greenwich Village, 1910–1920* (New York, 1972), p. 7.

15 Crystal Eastman, 'Now We Can Begin', *The Liberator* (December 1920), p. 23.

16 Ibid.

17 Goldman expounded this argument at length in 'The Social Aspects of Birth Control', an essay in her journal, *Mother Earth* (April 1916).

18 Mabel Dodge, *Movers and Shakers* (New York, 1936), pp. 143–4.

19 Harry Hibbard, *More Miles: An Autobiographical Novel* (New York, 1926), pp. 85–6.

20 Judith Schwarz, *Radical Feminists of Heterodoxy: Greenwich Village, 1912–1940* (Lebanon, NH, 1942), p. 19.

21 Quoted ibid., p. 18.

22 Schwarz adds that, relative to members' groups of the time, she expected to find represented in Heterodoxy 'less diversity in racial, cultural and religious background', with the representation of Irish and Jewish women particularly surprising, in comparison. In this respect, Schwarz suggests that Heterodoxy was actually more 'diverse' than the women's groups she herself was a member of in the 1980s (at the time she was writing).

23 Schwarz, *Radical Feminists*, p. 19.

24 Faderman, *Odd Girls and Twilight Lovers*, p. 82.

25 In a letter to renowned theorist of sexuality Magnus Hirschfeld, Goldman described her sadness that society 'shows so little understanding for homosexuals and is so crassly indifferent to the various gradations and variations of gender'. She later described being 'condemned bitterly' by fellow anarchists 'because I had taken up the cause of the Homo Sexual and Lesbians as a persecuted faction in the human family', quoted in Terence Kissack, *Free Comrades: Anarchism and Homosexuality in the United States, 1895–1917* (Oakland, CA, 2008), pp. 27–8.

26 Dodge, *Movers*, p. 48.

27 Louis committed suicide in 1917 at Romany Marie's restaurant. Letters between O'Neill and his wife Agnes Boulton suggest a difficult relationship with Adele in the years after Louis's death; in 1920, O'Neill writes that Adele has requested a loan of $25 *'immediately . . . if I really believed that she needed it I'd give it to her in spite of her poisonous tongue'; see William Davies King, *A Wind Is Rising: The Correspondence of Agnes Boulton and Eugene O'Neill* (Vancouver, 2000), p. 79.

28 W. Adolphe Roberts, *These Many Years: An Autobiography*, ed. Peter Hulme (Kingston, 2015), pp. 131–2.

29 Agnes Boulton, *Part of a Long Story: Eugene O'Neill as a Young Man in Love*, ed. William Davis King (Jefferson, NC, 2011), p. 75.
30 Hutchins Hapgood, *A Victorian in the Modern World* (New York, 1939), p. 426.
31 Quoted by William Brevda, *Harry Kemp: The Last Bohemian* (London and Toronto, 1986), p. 83.
32 Roberts, *These Many Years*, pp. 132–3.
33 Anna Alice Chapin, *Greenwich Village* (New York, 1925), pp. 221–2.
34 *Rogue*, I/1 (March 1915), p. 3.
35 Dame Rogue, 'Philosophic Fashions', *Rogue*, I/1 (March 1915), pp. 17–18.
36 Dame Rogue, 'Philosophic Fashions', *Rogue*, II/2 (November 1916), p. 2.
37 Crystal Eastman, 'Short Hair and Short Skirts', in *On Women and Revolution*, ed. Blanche Wiesen Cook (London and New York, 1978), pp. 74–6.
38 Dame Rogue, 'Philosophic Fashions', *Rogue*, I/3 (April 1915), p. 15.
39 Ibid.
40 Gertrude Stein, *Autobiography of Alice B. Toklas* (London, 2001), p. 150.
41 Hanne Bergius, '"First International Dada-Fair": Catalog of the Exhibition and Its Reconstruction', in *Crisis and the Arts: The History of Dada*, ed. Stephen Foster (New Haven, CT, 1996), vol. V, p. 40.
42 'J. L. McCutcheon Obituary', *Pittsburgh Press* (17 July 1905), p. 3.
43 Louise and Allen Norton married on 12 October 1911 and Michael was born 21 May 1912.
44 Louise Varèse, *Varèse: A Looking-Glass Diary, 1883–1928* (New York, 1972), p. 126.
45 Accounts of the events exist in several memoirs and biographies of O'Neill and his Greenwich Village circle. See, for example, John Loughery and Blythe Randolph, *Dorothy Day: Dissenting Voice of the American Century* (New York, 2020), p. 65.
46 Varèse, *Looking-Glass Diary*, p. 136.
47 Quoted in Jacquelynn Baas, *Marcel Duchamp and the Art of Life* (Cambridge, MA, 2019), p. 151.
48 Louise Norton, 'Buddha of the Bathroom', *Blind Man*, 2 (1917), pp. 5–6.
49 Louse Varèse, 'Marcel Duchamp at Play', in *Marcel Duchamp* (Munich and New York, 1989), pp. 224–5.
50 Ibid.
51 Djuna Barnes, 'Becoming Intimate with the Bohemians', in *Vivid and Repulsive as the Truth: The Early Works of Djuna Barnes*, ed. Katharine Maller (New York, 2016), pp. 69–77.
52 Ibid., p. 76.
53 Ibid.
54 Djuna Barnes, 'Greenwich Village as It Is', in *Vivid and Repulsive as the Truth*, ed. Maller, pp. 63–9.
55 Mary Unger, '"Dropping Crooked into Rhyme": Djuna Barnes' Disabled Poetics in *The Book of Repulsive Women*', *Legacy: A Journal of American Women Writers*, XXX/1 (2013), pp. 124–50, p. 138.
56 Barnes, 'Becoming Intimate', p. 73.

57 Djuna Barnes, *Interviews*, ed. Alyce Barry (Washington, DC, 1985), p. 388.

58 In her notes to the collected edition of Barnes's New York journalism, Alyce Barry comments that racism spurred a white middle-class interest in boxing in the 1910s, as white audiences sought a white fighter who could defeat Jack Johnson, the first African American world heavyweight champion.

59 Djuna Barnes, 'Commissioner Enright and M. Voltaire', in *New York*, ed. Alyce Barry (Los Angeles, CA, 1989), p. 301.

60 Thomas Heise, 'Degenerate Sex and the City: Djuna Barnes's Urban Underworld', *Twentieth Century Literature*, LV/3 (2000) pp. 287–321, p. 311.

61 Djuna Barnes, 'How the Villagers Amuse Themselves', *New York Morning Telegraph* (26 November 1916), p. 1.

62 'She Wore Men's Clothes', *New York Times* (17 September 1910), p. 6.

63 Baroness Elsa von Freytag Loringhoven, 'Caught in Greenwich Village', in *Body Sweats: The Uncensored Writing of Baroness Elsa von Freytag Loringhoven*, ed. Irene Gammel and Suzanne Zelazo (Cambridge, MA, 2011), pp. 108–9.

64 In Francis Naumann's assessment, the baroness likely came up with the concept and gave the piece its title, while Schamberg assembled and photographed it. See Francis Naumann, *New York Dada, 1915–23* (New York, 1994), p. 128.

65 Ezra Shales, '"Decadent Plumbers' Porcelain": Craft and Modernity in Ceramic Sanitary Ware', *Ostracon Journal of Criticism + Issues* (October 2017), pp. 211–42.

66 Jane Heap, 'Dada', *Little Review*, 6 (1919), p. 46.

67 This location of the draft in the archives of the *Little Review* suggests that the baroness intended 'Graveyard Surrounding Nunnery' to be printed in this graphic form.

68 Baroness Elsa von Freytag Loringhoven, 'Graveyard Surrounding a Nunnery', in *Body Sweats*, ed. Gammel and Zelazo, p. 201.

69 Ibid.

70 William Carlos Williams, *Autobiography of William Carlos Williams* (New York, 1967), p. 168.

71 Ibid.

72 George Biddle, *An American Artist's Story* (Boston, MA, 1939), p. 140.

73 Chapin's guidebook suggests that 'if you have not smoked Sonia's Art Cigarettes, it is like – "the sky without stars, the dance without music, or summer without sunshine, or life without love".' Chapin, *Greenwich Village*, p. 25.

74 Barnes, 'Becoming Intimate', p. 244.

75 Quoted in 'The Bob and Chop', *Bryn Mawr Alumnae Bulletin* (Summer 2017), p. 11.

76 Van Loon won the Newbery medal in 1921 for his children's history book and later played a role in Franklin D. Roosevelt's 1940 presidential campaign. His relationship with Criswell was tumultuous – they divorced and he remarried, then divorced again – but had reunited by the time of van Loon's death, and she inherited his estate. The Van Loon papers (including Criswell's) are now held at Cornell University.

77 Gina Modero, 'Jessie Tarbox Beals, Pioneering Woman Photographer', *New York Historical Society*, www.nyhistory.org, 12 December 2021.
78 'Greenwich Village', *Ladies' Home Journal* (March 1920), p. 5.
79 'Where Is the Artist Rich Enough to Rent a Studio?', *New York Tribune* (28 August 1921), p. 3.
80 Eleanor's experiences in the Village complicated her marriage to Franklin D. Roosevelt (free to experiment with her sexuality, she began a relationship with Lorena Hickok in the 1930s), but her biographer suggests that 'one might even legitimately wonder if FDR ever would have become president were it not for Eleanor's ongoing and transformative experiences in the Village'. See Jan Jarboe Russell, *Eleanor in the Village: Eleanor Roosevelt's Search for Freedom and Identity in New York's Greenwich Village* (New York, 2022).

3 CLARA TICE: *Belle of the Ball, Bohemian Queen*

1 Frank Crowninshield, *'Who Is Clara Tice?' Animals and Nudes by Clara Tice*, exh. cat., The Anderson Galleries (New York, 1922), p. 1.
2 Clara Tice, 'How You Looked to Clara Tice That Day on the Meramec', *St Louis Star and Times* (3 July 1921), p. 43.
3 Marie T. Keller suggests that, in later life, Tice alluded to having lived with Duchamp for a period in the 1910s. She also appears in notorious womanizer Henri-Pierre Roché's diary, with Roché noting down several trips to the opera, restaurants and the Arensberg salon with Tice, as well as overnight stays at her apartment. See Marie T. Keller, 'Clara Tice, "Queen of Greenwich Village"', in *Women in Dada*, ed. Naomi Sawelson-Gorse (Cambridge, MA, 1998), pp. 425–6.
4 Clara Tice, 'My Model World' (unpublished MS draft), Clara Tice Papers, 1922–1942. Pennsylvania State University Library.
5 Sarah Addington, 'Who's Who in New York', *New York Tribune* (14 November 1914), p. 2.
6 For more on this history and its legacy, see Jenny Brown, *Without Apology: The Abortion Struggle Now* (London, 2019).
7 Tice, 'My Model World'.
8 'Comstock Ban Brings Art Buyer', *New York Tribune* (14 March 1915), p. 1.
9 Crowninshield, *'Who is Clara Tice?'*, p. 3.
10 Carolyn Burke interview with Louise Norton Varise [*sic*], Box 6. Carolyn Burke Collection on Mina Loy and Lee Miller. Yale Collection of American Literature, Beinecke Rare Book and Manuscript Library.
11 Guido Bruno, *First Exhibit of Drawings and Paintings by Clara Tice*, exh. cat. (New York, 1915).
12 'Clara Tice Lights Guido Bruno Garret', *New York Times* (11 May 1915), p. 8.
13 Quoted in Francis Naumann, *New York Dada, 1915–1923* (New York, 1994), p. 118.
14 Tice, 'My Model World'.
15 'Vogue of Bobbed Hair: Of Course Greenwich Village Lassies Wear Short Locks, but Society's Doing It Too', *New York Times* (27 June 1920), p. 71.

16 'She Set the Fashion for Bobbed Hair', *St Louis Star and Times* (9 June 1921), p. 2.
17 *Cartoons Magazine*, XII/2 (August 1917).
18 The 1917 Espionage Act specifically targeted newspapers and magazines: postal officials were given authority to ban offending publications from the mail, and anyone found violating the Act could be fined $10,000 and given a twenty-year jail sentence. This was followed by the 1918 Sedition Act, passed to combat 'disloyal, profane, scurrilous or abusive language' about the government, the military and the American flag.
19 'Frank Crowninshield Obituary', *New York Times* (30 December 1947), p. 22.
20 Quoted in George H. Douglas, *The Smart Magazines: 50 Years of Literary Revelry at Vanity Fair, The New Yorker, Life, Esquire and the Smart Set* (New Haven, CT, 1991), p. 96.
21 'Where Is Greenwich Village?', *Vanity Fair* (July 1916), p. 65.
22 'The Smock Colony in Washington Square', *Vanity Fair* (May 1917), p. 76.
23 Ibid.
24 Ibid.
25 'Fashions of 1920', *Vanity Fair* (May 1916), p. 86.
26 'Scenes for Newport', *Vanity Fair* (July 1916), p. 58.
27 Tice, 'My Model World'.
28 Birmingham specifically refers to a 1911 performance in which Nijnsky scandalized the audience and the company he was dancing with by wearing tights with no modesty shorts. See Stephen Birmingham, 'Art That's Still Armed and Dangerous', *New York Times* (8 September 1996), p. 68.
29 Penny Farfan, *Performing Queer Modernism* (New York, 2017), p. 42.
30 *Tacoma Times* (12 December 1912), p. 1.
31 Tice, 'My Modern World'.
32 Ibid.
33 Ibid.
34 No photographs survive; this work is referenced in Keller, 'Clara Tice', pp. 431–2.
35 Helen Appleton Read, 'Clara Tice's Enticing Murals', *Brooklyn Daily Eagle* (23 December 1923), p. 13.

4 THE ARENSBERG SALON, HOME OF AMERICAN DADA

1 Gabrielle Buffet-Picabia, 'Some Memories of Pre-Dada Picabia and Duchamp', in *The Dada Painters and Poets*, ed. Robert Motherwell (Cambridge, MA, 1989), pp. 253–69.
2 Henri-Pierre Roché's semi-fictional novel *Victor* makes several references to Alice (Louise Arensberg) singing at the behest of Sabine (Mina Loy) and others.
3 Having bought *Nude Descending a Staircase, No. 2* for $324, Torrey would go on to sell the painting to the Arensbergs in 1919 for $1,000. For further information on Arensberg's purchases, see Bennard B. Perlman, ed., *American Artists, Authors, and Collectors: The Walter Pach Letters 1906–1958* (Albany, NY, 2002), pp. 31–53.
4 'Matisse at Montross', *American Art News* (23 January 1913), p. 1.

5 Clara Tice, 'Who's Who in Manhattan', *Cartoons* (August 1917), p. 178.
6 Allen Norton, 'Walter's Room', *The Quill*, IV/8 (June 1919), pp. 20–21.
7 Francis Naumann, 'Walter Conrad Arensberg: Poet, Patron, and Participant in the New York Avant-Garde, 1915–20', *Philadelphia Museum of Art Bulletin* (Spring 1980), pp. 2–32.
8 Louis Kaufman, *A Fiddler's Tale: How Hollywood and Vivaldi Discovered Me* (Maddison, WI, 2013), p. 152.
9 Katharine Kuh, *My Love Affair with Modern Art: Behind the Scenes with a Legendary Curator*, ed. Avis Berman (New York, 2006), p. 17.
10 Avis Berman and William McNaught, 'Interview with Katharine Kuh', *Archives of American Art Journal*, XXVII/3 (1987), pp. 2–36. It is worth pointing out that, in her later memoir, Kuh attributes the anxious hand-wringing that she recalls Louise constantly engaging in as linked to the pain caused by cancer, the illness that would kill her in 1953.
11 Arthur Miller, 'An Arensberg Profile', *Art Digest*, XXV/4 (February 1950).
12 Louise Stevens Arensberg, 'Poem/Thoughts Regarding Chagall's "Le Prete"', manuscript, 2 pp. with envelope, undated, Arensberg Archives, Philadelphia Museum of Art.
13 Louise Stevens Arensberg, 'Thoughts Regarding Modern Art', undated, Arensberg Archives, Philadelphia Museum of Art.
14 Norton, 'Walter's Room', p. 20.
15 Beatrice Wood, *I Shock Myself: The Autobiography of Beatrice Wood*, ed. Lindsay Smith (San Francisco, CA, 2006), p. 26.
16 Ibid.
17 Ibid.
18 McBride, 'The Walter Arensbergs', p. 156.
19 Wood, *Shock*, p. 22.
20 Quoted in *Pierre Cabanne; Dialogues with Marcel Duchamp*, trans. Ron Padgett (London, 1979), pp. 51–68.
21 William Carlos Williams, *The Autobiography of William Carlos Williams* (New York, 1967), p. 137.
22 Berman and McNaught, 'Interview with Katharine Kuh', p. 30.
23 Henri-Pierre Roché, Victor, in *Three New York Dadas and a Blind Man*, ed. Dawn Adès, trans. Chris Allen (London, 2014), p. 107.
24 Wood, *Shock*, p. 89.
25 For a detailed exploration of the Arensbergs in Hollywood, see Mark Nelson, William H. Sherman and Ellen Hoobler, *Hollywood Arensberg: Avant-Garde Collecting in Midcentury LA* (Los Angeles, CA, 2020).
26 Charles Demuth, 'Letter to Henry McBride', *Letters of Charles Demuth, American Artist, 1883–1935*, ed. Bruce Kellner (Philadelphia, PA, 2000), p. 6.
27 Quoted in Jacquelynn Baas, *Marcel Duchamp and the Art of Life* (Cambridge, MA, 2019), p. 148.
28 Louise Norton, 'Buddha of the Bathroom', *Blind Man*, 2 (1917), pp. 5–6.
29 Ibid.
30 'The Richard Mutt Case', *Blind Man*, 2 (1917), p. 5. The editorial is unsigned but understood to have been written by Wood.
31 Ibid.

32 Ezra Shales, '"Decadent Plumbers' Porcelain": Craft and Modernity in Ceramic Sanitary Ware', *Ostracon Journal of Criticism + Issues* (October 2017), pp. 211–42.

33 Charles Demuth, 'For Richard Mutt', *Blind Man*, 2 (1917), p. 6.

34 Advertisement, *Blind Man*, 2 (1917), p. 2.

35 Wood, *Shock*, p. 33.

36 'The Richard Mutt Case', p. 5.

5 BEATRICE WOOD: *Mama of Dada*

1 Beatrice Wood, 'Beatrice Wood diary, 1915–1919' and 'Beatrice Wood papers, 1894–1998'. Archives of American Art, Smithsonian Institution.

2 Beatrice Wood, *I Shock Myself: The Autobiography of Beatrice Wood*, ed. Lindsay Smith (San Francisco, CA, 2006), p. 19.

3 Letter from Beatrice Wood to Mary Mowbray-Clarke, 1912. Subseries B. Correspondence, 1903–1960, Sunwise Turn Papers. Harry Ransom Research Center, University of Texas at Austin.

4 Harold Loeb, *The Way It Was* (New York, 1959), pp. 27–9. For more on the Brocken group, see Allan Antliff, *Anarchist Modernism: Art, Politics, and the First American Avant-Garde* (Chicago, IL, 2007).

5 Letter from Caroline Wood to Beatrice Wood, undated. Third Party Correspondence, 1852–1964, Sunwise Turn Papers. Harry Ransom Research Center, University of Texas at Austin.

6 Letter from Beatrice Wood to Mary Mowbray-Clarke, 1912. Subseries B. Correspondence, 1903–1960, Sunwise Turn Papers. Harry Ransom Research Center, University of Texas at Austin.

7 Madge Jenison, *Sunwise Turn: A Human Comedy of Bookselling* (New York, 1923), p. 13. In an example of their radical ambitions, Mowbray-Clarke wrote to Sylvia Beach, owner of Shakespeare and Co. in Paris, to order copies of *Ulysses*, noting that they hoped to publish it but did not have the money (and possibly feared legal repercussions).

8 Interior-decoration designs and projects, 1917–1918, secondary records, 1904–1929. Sunwise Turn Papers, Harry Ransom Research Center, University of Texas at Austin.

9 Mary Mowbray-Clarke, manuscript of 'The Small Bookshop, The Substance of a Speech Made at the Class for Booksellers in the Public Library, 1922', Box 1, Sunwise Turn Papers. Harry Ransom Research Center, University of Texas at Austin.

10 Wood's diary entry for 22 January 1917 notes, 'Amy Lowell reads at Sunwise Turn. I recite "Patterns". Evening not marvellous.' Justin Duerr reveals the fallout from the evening, including an apologetic letter sent to Lowell by Jenison, and a terse reply from Lowell suggesting, 'had you contemplated asking other people to speak that same evening, it would have been better to have asked me beforehand if such a proceeding would be agreeable.' See Justin Duerr, 'Excerpt of a Plea for Loveliness: Life, Times, and Circle of Mary Mowbray-Clarke', https://justinduerr.medium.com, 10 October 2020.

11 Peggy Guggenheim, *Out of This Century: Confessions of an Art Addict* (New York, 1979), p. 23.

12 Wood, *Shock*, p. 26.

13 Ibid.

14 Ibid., pp. 22–3.

15 Ibid.

16 'The Richard Mutt Case', *Blind Man*, 2 (May 1917), p. 5.

17 'Letter from a Mother', *Blind Man*, 2 (May 1917), p. 8.

18 Wood, *Shock*, p. 32.

19 The original work is lost, but Wood created two copies in the 1970s. A reproduction drawing complete with bar of soap affixed is in the collection of the Whitney Museum of American Art. A glazed earthenware copy (1977) was also displayed at the 'Daughters of Dada' exhibition at Francis Naumann Fine Art in 2006 and is in the collection of Francis Naumann.

20 'The Independents Show', *American Art News* (21 April 1917), p. 4.

21 See Denise H. Sutton, *Globalizing Ideal Beauty* (New York, 2009), pp. 99–121.

22 Gertrude Stein, *The Autobiography of Alice B. Toklas* (London, 2001), pp. 50–51.

23 Wood, *Shock*, p. 20.

24 Wood's diary entry of July 14 1917 notes, 'Sick over break with Roche. Do not put[unclear] Cannot admit his going to Isadora Duncan's.'

25 Beatrice Wood, 'Beatrice Wood diary, 1915–1919', Beatrice Wood papers, 1894–1998, Archives of American Art, Smithsonian Institution.

26 Jenni Sorkin, 'Pottery in Drag: Beatrice Wood and Camp', *Journal of Modern Craft*, VII/1 (March 2014), pp. 53–66.

27 Anaïs Nin, 'Beatrice Wood at California Palace of the Legion of Honor', *Artforum*, www.artforum.com, 1 August 2020.

28 'Biography: Becoming a Potter', Beatrice Wood Center for the Arts, www.beatricewood.com, 15 November 2020.

29 Wood, *Shock*, p. 83.

30 Ibid., p. 126.

6 MINA LOY: *The Art of Modern Living*

1 Loy's first daughter, Oda, died in 1905, aged one. She and Stephan had a son, Giles (born in 1909), who died in 1923 while with his father in Bermuda. Her second daughter, Joella, was born in 1906, shortly after Loy's affair with her doctor, Henry Joel Le Savoureaux; Joella is presumed to be the result of this relationship, although she was given the Haweis name.

2 Gertrude Stein, *Autobiography of Alice B. Toklas* (London, 1990), p. 132.

3 Mina Loy, 'Letter to Carl Van Vechten', undated, Van Vechten Papers, Beinecke Rare Book and Manuscript Library.

4 The first two sections of the poem appear in the *Little Review*, with the third included in Robert McAlmon's *Contact Collection of Contemporary Verse* (1925). The sections were brought together by Loy's editor and executor Roger Conover in the collection *The Last Lunar Baedeker* (1982), which it is now out of print.

5 Reproduced in Barbara Spackman, *Fascist Virilities: Rhetoric, Ideologies, and Social Fantasies in Italy* (Minneapolis, MN, 1996), p. 12.

6 Quoted in Carolyn Burke, *Becoming Modern: The Life of Mina Loy* (New York, 1996), p. 157.

7 Suzanne Churchill, '5. Collision and Cittàbapini', *Mina Loy: Navigating the Avant-Garde*, https://mina-loy.com, 2 March 2021.

8 Mina Loy, 'Letter to Van Vechten' (*c.* 17 May 1915), Van Vechten Papers, Beinecke Rare Book and Manuscript Library.

9 Suzanne Churchill, *The Little Magazine 'Others' and the Renovation of Modern American Poetry* (Burlington, VT, 2006), p. 48.

10 Alfred Kreymborg, *Our Singing Strength: An Outline of American Poetry, 1620–1930* (New York, 1929), p. 489.

11 'Do You Strive to Capture the Symbols of Your Reactions? If Not You Are Quite Old Fashioned', *New York Evening Sun* (13 February 1917), pp. 10–12.

12 Kreymborg, *Our Singing Strength*, p. 488.

13 Djuna Barnes, 'Becoming Intimate with the Bohemians', *New York Morning Telegraph Sunday Magazine* (19 November 1916), in Djuna Barnes, *New York* (Los Angeles, CA, 1989), pp. 233–45, p. 242.

14 Marianne Moore, 'Letter to H.D.' (January 1921), in *Selected Letters of Marianne Moore*, ed. Bonnie Costello (London, 1998), p. 140.

15 Ibid.

16 Mina Loy, draft letter to James Laughlin, undated, Carolyn Burke Collection on Mina Loy and Lee Miller, Beinecke Rare Book and Manuscript Library, Yale University, YCAL MSS 778, Box 6. This draft is found on the back of a letter Laughlin sent to Loy requesting a biography (dated 21 June 1950).

17 Carolyn Burke interview with Louise Norton Varise [*sic*], Box 6. Carolyn Burke Collection on Mina Loy and Lee Miller. Yale Collection of American Literature, Beinecke Rare Book and Manuscript Library. And Pierre Caban, *Dialogues with Marcel Duchamp*, trans. Ron Padgett (London, 1979), p. 53.

18 Arthur Cravan, 'Letter to Mina Loy' (10 December 1917), published in the *New Yorker* (25 August 1997), p. 102.

19 Her grief over Cravan's disappearance would be further compounded by the loss of Giles, her only son; Stephen Haweis took him to the Caribbean while Loy was away in New York in 1921. He died there two years later.

20 'Would You Be "Different"? Madame Loy Shows How', *Orlean Evening Times* (16 March 1921), p. 6. Identical articles also appear in the *Richmond Item* (29 March) and the *Bismark Tribune* (13 April).

21 Sylvia Beach, *Shakespeare and Company* (Lincoln, NE, 1991), p. 113.

22 Burke, *Becoming Modern*, p. 410.

23 Quoted ibid.

24 Ibid.

25 See ibid., p. 433; Loy's friends Alex Blossom, Stevie Ferris and Julien Levy took care of the work for five years, until Duchamp and art dealer David Mann viewed the assemblages and arranged the Bodley Gallery exhibition.

26 Quoted in Roger Conover, 'Introduction', in *Lost Lunar Baedeker*, p. xviii.

27 Crystal Eastman, 'Birth Control in the Feminist Movement',

28 Loy, 'Gertrude Stein', *Lost Lunar Baedeker*, p. 297.

7 STETTHEIMER SALON:
Chateau Stettheimer and the Cellophane Sisters

1 Henry McBride, *Florine Stettheimer* (New York, 1946), p. 10.
2 Ibid.
3 Judith Brown, *Glamour in Six Dimensions: Modernism and the Radiance of Form* (Ithaca, NY, and London, 2009), p. 145.
4 Florine Stettheimer, 'Sweet Little Miss Mouse', in *Crystal Flowers*, ed. Irene Gammel and Suzanne Zelazo (Toronto, 2010), p. 44.
5 Ettie Stettheimer, 'Love Days', in *Memorial Volume of and by Ettie Stettheimer* (New York, 1951), p. 17.
6 Ettie Stettheimer letter to Alfred Stieglitz (1933). Alfred Stieglitz/Georgia O'Keeffe Archive, Yale Collection of American Literature. Beinecke Rare Book and Manuscript Library.
7 Florine Stettheimer, '[Paris – Living in the Latin Quarter]', in *Crystal Flowers*, ed. Gammel and Zelazo, p. 208.
8 Marcel Duchamp, 'Letter to Ettie Stettheimer' (9 August 1917), in *Affectionately, Marcel: Selected Correspondence of Marcel Duchamp*, ed. Hector Obalk (Brussels, 2000), p. 49. A letter Duchamp sent to Ettie in 1921, however, recalls the 'happy times' they spent in Tarrytown 'without flirting however. It's not easy, not flirting, not everyone can manage it.' (*Affectionately, Marcel*, p. 100).
9 Ettie Stettheimer, 'Pensée-cadeau', July 1922. The Florine and Ettie Stettheimer Papers, Yale Collection of American Literature, Beinecke Rare Book and Manuscript Library. (trans. 'I would like to be made to measure / for you, for you/ But I'm ready-made by nature/ For what, for what?/ As I don't know, I've made corrections/ For me')
10 Florine Stettheimer, 'To a Gentleman Friend', in *Crystal Flowers*, ed. Gammel and Zelazo, p. 90.
11 Henry McBride, 'Florine Stettheimer at the Independents', *The Sun* (April 1918), in *The Flow of Art: Essays and Criticism of Henry McBride*, ed. Daniel Catton Rich (New York, 1975), p. 152.
12 Georgia O'Keeffe, [On Florine Stettheimer (eulogy?)], undated. Alfred Stieglitz/Georgia O'Keeffe Archive, Yale Collection of American Literature. Beinecke Rare Book and Manuscript Library.
13 Marcel Duchamp, 'Letter to Ettie Stettheimer', in *Affectionately, Marcel*, p. 83.
14 'The Immigration Act of 1924 (the Johnson-Reed Act)', *Office of the Historian*, https://history.state.gov, 5 September 2021.
15 'Interview with Hasia Diner', *American Experience*, www.pbs.org, 5 September 2021.
16 See Patrick Weil, *The Sovereign Citizen: Denaturalization and the Origins of the American Republic* (Philadelphia, PA, 2012).
17 Barbara Bloemink, *Florine Stettheimer: A Biography* (Munich, 2022), p. 205.
18 Myerson, the daughter of Russian Jewish immigrants, faced pressure to change her name to something 'less Jewish' but refused. Her experiences are the subject of David Around's documentary *The One and Only Jewish Miss America* (2020).

19 While some critics cite naivety and ignorance on the part of 1930s figures like Dreier and Hartley, communist painter Alice Neel's 1936 painting *Nazis Murder Jews* (which depicts an anti-fascist protest in New York) offers a different perspective.

20 Robert Herbert, Eleanor Apter and Elise Kenney, *The Société Anonyme and the Dreier Bequest at Yale University: Catalogue Raisonné* (New Haven, CT, 1984), p. 20. The editors defend Dreier's Nazi apologism as naivety, yet it seems strange to imagine that such an astute and educated woman as Dreier (who was invested in Germany's affairs) could have remained 'naive' or 'gullible' though the 1930s.

21 Marsden Hartley, 'Letters from Germany, 1933–1938', *Archives of American Art Journal*, XXV/1–2 (1985), pp. 3–28.

22 Quoted in Townsend Ludington, *Marsden Hartley: The Biography of an American Artist* (Ithaca, NY, and London, 1992), p. 227. Ludington notes that Hartley wrote to Edith Halpert of his love for his Jewish friends, 'not [recognizing] that the argument that "some of my best friends are Jewish" was not an adequate response to the oppression that was rapidly mounting', and of which Hartley was well aware.

23 Donna M. Cassidy, *Marsden Hartley: Race, Religion, and Nation* (Hanover, NH, and London, 2005), p. 266.

24 Ibid., p. 362.

25 The tea room belonging to Eve Adams (also known as Eva Kotchever) was popular with a lesbian crowd, as well as working-class migrants and intellectuals. Adams's novel *Lesbian Love* (1925) was also used as part of the trial against her. Tragically, Kotchever was murdered in Auschwitz in December 1943. Jonathan Ned Katz, *The Daring Life and Dangerous Times of Eve Adams* (Chicago, IL, 2021).

26 Henry McBride letter to Florine Stettheimer (June 1927), in *An Eye on the Modern Century: Selected Letter of Henry McBride*, ed. Steven Watson and Catherine J. Morris (New Haven, CT, and London, 2000), p. 162.

27 Bloemink, *Biography*, p. 274.

28 It is important to note that although the Stettheimers and other modern women used Poiret's designs to subvert stereotypes, Poiret was deploying an orientalist stereotype that developed in the nineteenth century. Orientalism created an ahistorical, unspecific view of 'Asia' as 'always ancient, excessive, feminine, open for use, and decadent'; see Anne Anlin Cheng, *Ornamentalism* (Oxford, 2019) for more on orientalist, racist consumerism and Asiatic femininity.

29 Nancy Troy, *Couture Culture* (Cambridge, MA, and London, 2003), p. 124. Troy quotes a critic who decried the trousers for signalling 'the desire to break with the traditions of their sex, their race, of their country' and disparagingly linked the style to the 'Persian woman, the Jewess'.

30 John Richardson, *Sacred Monsters, Sacred Masters: Beaton, Capote, Dalí, Picasso, Freud, Warhol, and More* (New York, 2001), p. 77.

31 Marcel Duchamp, 'Letter to Carrie, Ettie, and Florine Stettheimer' (13 July 1919), in *Affectionately, Marcel*, p. 68.

32 Susan Stewart, *On Longing: Narratives of the Miniature, the Gigantic, the Souvenir, the Collection* (Durham, NC, and London, 1993), p. 69.

33 Carrie Stettheimer, 'Letter to Gaston Lachaise' (1931), Florine and Ettie Stettheimer Papers, Beinecke Rare Book and Manuscript Library.

34 'Florine Stettheimer Journal', Florine and Ettie Stettheimer Papers, Beinecke Rare Book and Manuscript Library.

35 Richard Hell, 'Andy Warhol: Everything Is Good', *Gagosian Quarterly* (Spring 2019), https://gagosian.com.; Andy Warhol, *Popism* (London, 1980), p. 16.

36 Georgia O'Keeffe, [On Florine Stettheimer (eulogy?)]. Alfred Stieglitz/ Georgia O'Keeffe Archive, Yale Collection of American Literature. Beinecke Rare Book and Manuscript Library.

37 Linda Nochlin, 'Florine Stettheimer – Rococo Subversive', *Art in America*, www.artnews.com, 5 May 2017.

38 Marcel Duchamp, 'Letter to Ettie Stettheimer' (9 July 1922), in *Affectionately, Marcel,* p. 118.

39 Stettheimer, '[Art Is Spelled with a Capital A]', in *Crystal Flowers*, ed. Gammel and Zelazo, p. 72.

40 Stettheimer, '[Look at My]', in *Crystal Flowers*, ed. Gammel and Zelazo, p. 111.

41 Stettheimer, 'Must One Have Models', in *Crystal Flowers*, ed. Gammel and Zelazo, p. 129.

42 Duchamp, 'Letter to Katherine Dreier', quoted in *The Société Anonyme: Modernism for America*, ed. Jennifer R. Gross (New Haven, CT, and London, 2006), p. 8.

43 Marcel Duchamp, 'Letter to Carrie, Ettie and Florine Stettheimer' (3 May 1919), in *Affectionately, Marcel*, p. 83.

44 Linda Dalrymple Henderson's *Duchamp in Context: Science and Technology in the 'Large Glass' and Related Works* (Princeton, NJ, 2006) offers a fascinating insight into Duchamp's interest in modern physics.

45 Stettheimer, '[The World Is Full of Strangers]', *Crystal Flowers*, ed. Gammel and Zelazo, p. 111.

46 Henry McBride, 'Florine Stettheimer: A Reminiscence', in *View: Parade of the Avant-Garde, an Anthology of 'View' Magazine (1940–1947)*, ed. Charles Henri Ford, Catrina Neiman and Paul Nathan (New York, 1991), pp. 155–60, p. 156.

47 Quoted in Calvin Tomkins, *Duchamp: A Biography* (New York, 1998), p. 344.

48 For more context on Carl Van Vechten's white voyeurism, see Laila Islam, 'Carl Van Vechten and the White Gaze', *PMA Stories*, https://blog.philamuseum.org, 4 February 2022.

49 Paul Rosenfeld, 'The World of Florine Stettheimer', *The Nation* (3 May 1933), pp. 522–3.

50 Julien Levy letter to Mina Loy (undated). Julien Levy Gallery Records, Philadelphia Museum of Art, Library and Archives.

51 Stettheimer, '[Art Is Spelled with a Capital A]', in *Crystal Flowers*, ed. Gammel and Zelazo, p. 72.

52 'Press Release: Large Exhibitions of Paintings by Florine Stettheimer', Museum of Modern Art. Museum of Modern Art Press Release Archive, New York.

CODA: *Make the World Your Salon*

1 Quoted in Jori Finkel, '"Gender Alchemy" Is Transforming Art for the 21st Century', *New York Times*, www.nytimes.com, 8 September 2021.

SELECT
BIBLIOGRAPHY

Barnes, Djuna, *New York*, ed. Alyce Barry (Los Angeles, CA, 1989)

Berman, Avis, *Rebels on Eighth Street: Juliana Force and the Whitney Museum of American Art* (New York, 1990)

Bloemink, Barbara, *Florine Stettheimer: A Biography* (Munich, 2022)

Burke, Carolyn, *Becoming Modern: The Life of Mina Loy* (New York, 1996)

Cheng, Anne Anlin, *Ornamentalism* (New York, 2019)

Cooke, Jennifer, *Contemporary Feminist Life-Writing: The New Audacity* (Cambridge, 2020)

Dodge, Mabel, *Movers and Shakers* (New York, 1936)

Faderman, Lillian, *Odd Girls and Twilight Lovers: A History of Lesbian Life in Twentieth-Century America* (New York, 2011)

Freytag-Loringhoven, Elsa von, *Body Sweats: The Uncensored Writings of Elsa von Freytag-Loringhoven*, ed. Irene Gammel and Suzanne Zelazo (Cambridge, MA, 2011)

Gammel, Irene, *Baroness Elsa: Gender, Dada, and Everyday Modernity* (Cambridge, MA, 2003)

Hartman, Saidiya, *Beautiful Lives, Wayward Experiments: Intimate Histories of Riotous Black Girls, Troublesome Women and Queer Radicals* (London, 2021)

Jones, Martha S., *Vanguard: How Black Women Broke Barriers, Won the Vote, and Insisted on Equality for All* (New York, 2020)

Kuh, Katharine, *My Love Affair with Modern Art: Behind the Scenes with a Legendary Curator*, ed. Avis Berman (New York, 2006)

Loy, Mina, *The Lost Lunar Baedeker*, ed. Roger Conover (Manchester, 1997)

—, *The Stories and Essays of Mina Loy*, ed. Sara Crangle (London, 2011)

McBride, Henry, *The Flow of Art: Essays and Criticism of Henry McBride*, ed. Daniel Catton Rich (New York, 1975)

Maller, Katharine, ed., *Vivid and Repulsive as the Truth: The Early Works of Djuna Barnes* (New York, 2016)

Naumann, Francis, *New York Dada, 1915–23* (New York, 1994)

Nochlin, Linda, *Why Have There Been No Great Women Artists? 50th Anniversary Edition* (London, 2021)

Obalk, Hector, ed., *Affectionately, Marcel: Selected Correspondence of Marcel Duchamp* (Brussels, 2000)

Palken Rudnick, Lois, *Mabel Dodge Luhan: New Woman, New Worlds* (Albuquerque, NM, 1987)

Pyne, Kathleen, *Modernism and the Feminine Voice: O'Keeffe and the Women of the Stieglitz Circle* (Berkeley and Los Angeles, CA, 2007)

Sawelson-Gorse, Naomi, ed., *Women in Dada* (Cambridge, MA, 1998)

Schulman, Robert, *Romany Marie: The Queen of Greenwich Village* (Nashville, TN, 2006)

Schwarz, Judith, *Radical Feminists of Heterodoxy: Greenwich Village, 1912–1940* (Lebanon, NH, 1982)

Sochen, June, *The New Woman: Feminism in Greenwich Village, 1910–1920* (New York, 1972)

Stein, Gertrude, *Autobiography of Alice B. Toklas* (London, 2001)

Stettheimer, Florine, *Crystal Flowers*, ed. Irene Gammel and Suzanne Zelazo (Toronto, 2010)

Swinth, Kirsten, *Painting Professionals: Women Artists and the Development of Modern American Art, 1870–1930* (Chapel Hill, NC, and London, 2001)

Varèse, Louise, *Varèse: A Looking-Glass Diary, 1883–1928* (New York, 1972)

Wood, Beatrice, *I Shock Myself: The Autobiography of Beatrice Wood*, ed. Lindsay Smith (San Francisco, CA, 2006)

Zorach, William, *Art Is My Life: The Autobiography of William Zorach* (Cleveland, OH, 1967)

ACKNOWLEDGEMENTS

Thank you to the team at Reaktion – especially Vivian Constantinopoulos for seeing potential in this project and being patient and supportive throughout the process. This book wouldn't have been possible without innumerable writers and scholars whose work on women's art and creative practice has paved the way for present-day efforts to challenge the canon and provide new perspectives on art and cultural history – I hope anyone who enjoys this book will dig deeper into writing on Mina Loy, Florine Stettheimer, the women of New York Dada, and early twentieth-century feminism.

I'm indebted to several scholars, researchers and archivists who've given their time to answer questions and help with archival materials – many thanks to Francis Naumann, Barbara Bloemink, Kevin Wallace, Katherine Prater and the staff at the Avery Library, Columbia University; Justin Duerr, for offering insights into Mary Mowbray-Clarke and sharing research material; Peter Zorach kindly shared memories and photographs of the Zorach family; Francesca Mancino, who generously gave access to the Clara Tice collection.

Thank you to my PhD supervisor Professor Suzanne Hobson for sparking my interest in Mina Loy and encouraging me on the long journey to this book. Thanks to Hannah Hutchings-Georgiou of Lucy Writers for her incredible generosity in championing and supporting me and other new writers. A special thank you to Dr Jade French, who I'm honoured to know as a colleague and a friend, for her support and advice – our conversations and our work on Decorating Dissidence are a constant source of motivation and inspiration.

This book is for the radicals and rogues in my family and their quiet, everyday acts of resistance and rebellion – I'm grateful to them for encouraging me to leap into the unknown. Deepest gratitude to my mum, for endless belief in me, unconditional support, strength and wisdom. This is also for Dexter, for the kindness, the caring, the understanding, the keeping everything going while I read/write/despair – couldn't do it without you.

PHOTO ACKNOWLEDGEMENTS

The author and publishers wish to express their thanks to the sources listed below for illustrative material and/or permission to reproduce it. Some locations of artworks are also given below, in the interest of brevity:

Archives of American Art, Smithsonian Institution, Washington, DC: p. 93 (Jean Crotti papers, 1913–1973); Avery Architectural and Fine Arts Library, Columbia University, New York: pp. 241, 264; Beatrice Wood Center for the Arts/Happy Valley Foundation, Ojai, CA: p. 174; Beinecke Rare Book and Manuscript Library, Yale University, New Haven, CT: pp. 27, 42, 87, 89, 91, 187, 200; Cleveland Museum of Art, OH (Edwin R. and Harriet Pelton Perkins Memorial Fund, 2020.261): p. 54; collection of Justin Duerr: pp. 177, 178, 180; Library of Congress, Washington, DC: pp. 66, 70, 71, 74, 78, 101, 224, 238, 252; collection of Francesca Mancino: pp. 69 (above and below), 116, 126, 129, 130, 131, 168; The Museum of Fine Arts, Houston, TX: p. 103; National Gallery of Art, Washington, DC: p. 40; collection of Francis M. Naumann and Marie T. Keller, Yorktown Heights, NY: p. 196; New-York Historical Society: p. 73; Philadelphia Museum of Art, PA: pp. 142, 161 (photo Art Resource, NY), 164 (photo Art Resource, NY); private collection: p. 259; Schlesinger Library, Radcliffe Institute for Advanced Study, Harvard University, Cambridge, MA: pp. 109 (PC60-60F-14), 112 (PC60-63-12); Smithsonian American Art Museum, Washington, DC (gift from the collection of Tessim Zorach, 1968.87.1): p. 48; Yale University Art Gallery, New Haven, CT: pp. 257, 262; © Estate of Marguerite Thompson Zorach, photo Brooklyn Museum (gift of the collection of the Zorach children, 84.45.8): p. 52.

INDEX

Page numbers in *italics* indicate illustrations